Brickwork

A Practical Guide for Level 1

Dr Joseph Durkin

Nelson Thornes

a Wolters

Published in 2006 by:
Nelson Thornes Ltd
Delta Place
27 Bath Road
CHELTENHAM
GL53 7TH
United Kingdom

06 07 08 09 10 / 10 9 8 7 6 5 4 3 2 1

A catalogue record for this book is available from the British Library

ISBN 0 7487 9685 1

Cover photograph George Demetri
Illustrations by Peters and Zabransky
Page make-up by Florence Production Ltd, Stoodleigh, Devon

Printed and bound in Croatia by Zrinski

Contents

Introduction

This book has been written with the objective of assisting those students who are studying for the National Vocational Qualification Level 1 certificate in Trowel Occupations (Construction). The contents are based on the new Magenta Scheme syllabus in brickwork, and should prove useful to both students and tutors alike.

Having felt the need of such a publication in my own apprenticeship days, I hope that this book will do much to help and guide all those who wish to study and maintain the genuine craft of brickwork.

Work-based Evidence

Each chapter will from time to time give you instructions on what type of evidence to gather from work. Remember, that if you are undertaking NVQ training, it is your responsibility to collect and record evidence of the tasks carried out in the workplace, then to map and record it against the syllabus.

Quick Quiz

There will usually be a quick quiz after each section. The quizzes are designed to test your knowledge of the work recently undertaken. They can be attempted at any time after reading the relevant section. If you do not do well first time, try again later.

Try This Out

Try This Out activities will be of a more demanding nature than the quick quizzes and are designed to assist students who are preparing for exams at Level 1. The contents of the questions and tasks are based on examinations of recent years and should prove useful for revision purposes.

Note: Some of the tasks are to test practical ability and need to be carried out in a workshop or on site. It would be useful therefore if you liaise with your tutor about these.

Magenta Scheme – Level 1 – Brickwork

Qualification Structure

The NVQ qualification structure for Trowel Occupations (Construction) Level 1 (Magenta Scheme) is as follows.

Mandatory Units

Unit No. VR 01 Conform to General Workplace Safety

Unit No. VR 03 Move and Handle Resources

Unit No. VR 36 Prepare and Mix Concrete and Mortar

Unit No. VR 37 Lay Bricks and Blocks to Line

Plus
Optional Units (any one unit from the following)

Unit No. VR 38 Contribute to Setting Out Basic Masonry Structures

Unit No. VR 39 Joint Brick and Block Structures

Note. This book covers both the mandatory and optional units.

National Vocational Qualifications

Construction National Vocational Qualifications (NVQs) are qualifications designed to reflect accurately what is expected of people working in the construction industry. An NVQ reflects a typical kind of job, in your case bricklaying. Therefore, the best place to be assessed to see whether you have reached the standard required for an NVQ, is at work. Only at work can it be seen that you carry out your job competently – to the national standard.

Such qualifications are accessible to everyone. Traditional barriers such as age, the length and type of training, and where and how skills have been acquired are removed.

NVQs are not like traditional courses of study, where you sit an exam paper and never meet the examiner. For an NVQ the learner or candidate has responsibility for proving they have the necessary skills and competence to carry out the work expected of them.

Awarding Bodies

CITB-ConstructionSkills and City & Guilds is one of several awarding bodies. CITB-ConstructionSkills, formerly the Construction Industry Training Board, and City & Guilds is a joint awarding body for the construction industry. CITB-ConstructionSkills is responsible for the setting of standards for the craft and operative routes into gaining an NVQ. In order to do this effectively it works closely with representatives from the industry to ensure that the NVQ reflects the needs of the workplace and the requirement for training a competent, numerate and literate workforce.

What Makes Up an NVQ?

An NVQ is made up of a number of individual units of competence.

Unit Title

This relates back to outcomes contained within the Functional Map of the industry, but is expressed in industry language.

Performance Criteria

These define the acceptable level of performance required for employment, expressed in outcome terms.

Scope of Performance

This details the evidence necessary to meet the requirements of each performance criterion, this is usually work based; simulation is only allowed where indicated in the standards.

Knowledge and understanding

This links, in generic terms, the knowledge and understanding requirement directly to the performance criteria.

Scope of Knowledge and Understanding

This takes key words contained in the knowledge and understanding (identified in bold type) and expands them to cover the scope of knowledge required by the industry for competence in the workplace.

The NVQ Process

A number of people work closely together in order to see that the NVQ process works effectively. They are:

- Candidates
- Assessors
- Work-based recorders
- Internal verifiers
- External verifiers.

Magenta Scheme – Key Points

The Magenta Scheme went live on 1 September 2005.

Candidate Registration

All registrations from the above date must be for the new Magenta Scheme.

Magenta CQS 001 forms are available from the NVQ helpline on 0870 4176874 or email nvq.product@citb.co.uk . Alternatively, they can be downloaded from the CITB website www.citb.co.uk

CQS004 Pads

CITB are currently taking orders for the Magenta CQS004 pads as these will not automatically be distributed to centres or assessors. To order email nvq.product@citb.co.uk

Unit Builders

The Magenta Unit Builder, showing the structures of the qualifications including the mandatory, optional and additional units, will be available On-line during September 2005. The web address is www.citb-constructionskills.co.uk

Question and Answer Packs

The Magenta packs can be ordered from CITB Publications Department in the usual way. Go to www.citb-constructionskills.co.uk to order on-line or call 01485 577800.

Centre Assessment Guidelines and Assessor Recording Packs

These Magenta publications have been available to view and download on-line since early this year in the NVQ Support material section of the website www.citb-constructionskills.co.uk. They can also be purchased from the Publications Department and are priced at £25 each.

General Enquiries

For general enquiries regarding the magenta launch for example, registration, centre/assessor approval and so on, please email nvq.product@citb.co.uk

Magenta Occupation Enquiries

For specific enquiries regarding the National Occupational Standards (NOS) for the Magenta Scheme, email magenta@questions.co.uk. CITB endeavour to reply within 10 working days.

Qualification Details

Details of all current qualifications (NVQ 2000 and Magenta) can be found on the QCA website www.qca.org.uk/openquals. The website shows the end registration and certification dates and the full structure of each qualification.

NVQ Helpline

For all enquiries regarding Magenta and NVQs, Tel: 0870 417 6874.

Key Terms ▮▬▬▬

Assessor – Person appointed to carry out judgement of a candidate's evidence of competence.

Candidate – The person undertaking an NVQ.

Competence – The proven ability to work to the national standard for brickwork.

Evidence – Proof of competence.

Knowledge and understanding – Links, using generic terms, the knowledge and understanding to the performance criteria.

Level – Degree of difficulty.

National Vocational Qualification (NVQ) – Competence-based qualification focused on the workplace.

Performance Criteria – Define the acceptable level of performance required for employment expressed in outcome terms.

Scope of Knowledge and Understanding – Expands key words contained in the knowledge and understanding to cover the scope of knowledge required for competence in the workplace.

Scope of Performance – Details the evidence needed to meet the requirements of each performance criterion, it is usually work based, unless indicated in the standards.

Standards – The entire collection of units and elements developed for an NVQ in brickwork.

Transferable – May be applied in circumstances additional to those in which the candidate is assessed.

Unit title – Relates to outcomes contained within the Functional Map of the industry, expressed in industry language.

Key Skills ▮▬▬▬

The assessment of Key Skills is an important feature of vocational qualifications and helps students to improve their individual learning. The key skills required for a bricklayer are Application of Number and Communication.

The Essential Skills of Communication and Application of Number can be taken individually or combined to form the Essential Skills qualification. The awarding bodies provide a range of support material for the delivery and assessment of Essential Skills. The details are included in the list of useful addresses and websites at the end of this section. It is for these reasons that such emphasis has been placed on ensuring that there are essential skills tasks in the syllabus.

Work-based Evidence

The main source of evidence needed by a candidate is work-based and confirms that practical skills meet the appropriate performance criteria and range statements. Work-based evidence covers the carrying out of naturally occurring activities – with all the attendant relationships, constraints, time and other pressures, within the total working environment of a construction company.

Work-based evidence is of activities frequently carried out. Where the evidence is considered insufficient in quality or quantity by an assessor, the candidate can be asked to demonstrate competence by simulated activities. Activities that are infrequently carried out in the workplace can also be simulated to provide evidence of a candidate's skill.

Note: There is very little scope for simulated activities within the Magenta Scheme; tutors must study the National Occupational Standards closely before accepting any form of simulated activity from a candidate.

Without evidence from the workplace, a candidate will be unable to obtain an NVQ. The NVQ demands that candidates prove they can carry out tasks in a real work environment.

Gathering Evidence

Work-based evidence, as has already been stated, is an extremely important part of an NVQ course. You are required to provide this evidence in order to gain an NVQ. If you think you will be unable to gather any part of the work-based evidence required, it is important that you speak to your course tutor at the first possible opportunity. Your tutor will then speak to your employer and managing agent in order to resolve the problem.

Suitable Evidence

A site diary or time sheets would provide evidence for most of the units in this NVQ, provided it is presented in the correct manner. For the site diary or time sheets to count as evidence they would need to be signed by yourself and countersigned by your work-based recorder. He could substantiate it further, by noting in the site diary or time sheets any relevant conversations that you have had, such as seeking advice or help from another member of the site team.

Photographs are also an important form of evidence. The main good practice principles are:

1. Candidates should ideally be in the photograph for identification.
2. Photographs should:
    (a) be accompanied by a brief description of the work activity
    (b) include the job/site address and the date the work was carried out

(c) be signed by the candidate and work-based recorder or site foreman

(d) be referenced by the assessor/candidate to the occupational unit's performance criteria.

Photographic evidence as used above can be strong and credible supporting evidence, but observation by an assessor of some aspects of a candidate's work performance is still required to be sure of competence.

Remember VACS!

Valid – Is the work/evidence relevant to the NVQ unit content?

Authentic – Can you be sure the work shown in the photograph is the candidate's?

Current – How old is the evidence and is it still relevant?

Sufficient – Is it sufficient on its own, or is some other evidence required?

Therefore, photographic evidence must meet the VACS rule as explained above.

Copies of drawings, specifications or job sheets that you have used during the dates on the timesheet can also be cross-referenced in order to provide evidence.

Besides the evidence already mentioned, other items can also be used, such as holiday forms, employment contracts, delivery notes, invoices, receipts, requisitions, company procedures or policies, for such things as health and safety, training procedures, acceptable behaviour and so on.

Note: Always get permission to take away any paperwork from site, as certain documents are confidential.

Witness Testimonies

Witness testimonies are an essential part of your work-based evidence. They can take several forms, from a simple statement confirming that you have undertaken all the work in your portfolio, to complex descriptions of work that you have carried out on site. Witness testimonies should be written by a person in a responsible position, examples of these are:

Work-based recorder
Skilled tradesperson
Manager or supervisor
Your employer
The client.

Witness testimonies should be signed and dated by any of the above, with the relevant contact details such as address and telephone number. Whenever possible, it should be on letter headed paper, it should also include the position of the person writing the testimony.

Witness Testimony Example ▬

To whom it may concern

I would like to confirm that between the 1st September 2005 and the 10th of September 2005 Diana Whatmough was employed by Hopwood Building Company on a short term contract as a bricklayer. During this time she completed several jobs for us, I have signed and dated any relevant photographs of her work, along with copies of the original documentation that she was given (drawings, specifications, job sheets and so on) I have also signed and dated these.

During her time with us, Diana was always punctual, her work-station was always kept tidy, and she followed company policies in all areas, including health and safety. The work that she carried out for us was to a high standard and was completed in the allocated time span. We would have no problem in employing Diana again in the future.

Yours faithfully

Ravi Singh (site supervisor)

As you can see in the example, the person writing the witness testimony has not put a detailed description of the work carried out, this is not necessary in this particular case, as the photographs and the other documentation provides a very clear picture of the work that Diana has carried out. The important point is that the documentation has all been authenticated by the site supervisor.

The Role of the Candidate ▬

The role of the candidate in studying for an NVQ in brickwork is as follows:

Agree an assessment plan with your assessor, ensuring that you have the following:

■ Details of the relevant NVQ

■ Understanding of what units you are to be assessed on

■ Understanding of what type of evidence you need to produce

■ Agreement on how the units are going to be assessed

■ Agreement on the review process.

Carry out the following:

■ Ensure that all the work-based evidence that you produce is recorded and mapped in a form agreed with your assessor.

■ Ensure that you work closely with the work-based recorder if different from the assessor to decide if you are collecting and recording the correct evidence.

■ Gather as much supplementary supporting evidence as possible.

- Always obtain signatures and dates from the work-based recorder to authenticate your evidence.
- Present your work-based evidence to your assessor for guidance and answer any job-knowledge questions asked or set by the assessor.

Supplementary Evidence

Supplementary evidence can be any of the following:
- Photographs of the task and possibly you carrying it out
- Site drawings you might be using
- Time sheets and day work sheets
- Details of the jobs worked on
- A video of you carrying out various tasks
- Witness testimony sheets signed and dated by your supervisor, client, architect, site manager and so on
- Your contract of employment and job-description
- Reports from colleges or training providers
- Details of your experience to date in the form of a c.v.

Work-based Recorders

Work-based recorders have the role of:
- Observing you and the work you carry out at the workplace
- Ensuring that you carry out all work in a safe manner and that the tasks meet the industrial standard required
- Authenticating your work-based evidence by signing and dating it as necessary
- Meeting with the assessor as required monitoring your performance
- Ensuring whenever possible that you are being given every opportunity to gain the relevant work experience.
- Providing support and guidance to you on the gathering and recording of evidence.

The Assessment Process

The joint awarding body CITB-ConstructionSkills and City & Guilds approves organizations to carry out assessment of candidates or learners for the granting of NVQs. Usually these organizations are:
- Further education colleges
- Private training centres
- Construction companies.

Once approval has been granted they are known as assessment organizations. These organizations employ staff to carry out assessment and verification. These people are known as assessors and internal verifiers.

Assessors

Assessors are occupationally competent in that they will have been a bricklayer and are qualified in the assessment process. They are responsible for deciding whether you are competent in the tasks which you are set.

Internal Verifiers

Internal verifiers are people responsible for ensuring that the quality of the assessment carried out by the assessor is to an acceptable standard. They fulfil the same role as quality control in your own organization.

The joint awarding body for Construction of CITB-ConstructionSkills and City & Guilds employs a number of people to monitor the whole assessment process and to ensure that all aspects of it are carried out correctly. These people are known as external verifiers.

External Verifiers

External verifiers are there to ensure that all assessment centres are working to the standards set by the awarding bodies.

The Assessment Process and Work-based Recorders

How does the work-based recorder fit into this process? It should be understood that work-based recorders cannot carry out assessment themselves; only an accredited assessor can do that. However, they are the important link between the assessor and the candidate. Usually they are given the task by their employer in order to authenticate the evidence that a candidate is gathering from the workplace and to ensure that it is valid and to the standard and quality required. Assessors and work-based recorders are usually known to each other and will be confident of each other's ability to decide whether a candidate is competent in the work he/she is set.

The Assessor's Role

It is for the assessor to:

- Direct and advise a candidate on the correct NVQ for him/her usually in agreement with the employer.
- Carry out an assessment plan for the candidate.
- Observe the candidate on a regular basis at the workplace to ensure he/she is carrying out a full range of necessary activities to create an evidence portfolio.
- Carry out regular reviews with the candidate relating to the assessment plan and adjust it if required.
- Decide on whether the candidate has the necessary knowledge and understanding required to complete an NVQ programme of study.

It should be understood that candidates can take internal exams and tests either orally or in written form

■ Make a decision on all the evidence that the candidate provides to support their claim of competence.

Role of the Company

The majority of companies unless they have their own training division will use an assessment organization, for example a college of further education. In this case the assessor will visit the company usually on an eight-week cycle to see the candidate. In this situation, the work-based recorder carries out the majority of the observations of the candidate and confirms to the assessor whether he/she has carried out the work to the industrial standard.

Source : CITB-ConstructionSkills. Candidate's Guide to Construction NVQs. 2005.

Acknowledgements

Any book is a shared effort and without the support of others would never get to publication. I would like to thank all the people at Nelson Thornes who have been involved with the process, particularly my editors, Jess Ward, Eve Thould and Chris Wortley. As ever though, for their patience and support, my thanks go out to my wife Caroline and daughter Katie.

The authors and publishers gratefully acknowledge the owners of any copyright material reproduced herein. Material reproduced from HSE on pages 4, 59 and other quotes are © Crown copyright.

The safety signs that appear in the book are from Instant Art/Magnum (NT).

Cover Image: Courtesy of the Brick Development Association.
Student Halls of residence, Aston university, Birmingham
Architect: Feilden Clegg Bradley
Photography: George Demetri

Inside Cover Images: Courtesy of the Brick Development Association

Geffrye Museum, London
Architect: Branson Coates
Photography: Locations Photography

Grand Shaft, Dover
Architect: Roger Joyce Associates

Keyworth Centre, London South Bank University.
Architect: Building Design Partnership.
Photography: Craig Auckland.

Housing at Ashwood Place, Woking, Surrey
Architect: Michael J. Wilson & Prime Meridan
Photography: Nigel Spreadbury

Every effort has been made to reach the copyright holders, but the publisher would be grateful to hear from any source whose copyright they have unwittingly infringed.

Chapter one

Conform to General Workplace Safety

NVQ Level 1   Unit No. VR 01   Conform to General Workplace Safety

This unit, in the context of brickwork and the construction industry work environment, is about:

- awareness of relevant current statutory requirements and official guidance
- personal responsibilities relating to workplace safety, wearing appropriate personal protective equipment (PPE) and compliance with warning and safety signs
- personal behaviour in the workplace
- security in the workplace.

There are six sections in this chapter: emergency procedures, fire extinguishers, hazards, notices, personal protective equipment and security.

This chapter will now cover methods that conform to general workplace safety.

EMERGENCY PROCEDURES   1.1

In this section you will learn about emergency procedures in accordance with organizational policy:

- accidents and emergencies associated with the type of work being undertaken and the work environment.

When you have completed this section you will be able to:

- comply with all emergency procedures in accordance with organizational policy.

Know and understand:

- what the organizational emergency procedures are.

Emergencies

Emergencies require immediate action. Some examples of emergencies are fire, uncontained spillage or leakage of chemicals or other hazardous substances, scaffold failure, bodily damage and health problems.

Procedures

If an evacuation alarm sounds, it must be assumed that it is a genuine alarm, unless prior notice of a system test has been given. In the event of an alarm sounding, all personnel should be aware of:

- the location of the assembly point at which to report
- the name of the person to whom they report
- the procedures to be followed after reporting at the assembly point.

Note: Under no circumstances should you re-enter the site or work area until authorized by the emergency services or your supervisor.

Roles and Responsibilities of Personnel

The operative's role in dealing with incidents and emergencies is limited to:

- Recognizing and reporting details of the incident or emergency to the person in charge
- Following all evacuation procedures as instructed
- Obtaining help from trained staff in situations requiring first-aid
- Recording details of accidents in the accident book.

Common Types of Accident and Emergency

In the European Union, the construction industry is the industry most at risk from accidents, with more than 1300 people being killed in construction accidents every year.

Source: European Agency for Safety and Health at Work, Facts, 2003.

Risks and Procedures

Common accident risks are:

- Slipping on uneven, slippery surfaces
- Trapping limbs
- Injuries caused by falling objects
- Inhalation of toxic fumes
- Burns/skin problems from chemical substances
- Electrical faults
- Strains from faulty lifting.

The law requires employers to provide:

- Adequate first-aid equipment and facilities
- A trained and qualified person to give first-aid (dependent on the size of the workforce)

The role of site personnel at the scene of an accident or emergency is to:

- Ensure that their own safety is not at risk
- Remove the hazard if safe to do so
- Call for help, for example, a first-aider
- Call for an ambulance if necessary

While awaiting the arrival of the first-aider or ambulance the operative should:

- Not move the casualty, unless in immediate danger
- Not give food or drink to the casualty
- Not allow the casualty to smoke
- Remain with the casualty and give reassurance
- Make the casualty as comfortable as possible
- Keep the casualty warm

Reporting Accidents and Near Misses

All accidents and near misses must be reported by site personnel to their supervisor and recorded. It is a legal requirement for details of an accident to be recorded in an Accident Book, which must be kept on each construction site for that purpose.

Accident Book

There is no set place to keep an Accident Book. It needs to be readily available to all site personnel. It is an employer's duty to inform all site personnel where the Accident Book is kept, usually by displaying the location on a site notice board. The company safety policy may also say where it is kept.

A site operative who has sustained an injury or taken part in dealing with an accident involving other people must enter relevant details in the Accident Book. These details will include:

- The date and time of the accident
- Where the accident took place and how it happened
- The cause of the accident
- The method of treating the accident
- Other people involved
- Own signature and date of entry.

The Health and Safety Executive (HSE) will also need to be informed if a major injury or dangerous occurrence takes place, or if the employee is off work for more than three days – see Figure 1.1.

Source: HSE, *RIDDOR Explained*, 2002.

Note – The Health and Safety Executive introduced a new accident record book in May 2003. the new publication ensures companies comply with legal requirements to record accidents at work, and it has been revised to take into account the requirements of the Data Protection Act 1998.

HSE Health & Safety Executive

Health and Safety at Work etc Act 1974
The Reporting of Injuries, Diseases and Dangerous Occurrences Regulations 1995

Report of an injury or dangerous occurrence

Filling in this form
This form must be filled in by an employer or other responsible person.

Part A
About you
1 What is your full name?
2 What is your job title?
3 What is your telephone number?

About your organisation
4 What is the name of your organisation?
5 What is its address and postcode?
6 What type of work does the organisation do?

Part B
About the incident
1 On what date did the incident happen?
2 At what time did the incident happen? (Please use the 24-hour clock eg 0600)
3 Did the incident happen at the above address?
Yes — Go to question 4
No — Where did the incident happen
- elsewhere in your organisation – give the name, address and postcode
- at someone else's premises – give the name, address and postcode
- in a public place – give details of where it happened

If you do not know the postcode, what is the name of the local authority
4 In which department, or where on the premises, did the incident happen?

F2508 (01/96)   Continued overleaf

Part C
About the injured person
If you are reporting a dangerous occurrence, go to Part F.
If more than one person was injured in the same incident, please attach the details asked for in Part C and Part D for each injured person.
1 What is their full name?
2 What is their home address and postcode?
3 What is their home phone number?
4 How old are they?
5 Are they
- male?
- female?
6 What is their job title?
7 Was the injured person (tick only one box)
- one of your employees?
- on a training scheme? Give details
- on work experience?
- employed by someone else? Give details of the employer?
- self-employed at at work?
- a member of the public?

Part D
About the injury
1 What was the injury? (eg fracture, laceration)
2 What part of the body was injured?

3 Was the injury (tick the one box that applies)
- a fatality?
- a major injury or condition? (see accompanying notes)
- an injury to an employee or self-employed person which prevented them doing their normal work for more than 3 days?
- an injury to a member of the public which meant they had to be taken from the scene of the accident to a hospital for treatment?
4 Did the injured person (tick all the boxes that apply)
- become unconscious?
- need resuscitation?
- remain in hospital for more than 24 hours?
- none of the above.

Part E
About the kind of accident
Please tick the one box that best describes what happened, then go to Part G.
- Contact with moving machinery or material being machined
- Hit by a moving, flying or falling object
- Hit by a moving vehicle
- Hit something fixed or stationary
- Injured while handling, lifting or carrying
- Slipped, tripped or fell on the same level
- Fell from a height How high was the fall? ___ metres
- Trapped by something collapsing
- Drowned or asphyxiated
- Exposed to, or in contact with, a harmful substance
- Exposed to fire
- Exposed to an explosion
- Contact with electricity or an electrical discharge
- Injured by an animal
- Physically assaulted by a person
- Another kind of accident (describe it in Part G)

Part F
Dangerous occurrences
Enter the number of the dangerous occurrence you are reporting. (The numbers are given in the Regulations and in the notes which accompany this form.)

For official use
Client number   Location number   Event number
INV REP Y N

Part C
Describing what happened
Give as much detail as you can. For instance
- the name of any substance involved
- the name and type oof any machine involved
- the events that led to the incident
- the part played by any people.
If it was a personal injury, give details of what the person was doing. Describe any action that has since been taken to prevent a similar incident. Use a separate piece of paper if you need to.

Part H
Your signature
Signature
Date
Where to send the form
Please send it to the Enforcing Authority the place where it happened. If you do not know the Enforcing Authority, send it to the nearest HSE office.

Fig 1.1 Official HSE report form
Source HSE

Work-based Evidence Required

■ Organizational procedures in case of accident and/or fire

To meet this requirement, obtain a witness testimony sheet from your supervisor stating that you carried out your company's organizational procedures in respect of an accident and/or fire on site. Place the evidence in your work-based evidence portfolio when next in college and map and record it against the syllabus.

Note: This item may be simulated if required.

Common Words and Meanings

Health and safety has a lot of terms and meanings that need to be read, understood and remembered.

Accident

This is an unplanned or unwanted event or occurrence that may result in injury to a person and/or damage to property.

Competent Person

This is someone who has carried out training in a certain task and is able to carry it out unsupervised.

First Aid

This is the method of treating minor injuries where other treatment is not needed. This minimizes any chance of further injury or illness until a doctor, nurse or paramedic arrives.

Hazard

This is something that can cause harm, illness or damage to health or property.

Improvement Notice

This is issued by the HSE to state what is wrong and what is required to be put right, usually to a given timescale.

Kinetic Lifting

This is the term used to describe the correct method of lifting.

Mandatory/Compulsory

This must be done. For example, a circular sign with a blue background, such as wear a hard hat.

Prohibition Notice

This is issued by the HSE on employers or employees where, in their opinion, there is an imminent risk of an accident. The work must stop immediately. Matters must be corrected before the notice is lifted.

Regulations

These are rules that have been put in place to ensure work is carried out both correctly and safely.

Risk

This is the likelihood or chance that harm, illness or damage will occur and the degree of harm (how many people might be affected and how badly).

Risk Assessment

This is mainly carried out by an employer to identify risks to his or her employees (and others) and decide what is necessary to control these risks to the standards required under the law.

Source: **Department for Education and Skills,** *Improving Teaching and Learning in Construction,* **2004.**

Emergency Procedures

A common emergency on construction sites is fire. Described below are the procedures for dealing with such an occurrence.

If you discover a fire:

- Raise the alarm and then call the Fire Brigade
- Close doors and windows to prevent the spread of fire
- Evacuate the building or area where you are working
- Fight the fire, if you have been trained to do so, but avoid endangering life
- Fight the fire with an appropriate fire extinguisher, fire blankets, water or sand, but do not put yourself at risk.

In order to save lives and reduce the risk of injury occurring, all site personnel must be informed of the current safety and emergency procedures. All site personnel must be aware of what to do in the event of a fire or accident.

What Fires Need

In order for a fire to start the following must be present:

Fuel – This can be anything that will burn, for example wood, furniture, flammable liquid, gas and so on.

Oxygen – or air in normal circumstances, will allow a fire to burn.

Heat – A minimum temperature is required but a naked flame, match or spark is enough to start a fire especially if in contact with something flammable – see Figure 1.2.

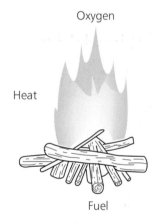

Oxygen

Heat

Fuel

Fig 1.2 **Things that feed fires (wood, furniture, flammable liquid, etc.)**

TRY THIS OUT

- Prepare a list of at least eight common types of accident or health emergency that could be encountered on a building site or in the workplace.
- Describe three things you should do in carrying out your roles and responsibilities in dealing with incidents or emergencies.

Prevention of Fires

Some actions that can be taken to prevent the risk of fire occurring are as follows:

- Not smoking at work
- Maintaining all electrical appliances in a safe manner
- Removing burnable materials to a safe place
- Storing flammable materials in metal cupboards
- Putting up signs and notices so personnel know what to do
- Training all personnel in health and safety.

Source: **Department for Education and Skills,** *Trowel Occupations,* **2004.**

Quick quiz Quick quiz Quick quiz Quick quiz Quick quiz

❶ What code is used for an accident report form?
❷ Give the three elements that are required to start a fire.
❸ Name three specific types of emergency.
❹ Name three common accident risks.
❺ What is an accident book used for?
❻ What do the initials HSE stand for?
❼ What is the biggest cause of death in accidents in the UK?
❽ What two things does the law require employers to provide?
❾ Where should all accidents be reported?

FIRE EXTINGUISHERS   1.2

In this section you will learn about the following types of fire extinguishers, water, CO_2, foam, powder, vaporizing liquid and their uses.

When you have completed this section you will be able to:

■ comply with all emergency procedures in accordance with organizational policy.

Know and understand:

■ what types of fire extinguishers are available and how they are used.

Fire Extinguishers

There are five different types of fire extinguisher for use in the fighting of fires. You will need to learn to choose the correct one. Each type of fire extinguisher is designed to put out fires that are caused by specific circumstances. It can be extremely dangerous to use the wrong type of extinguisher.

The standard colour for fire extinguishers is red, with the contents indicated by a contrasting colour band or panel on the extinguisher. There are also pictograms showing what type of fire it can be used on.

Colour Codes for Fire Extinguishers

Type of extinguisher – Water
Colour Code – Red
For use on – Solid fuels, e.g. wood, paper and textiles
Do not use on – Flammable liquids or live electrical equipment – see Figure 1.3.

Type of extinguisher – Foam
Colour Code – Cream
For use on – Wood, paper, textiles and flammable liquids.
Do not use on – Live electrical equipment – see Figure 1.3.

Type of extinguisher – Dry Powder
Colour Code – Blue
For use on – Wood, paper and textiles, flammable liquids, gaseous fires and live electrical equipment – see Figure 1.3.

Type of extinguisher – Carbon Dioxide
Colour Code – Black
For use on – Flammable liquids and live electrical equipment.
Do not use this type of extinguisher in a confined space – see Figure 1.3.

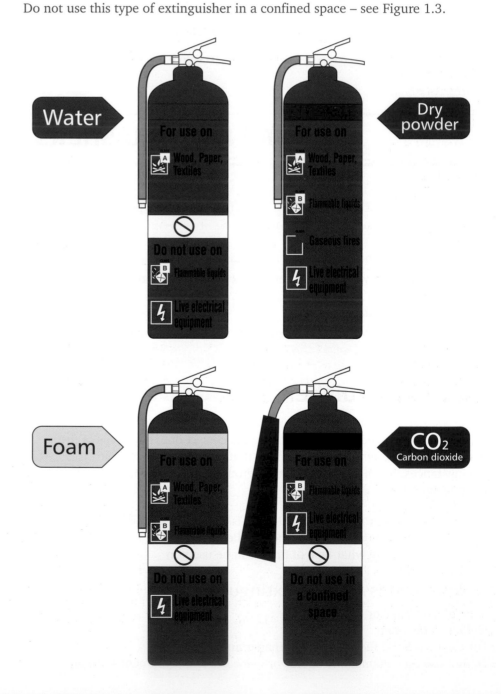

Fig. 1.3 **Know your fire extinguisher colour codes**

Type of extinguisher – Halon
Colour Code – Green
For use on – Flammable and liquefied gases and electrical hazards.
Note: Halon extinguishers are being phased out for environmental reasons.

Source: Department for Education and Skills. *Improving Teaching and Learning in construction*, 2004.

Fire Blankets

In addition to the various types of fire extinguisher, there are fire blankets. These are fireproof blankets which, when laid on a fire, cut off the oxygen supply and prevent further burning of the substance. They can be used on all types of fires.

Using a Fire Extinguisher

Every fire extinguisher has brief instructions on how it should be used. The method of use varies across the range of types and makes of extinguisher.

Fire extinguishers are pressurized so that by operating a trigger, the contents will be forced out of the extinguisher, at a high speed, towards the source of the fire. The contents and pressure of the extinguisher should be checked regularly and each extinguisher should have a label certifying that it has been inspected and meets the requirements.

The jet from a fire extinguisher should only be directed at the centre of the fire because of the pressure at which the contents are ejected. The pressure could cause burning debris to spread and create a wider hazard. Instead, the jet should be aimed around and over the fire, gradually containing it to the point where it is extinguished totally.

Fire extinguishers should only be used when it is safe to do so and the user is properly trained. Smoke and toxic fumes are as dangerous as the fire itself and, in general, the fighting of fires is best left to the fire service. Small fires can be dealt with if there are clear escape routes and if they can be extinguished quickly, thereby preventing the spread of fire.

> *Point to note*
>
> Fire extinguishers should only be used if the user is properly trained. Untrained users could make the situation worse.

Work-based Evidence Required

■ Safe use of fire extinguishers, as appropriate to the fire.

To meet this requirement, obtain a witness testimony sheet from your supervisor stating that you safely used fire extinguishers that were appropriate to the fire. Place the evidence in your work-based evidence portfolio when next in college and map and record it against the syllabus.

Note: This item may be simulated if required.

Quick quiz Quick quiz Quick quiz Quick quiz Quick quiz

❶ List four types of fire extinguisher.

❷ What is the standard colour code for a fire extinguisher?

❸ What are the colour codes for the contents of a fire extinguisher?

❹ What type of fire extinguisher is being phased out, and why?

❺ How many different types of fire extinguisher are there for use in the fighting of fires.

❻ What is the colour code for a dry powder extinguisher?

❼ What type of fire extinguisher would you use on a wood, paper or textile fire?

❽ What type of fire would you fight with an extinguisher with the colour code black?

HAZARDS 1.3

In this section you will learn about hazards associated with the work area. These include:

◼ Resources, workplace, environment, substances, equipment, obstructions, storage, services and work activities.

When you have completed this section you will be able to:

◼ Identify hazards associated with the workplace and record and report in accordance with organizational procedure

◼ Recognize potentially hazardous situations in the workshop or work area

◼ Plan, organize and maintain a safe working environment for site personnel.

Know and understand:

◼ The hazards associated with the work area.

Hazards in the Workplace

On the majority of construction sites in the UK, there is great emphasis on protecting construction personnel and the general public from hazards associated with the work area and certain types of work practice.

Head Protection

Falling materials or tools on building sites can cause injury to the head and other parts of the body. It is not only essential but the law dictates protective headgear be worn at all times by all site personnel and visitors in order to minimize the hazard (see Figure 1.4).

key terms

Hazard – A hazard is something with the potential to cause harm.

Noise

Excessive noise levels from site machinery can cause damage to hearing if workers are exposed to it continually. Therefore ear defenders must be worn to protect the ear drums. Young people's hearing can be damaged as easily as that of the old and premature deafness is even worse. Sufferers often first start to notice hearing loss when they cannot keep up with conversations in a group, or for example when the rest of their family complain they have the television on too loud. Deafness that can make people feel isolated from their family, friends and colleagues (see Figure 1.5).

Fig. 1.4 **Bricklayer wearing a hard hat**

**EAR DEFENDERS
BS 6344 EN 352-2**

A wide range of equipment on site can be harmful to your ears. Even if you are not using the equipment, you can still be affected when someone is using it close by.

If you have to shout to be heard then ear defenders should be worn

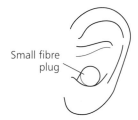

Small fibre plug

Small fibre earplugs can be used where noise is not too severe

Hands should be clean before inserting plugs and plugs should be disposed of after one use.

Where excessive noise is encountered full earmuffs should be used.

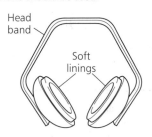

Head band

Soft linings

Fig. 1.5 **Ear muffs and information**

Manual Handling

Manual handling is transporting or supporting loads by hand or using bodily force. Many people hurt their back, arms, hands or feet lifting everyday loads, not just when the load is too heavy. More than a third of all over-three-day injuries reported each year to the Health and Safety Executive and to local authorities are the result of manual handling. These can result in those being injured taking an average of 11 working days off each year.

Most cases of injury can be avoided by providing suitable lifting equipment, which is regularly maintained, together with relevant training on both manual handling techniques and safe use of the equipment.

Electricity

Electricity can kill. Most deaths are caused by contact with overhead or underground power cables. Even non-fatal shocks can cause severe and permanent injury. Shocks from equipment may lead to falls from ladders, scaffolds or other work platforms. Those using electricity may not be the only ones at risk. Poor electrical installation and faulty electrical appliances can lead to fires which can also result in death or injury to others.

Work Equipment

Work equipment covers an enormous range, including process machinery, machine tools, office machines, lifting equipment, hand tools and ladders. Important points include:

    selecting the right equipment for the job

- making sure equipment is safe to use and keeping it safe through regular maintenance
- inspection and, if appropriate, thorough examination
- training of personnel to use equipment safely and following manufacturers' or suppliers' instructions.

Accidents involving work equipment happens all the time – many serious, some fatal (see Figure 1.6).

Workplace Transport

Every year about 70 people are killed and about 2500 seriously injured in accidents involving vehicles at the workplace. Being struck or run over by moving vehicles, falling from vehicles, or vehicles over-turning are the most common causes. Vehicles operating in the workplace include cars and vans, lift trucks, heavy goods vehicles, dumpers, specialized vehicles or plant. Often there is significantly more danger from vehicles in the workplace than on the public highway since the operating conditions are different.

Fig. 1.6 **Worker using power tools**

Slipping and Tripping

The most common cause of injuries at work is the slip or trip. Resulting falls can be serious. They happen in all kinds of business, with the construction industry reporting higher than average numbers. These cost employers over £300 million a year in lost production and other costs.

Hazardous Substances

Thousands of people are exposed to all kinds of hazardous substances at work. These can include chemicals that people make or work with directly, and also dust, fumes and bacteria which can be present in the workplace. Exposure can happen by breathing them in, contact with the skin, splashing them into the eyes or swallowing them. If exposure is not prevented or properly controlled, it can cause serious illness, including cancer, and dermatitis, trigger asthma and sometimes even cause death.

Asbestos

Asbestos is the largest single cause of work-related fatal disease and ill health in the UK. Almost all asbestos-related deaths and ill health are from exposure several decades ago, but if you work with asbestos, or come into contact with it during repair and maintenance work, you are at risk. You should avoid working with asbestos if possible, but if you can't you must do so safely. Asbestos can be found in buildings built from 1950 to 1985 in many forms.

Flammable Substances

Small quantities of dangerous goods can be found in most workplaces. Whatever they are used for, the storage and use of such goods can pose a serious hazard unless basic safety principles are followed. If you use one particular group of dangerous goods – flammable and explosive – this section will be of help to you.

Safety Principles

If your employers apply the following five principles recommended by the Health and Safety Executive, they will be well on the way to making sure you are working safely with flammable substances. All workers should be aware of the principles.

Ventilation

Is there plenty of fresh air where flammable liquids or gases are stored and used? Good ventilation will mean that any vapours given off from a spill or leak, or released from any process, will be rapidly dispersed.

Ignition

Have all the obvious ignition sources been removed from the storage and handling area? Ignition sources can vary and include sparks from electrical equipment or welding and cutting tools, hot surfaces, open flames from heating equipment, smoking materials, and so on.

Containment

Are your flammable substances kept in suitable containers? If you have a spill will it be contained and prevented from spreading to other parts of the working area? Use of lidded containers and spillage catchment trays, for example, can help to prevent spillages spreading.

Exchange

Can you exchange a flammable substance for a less flammable one? Can you eliminate flammable substances from the process altogether? You may be able to think of other ways of carrying out the job more safely.

Separation

Are flammable substances stored and used well away from other processes and general storage areas? Can they be separated by a physical barrier, wall or partition? Separating your hazards in this manner will contribute to a safer workplace.

The Health and Safety Executive advise employers to apply these five principles wherever possible.

Emergencies

Staff are instructed in emergency procedures as an important part of their job training. Examples of things you will be made aware of are:

- the importance of preventing the mixing of incompatible chemicals
- the procedures to be followed if there is a leak or spill of flammable material
- how to use any special first-aid facilities or equipment.

Work at Height

Falls from a height account for around 70 fatalities and 4000 major injuries every year. One of the main causes is falls from ladders. To prevent falls, you should be provided with adequate training and suitable and safe equipment for tasks, which should be properly managed and supervised. Suitable and sufficient personal protective equipment should be in place when you are working at height.

Control of Substances Hazardous to Health Regulations 2002 (COSHH)

Using chemicals or other hazardous substances at work can put people's health at risk. So the law requires employers to control exposure to hazardous substances to prevent ill health. Employers have to protect both site personnel and others who may be exposed, by complying with COSHH.

Hazardous Substances

Hazardous substances include:

- substances used directly in work activities, for example, adhesives, paints, cleaning agents
- substances generated during work activities, for example, fumes from soldering and welding
- naturally occurring substances, for example, grain dust
- biological agents such as bacteria and other micro-organisms.

REMEMBER

Keep a check on your workplace safety.

Where are hazardous substances found? In nearly all work environments, for example:

➤ factories

➤ shops

➤ mines

➤ farms

➤ construction sites

Examples of the effects of hazardous substances include:

➤ skin irritation or dermatitis as a result of skin contact

➤ asthma as a result of being overcome by toxic fumes

➤ losing consciousness as a result of being overcome by toxic fumes

➤ cancer, which may appear long after the exposure to the chemical that caused it

➤ infection from bacteria and other micro-organisms (biological agents).

Substances Hazardous to Health

What is a substance hazardous to health under the COSHH regulations? Under COSHH there are a range of substances classified as dangerous to health under the Chemical Regulations 2002. These can be identified by their warning label and the supplier must provide a safety sheet for them. Many commonly used dangerous substances are listed in the Health and Safety Executive's publication *Approved Supply List*. Suppliers must decide if preparations and substances that are not in the Approved Supply List are dangerous, and, if so, label them accordingly.

Substances with occupational exposure limits are listed in the HSE publication, *Occupational Exposure Limits*.

Biological agents (bacteria and other micro-organisms) are hazardous, particularly those that are directly connected with work, such as farming, sewage treatment, or healthcare, or if the exposure is incidental to work, for example, exposure to bacteria from an air-conditioning system that is not properly maintained.

Any kind of dust if its average concentration in the air exceeds the levels specified in COSHH.

For the vast majority of commercial chemicals, the presence (or not) of a warning label will indicate whether COSHH is relevant.

Advice and Information

If in doubt, contact your local HSE office (the address is in the phone book). The staff there can refer you to the appropriate inspector or the environmental health officer at your local authority.

First Aid

First aid arrangements will vary with the degree of risk on the site but should usually include as a minimum:

- first aid facilities placed in a convenient location (see Figure 1.7)
- a trained first aider, though for small sites it is sufficient to appoint a person to take charge of the first aid box and any situation where serious injury or major illness occurs
- information for site personnel about first aid arrangements, including the location of the nearest telephone.

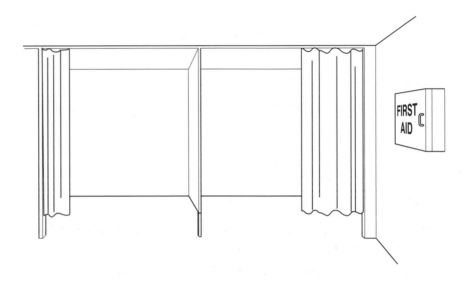

Fig. 1.7 **First aid box**

Through the initial management of injury or illness suffered at work, lives can be saved and minor injuries prevented from becoming major ones.

The objectives of first aid are to:

- save life
- prevent the casualty's condition from getting worse
- access medical help as soon as possible.

Before first aid is required ensure that:

- you know where the first aid box is kept
- you know who the first-aider and appointed persons are
- anything used from the first aid box has been replaced
- if you are working in a small group away from the main site you have a small travelling first aid kit.

When first aid is required:

- call for help from someone knowledgeable, preferably the first-aider
- send someone to telephone for an ambulance if necessary
- do not move the casualty, unless in immediate danger
- remain with the casualty and give reassurance
- make the casualty as comfortable as possible

- do not give drinks or food to the casualty, moisten lips only
- do not allow the casualty to smoke.

Source: HSE. First Aid at Work. 2002

Safety Organization

Large construction sites should have a safety officer employed by the contractor to ensure that all work areas are safe. On smaller building sites where there is no safety officer, the foreman or supervisor is usually responsible for the implementation of site safety.

Safety programmes and laws are only effective if:

- they are enforced on site
- they are legally enforceable
- all members of staff are aware of safety.

The Health and Safety at Work Act 1974 (HASAWA)

HASAWA covers the health and safety of almost everyone in the workplace. The main objectives of HASAWA are:

- to secure the health and safety and welfare of all persons at work
- to protect the general public from risk to health and safety arising out of work activities
- to control the use, handling, storage and transporting of explosives and highly flammable substances
- to control the release of noxious or offensive substances into the atmosphere.

HASAWA is enforced by inspectors, employed by the Health and Safety Executive (HSE). Their authority permits them to:

- enter premises to carry out investigations involving taking photographs, recording and samples
- take statements
- check records
- give advice and information
- seize, dismantle, neutralize or destroy material, equipment or substances that are likely to cause immediate serious personal injury
- issue prohibition notices – put right within a specified period of time any minor hazard or infringement of legislation
- prosecute all persons who fail to comply with their duty under HASAWA.

TRY THIS OUT

- Analyse the reasons why accidents occur.
- Think about the reasons and draw conclusions about the ways in which accidents can be prevented.
- Present your findings in report form.

Work-based Evidence Required

- **Hazards, associated with the workplace and occupations at work, are recorded and/or reported.**

Meeting the Requirements

To meet this requirement, obtain a witness testimony sheet from your supervisor stating that you recorded and reported a hazard at work. Place the evidence in your work-based evidence portfolio when next in college and map and record it against the syllabus.

Quick quiz Quick quiz Quick quiz Quick quiz Quick quiz

1. Define the term hazardous substance.
2. Explain the term manual handling.
3. What is the most common cause of injuries at work?
4. Define risk assessment.
5. List the types of fire protection equipment.

NOTICES   1.4

In this section you will learn about notices, statutory requirements and official guidance for construction and the work area.

When you have completed this section you will be able to:

- comply with all workplace safety requirements at all times.

Know and understand:

- what safety legislation notices are relevant to the work area.

The Health and Safety (Safety Signs and Signals) Regulations 1996

These regulations bring into force the European Community Safety Signs Directive on the provision and use of safety signs at work. The purpose of the Directive is to encourage the standardization of safety signs throughout the member states of the European Union so that safety signs have the same meaning wherever they are seen.

Identification of Safety Signs and Notices

All employers have to provide safety signs in a variety of different situations that do, or may, affect health and safety.

Safety signs and notices give warnings of possible danger and must always be obeyed. To be safe on a construction site you will need to recognize, understand and respond to a lot of different safety signs.

Safety signs fall into five separate categories. These can be recognized by their shape and colour. This is to make sure that everyone understands health and safety information in a simple, bold and effective way, with little or no use of words.

The five categories for basic safety signs are as follows:

Fig. 1.8 **Prohibition sign**

Prohibition Signs

Shape – They are circular

Colour – They have a red border and cross bar with a black symbol on a white background.

Meaning – They show people what must not be done. For example, no smoking in college (see Figure 1.8).

Mandatory Signs

Shape – They are circular

Fig. 1.9 **Mandatory sign**

Colour – They have a white symbol on a blue background

Meaning – They show you what must be done. For example, wear your safety helmet (see Figure 1.9).

Warning Signs

Shape – They are triangular

Fig. 1.10 **Warning sign**

Colour – They have a yellow background with a black border and symbol

Meaning – They warn you of hazard or danger. For example, caution, there is a risk of an electric shock (see Figure 1.10).

Information Signs

Shape – They are square or oblong

Colour – They have white symbols on a green background

Fig. 1.11 **Information sign**

Meaning – They indicate or give information about safety provision. For example, location of the first aid point (see Figure 1.11).

Fire Safety Signs

Shape – They are square or rectangular

Colour – They have white symbols on a red background

Meaning – They give the location of fire information, fire alarms or fire-fighting equipment. For example, location of a fire extinguisher or fire hose reel (see Figure 1.12)

Examples of Safety Signs

To be safe at work you will need to recognize, understand and respond to a lot of different safety signs. The signs in Figure 1.13 help you to recognize the types of safety signs and their meaning and to understand how and where to use the signs.

Fig 1.12 **Fire safety sign**

> REMEMBER
>
> You can recognize signs from their shape. Write in the type of sign, the colour and the general meaning of each of the signs in Figure 1.13.

Ear protectors must be worn in this area

Eye protection must be worn

Foot protection must be worn

Hand protection must be worn

Head protection must be worn

Caution Risk of fire

DANGER Corrosion risk

Fig. 1.13 **Safety signs**

Signs with Supplementary Text

Any information signs may be supplemented by text. A number of examples of supplementary signs are illustrated in Figure 1.14

Source: HSE, Safety signs and signals, 2002.

> *Points to note*
>
> Remember always look out for and obey safety signs, they are there for your protection.

Fig. 1.14 Signs with supplementary text

TRY THIS OUT

- Prepare a list of safety considerations that site personnel need to observe when erecting, taking down and dismantling access equipment.
- Present the list to your supervisor and ask for it to be compared with the official procedures in order to check the correctness of your findings.

Work-based Evidence Required

■ **Adherence to statutory requirements and/or safety notices and warning signs displayed in the workplace.**

To meet this requirement, obtain a witness testimony sheet from your supervisor stating that you have adhered to statutory requirements, safety notices and warning signs on site. Place the evidence in your work-based evidence portfolio when next in college and map and record it against the syllabus.

Quick quiz Quick quiz Quick quiz Quick quiz Quick quiz

❶ What regulations govern safety signs?

❷ What shape is a mandatory sign?

❸ What colours are used for warning signs?

❹ How many different categories of safety sign are there?

❺ What type of sign would you find near a fire exit?

❻ What colours are used on information signs?

❼ What shape is a prohibition sign?

❽ Name the different categories of safety sign.

❾ Draw four types of safety sign, each from a different category using the correct colours.

❿ What instruction is given on a mandatory sign?

PERSONAL PROTECTIVE EQUIPMENT (PPE)   1.5

In this section you will learn about PPE as required for the general work environment that includes:
- helmets, ear defenders, overalls, safety footwear, and high visibility vests and jackets.

When you have completed this section you will be able to:
- comply with all workplace safety legislation requirements at all times
- identify building site or work conditions which require special safety precautions
- identify, select and use protective clothing correctly
- identify, select and use safety equipment correctly.

Know and understand:
- why and where personal protective equipment should be used.

Introduction

The use of personal protective equipment (PPE) is not the solution to preventing accidents. It is more important to identify possible hazards and take the necessary steps to eliminate them.

Safety footwear will, for example, protect against nails penetrating the foot. Ordinary shoes will probably not do so. However, the initial problem is the nail hazard, not the lack of safety footwear. The wearing of PPE is therefore a back-up for an effective site safety programme (see Figure 1.15).

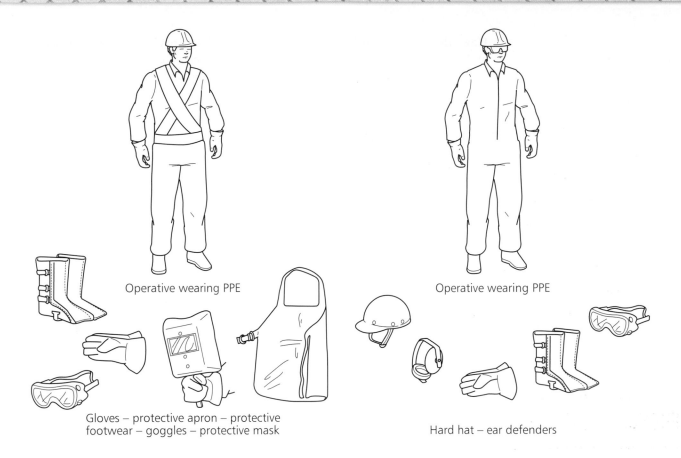

Operative wearing PPE

Operative wearing PPE

Gloves – protective apron – protective footwear – goggles – protective mask

Hard hat – ear defenders

Fig. 1.15 **Items of personal protective equipment**

Safety Provisions

- All personnel must be provided with protective clothing and other PPE
- national standards regarding PPE must be observed
- all personnel must be instructed in the use of the PPE provided
- personnel should make proper use and take proper care of the PPE provided
- all PPE should be kept fit for immediate use
- all necessary measures should be taken by the employer to ensure that protective clothing and the PPE are effectively worn.

Personal Protective Equipment

A wide range of safety clothing and equipment is available to safeguard the health and safety of people at work. It is therefore important when working to know the different types of protective clothing and PPE required for separate tasks.

Head and Neck Protection

Safety helmets – must be worn at all times when working on a construction site.

Hazards – Helmets are worn to protect the head and neck from falling objects and from knocks against obstructions, and where necessary to protect the head from possible electric shocks. The proctective helmets should be insulated or made of insulating material.

Personnel working in the sun in hot weather should wear a suitable head covering.

Choices – helmets; hats; caps; and cape hoods.

Eye Protection

Eye protection must be worn when carrying out operations that are likely to produce dust, chips or sparks, for example cutting bricks and blocks (see Figure 1.16).

Hazards – chemical or metal splash; dust projectiles; gas and vapour; radiation.

Choices – spectacles; goggles; face-screens.

Fig. 1.16 **Eye protection, e.g. goggles, spectacles, face screens**

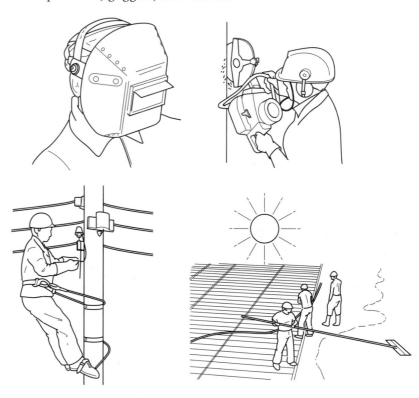

Breathing

Dust masks – must be worn when carrying out operations that produce dust, for example, sweeping up after the day's work. The dust masks used on a construction site are lightweight and reasonably comfortable. They should under no circumstances be worn by more than one person and should be disposed of after use (see Figure 1.17)

Hazards – dust; vapour; gas; oxygen deficient atmospheres.

Choices – disposable filtering face-piece or respirator; half/full face respirators; air-fed helmets; breathing apparatus.

**DUST MASKS
BS 2091**

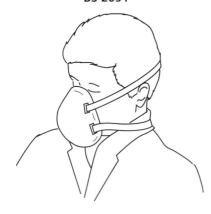

Fig. 1.17 Dust masks

Hand and Arm Protection

Gloves – Different types of gloves are available for a variety of operations. Leather gloves are worn for general protection such as when handling timber, bricks, or bags of cement and lime. Rubber gloves should be worn when using chemicals, for example brick cleaning acid (see Figure 1.18).

Hazards – abrasion; temperature extremes; cuts and punctures; impact; chemicals; electric shock; skin infection; disease or contamination; vibration.

Choices – gloves; gauntlets; mitts; wrist-cuffs; armlets.

Foot and Leg Protection

Safety Footwear – Must be worn at all times on construction sites. Safety footwear offers protection from crushing or penetration injuries (see Figure 1.19).

Hazards – wet; electrostatic build-up; slipping; cuts and punctures; falling objects; metal and chemical splash; abrasion.

Choices – safety boots and shoes with steel toe caps and steel mid sole; gaiters; leggings.

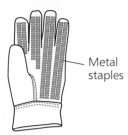

Metal staples

GLOVES ARMOURED WITH STAPLES
Use when handling heavy blocks, concrete and steel lintels

LIGHTWEIGHT TWILL GLOVES
Use when handling cement and timber

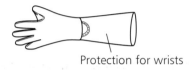

Protection for wrists

CHROME LEATHER GAUNTLET
Use when handling glass to give protection to the hand and wrist

Fig. 1.18 Gloves, e.g. leather gloves/rubber gloves

Foot protection

Workers should wear footwear of an appropriate type when employed at places where they might be exposed to injury from:
• falling objects
• hot, corrosive or poisonous substances
• sharp-edged tools (axes, etc.)
• nails
• abnormally wet surfaces
• slippery or ice-covered surfaces

Worker wearing protective footwear whilst cutting blocks

Worker wearing protective footwear whilst working in wet concrete

Fig. 1.19 Foot protection, e.g. safety footwear

Protecting the Body

Overalls and protective clothing should be worn at all times on construction sites. They are designed to protect you from dust and spillages and other hazards, and keep your daily clothes clean (see Figure 1.20).

Hazards – temperature extremes; adverse weather; chemical or metal splash; spray from pressure leaks or spray guns; impact or penetration; contaminated dust; excessive wear or entanglement of own clothing.

Choices – conventional or disposable overalls; boiler suits; donkey jackets; specialist protective clothing, e.g. chain-mail aprons; high visibility clothing.

Source: HSE, Personal Protective Equipment, 2002.

Fig. 1.20 **Safety clothing**

Protection Against Site Traffic

Operatives who are regularly exposed to danger from moving site vehicles should wear:

- distinguishing clothing, preferably bright yellow or orange in colour; or
- clothing of reflecting or otherwise conspicuously visible material (see Figure 1.21).

Vehicles such as earth moving equipment, fork lifts, trucks, ready mixed concrete lorries and so on, should have a distinct warning signal which activates automatically when the vehicle reverses (see Figure 1.22)

Source: International Labour Office, Geneva, Personal Protective Clothing and Equipment, 1989.

Equipment Checks

Frequent safety checks of workshop equipment, construction sites, scaffolding and safety equipment such as fire extinguishers and so on are mandatory on all building sites.

Fig. 1.21 Site traffic clothing

Fig. 1.22 Truck reversing

Work-based Evidence Required

■ **Safe use of general personal protective equipment (PPE) when in the work environment, in accordance with legislation and/or organizational requirements**

Fig. 1.23 Bricklayer working whilst wearing PPE

To meet this requirement, obtain photographs of yourself wearing personal protective equipment whilst carrying out bricklaying activities. The PPE might include the following: safety helmet; safety boots; high visibility vest; goggles; ear defenders; gloves, and so on.

When the photographs have been developed, place them on a photo evidence sheet, and get your supervisor to authenticate them by signing and dating them. Place the evidence in your work-based evidence portfolio, when next in college and map and record it against the syllabus. Figure 1.23 shows a bricklayer carrying out the actions mentioned above as an example of the type of evidence required.

Quick quiz **Quick quiz** Quick quiz Quick quiz Quick quiz

❶ What do the initials PPE stand for?

❷ List four items of PPE that should be worn when lifting heavy and sharp objects on to a platform.

❸ What does the abbreviation HSE stand for?

❹ List three safety provisions relating to the use of PPE.

❺ How would you safeguard site personnel against site traffic?

❻ Name the PPE that would be worn when cutting bricks.

❼ Why is the wearing of PPE not the solution to preventing accidents?

❽ What type of PPE should be worn when working in strong sunlight?

❾ List eight items of PPE.

❿ What measures should an employer take in relation to PPE?

SECURITY   1.6

In this section you will learn about organizational procedures relating to the general public, site personnel and resources.

When you have completed this section you will be able to:

- comply with and maintain all organizational security arrangements and approved procedures

know and understand:

- how security arrangements are implemented in the workplace.

Security Controls

It is very important that adequate security controls are established at the start of a building project. Materials and components stored on site are valuable items, as are the plant and equipment. Loss of equipment can involve the contractor in delays both in obtaining replacements and dealing with insurance enquiries, and the extra paperwork involved.

The majority of large companies employ their own security staff and have written information for site managers, outlining the standard security procedures. The site manager should establish basic security arrangements and maintain them throughout the project.

> **Points to note**
>
> There is no point having a complex security system on site if it is not adhered to or treated casually by site personnel.

Protection of the General Public

The main contractor is solely responsible for the safety of the general public either on the site or on land or workings immediately adjoining the site. Precautions taken to protect the general public from harm are as follows.

Hoardings

To prevent unauthorized access to the site, hoardings must be in place. They should be of suitably substantial construction and properly erected. Where a hoarding approaches a public footpath adjoining a road, the contractor must ensure the safety of pedestrians by constructing a walkway with a suitable barrier preventing road accidents. If there is overhead work within that area the walkway has to be covered. Adequate lighting must be installed for both day and night – see Figure 1.24.

Compounds

The site compound is vulnerable during working hours, particularly during breaks, and when hired vans and private vehicles are allowed to gain access to the site.

There are two basic types of site storage to consider:

- accommodation in site huts, where a storeman issues materials to authorized personnel

Fig. 1.24 **A site hoarding with lighting**

covered storage which contains bulk materials which cannot be left exposed to the weather or site personnel.

The former must be sited within the perimeter fence of the compound and provided with separate access through the fence, although the store itself must be sealed off from the compound – see Figure 1.25.

Access

Access on to and exit from the site varies according to the nature of the site, that is, the levels of any existing buildings and of those to be built. Exit from the site is preferably on a quiet side road free from traffic and pedestrians. Access around the site is made on temporary roads of consolidated hardcore and steel mats. The position of access roads depends upon sitings for storage, mixing points, and so on, see Figure 1.25.

All lorries, private vehicles and vans must be controlled from the time they enter the site until they leave. The services of a person to man the access and exit to the site may be more cost effective in the long term than the replacement of stolen materials.

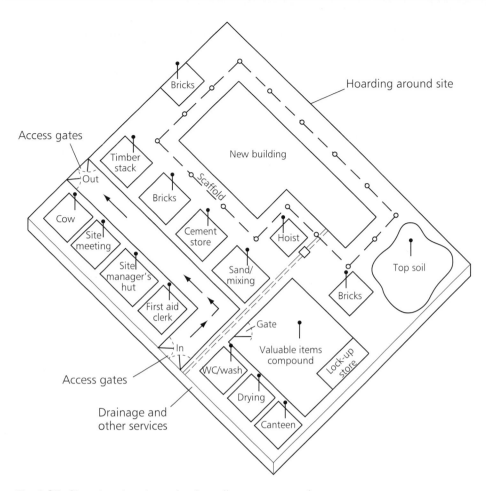

Fig. 1.25 Site plan showing exits, hoardings, compounds, etc.

Security of Resources

Security of materials generally poses a problem to site managers. A suitable system of materials control should be adopted to show: present stock; deliveries; amounts and so on. Controls are required to prevent theft from within the workplace as well as potential outside risks. These controls will monitor the materials used and hence, materials wastage. Site cleanliness and layout also give some indication of how well a site is being run.

Large amounts of materials and components should not be left unprotected on delivery vehicles overnight and when offloaded should be evenly distributed between various points on the site to discourage thieves. Materials should always be stored in an orderly manner and covered with protective sheeting.

Security Lighting

Good lighting of the site will help to reduce theft, vandalism and other intrusion, particularly by children. Lighting the stores and compound areas will discourage intruders at night, and help security patrols.

A purpose designed security lighting system should cover the perimeter, access routes, vehicle compounds, materials compounds and open areas. The degree of risk will determine the required standard of lighting, after allowing for the brightness of the surrounding area. Lighting costs depend on the shape and contours of the area to be lit, the level of illumination required, and the hours the system will be in use.

Fire Precautions

Despite the high cost of materials and components stored in site compounds, precautions against damage by fire are very limited on the average construction site, and in some cases non-existent.

To reduce the risk of the spread of fire, site stores, site offices and other temporary buildings should be positioned at least 6 metres away from main buildings, and temporary offices should be built with a reasonable distance between them of at least 3 metres. All areas around site offices and stores should be kept free from combustible materials, including grass or weeds. Similar precautions should be taken at the perimeter of compounds and next to site hoardings.

Fire Fighting Equipment

Water supplies and other fire fighting equipment should be convenient for use in the case of fire. All fire fighting equipment should be located and marked with a prominent notice close to the site entrance and other high risk areas and must be kept free from obstructions at all times. Notices should also be displayed in prominent places around the site drawing the attention of all site personnel to the dangers of fire, quoting the telephone number of the nearest fire station.

Flammable Substances

Small supplies of flammable substances should be kept in clearly marked containers with securely fastened caps or lids in a well ventilated store built with brick walls, concrete floor and non-combustible roof. This store should be sited well away from other buildings and marked with a prominent notice, stating that the contents are highly inflammable see Figure 1.26.

Toxic

Corrosive

Risk of explosion

Flammable

Fig. 1.26 Hazard signs

TRY THIS OUT

Using your knowledge of safety information sources, mention organizations that could provide information on, for example,

- asbestos precautions,
- flammable substances,
- fire prevention,
- scaffolding safety
- guards for machines.

Work-based Evidence Required

■ **Organizational procedures for maintaining the security of the workplace:**

■ during the working day

■ on completion of the days work

■ from unauthorized personnel (other operatives and/or the general public)

■ from theft.

To meet this requirement obtain a witness testimony sheet from your supervisor stating that you carried out the organizational procedures for maintaining the security of the workplace, as described above.

When you have received the signed and dated witness testimony sheet from your supervisor, place them in your work-based evidence portfolio when next in college and map and record it against the syllabus.

Quick quiz Quick quiz Quick quiz Quick quiz Quick quiz

❶ Why is it important to have security controls?
❷ What is the purpose of hoardings?
❸ Where should flammable substances be kept?
❹ Name two types of site storage.
❺ What does good lighting of the site help to reduce?

Health and Safety

For more information about words and meanings and information on all aspects of health and safety why not visit the Department for Education and Skills, Success for All website?

http://www.successforall.gov.uk

Accident Procedures

For more information about accident procedures, why not visit the following websites.

The Health and Safety Executive

www.hse.gov.uk

European Agency for Safety and Health at Work

http://osha.eu.int/

Good safety management practice is available from the Agency's website. All Agency publications can be downloaded free of charge. The Agency site links to member states' sites where national legislation and guidance on construction may be found.

United Kingdom

http://uk.osha.eu.int/

For more information about fire extinguishers why not visit the following websites or visit your local fire station.
www.firestat.co.uk
www.staylegal.net
www.safelines.co.uk

The Health and Safety Executive

www.hse.gov.uk

For more information about hazards in the construction industry why not visit the following websites.

Health and Safety Executive

www.hse.gov.uk

Of great help in the writing of this section was the booklet, *An Introduction to Health and Safety*, published by the HSE and from which all sources have been taken.

HSE priced and free publications are available by mail order from HSE Books, PO Box 1999, Sudbury, Suffolk CO10 2WA.
Tel: 01787 881165 Fax 01787 313995.
www.hsebooks.co.uk

HSE priced publications are also available from bookshops and free leaflets can be downloaded from the HSE website.

Common Abbreviations and Meanings

Health and safety has a lot of terms that need to be read, understood and remembered. The list that follows is to remind you of them and to help you remember their meanings.

HASAWA – Health and Safety at Work Act 1974

The Act lists the main rules which govern health and safety in the construction industry and elsewhere in the workplace. They are there to provide health and safety in the workplace. The Act protects visitors and members of the public on construction sites and elsewhere.

HSE – Health and Safety Executive

The HSE enforces the law in the workplace. It has powers to inspect premises and construction sites to ensure employers and employees are not breaking the law.

PUWER – Provision and Use of Work Equipment Regulations

The regulations help to provide guidance to protect people's health and safety from equipment that they use at work. This equipment might include, ladders, lifting equipment, earth-moving machinery, powered hand tools, cutting and drilling machines and so on.

COSHH – Control of Substances Hazardous to Health

This covers dangerous solids, liquids or gases and gives guidelines on how they should be used and stored. It gives details of actions the employer and employees must take to protect the health of the individual and others.

CDM – Construction (Design and Management) Regulations

These are rules laid down by the main contractor on a construction site which must be observed by all sub-contractors and employees on the site.

ACoP – Approved Codes of Practice

These rules provide general guidance for employers on the most suitable and safest way to carry out activities on site.

RIDDOR – Reporting of Injuries, Diseases and Dangerous Occurrences Regulations

Certain events must be reported to the HSE, for example, major injuries and deaths that occur on a construction site, or accidents in which employees are unable to work for more than three days, as well as diseases and dangerous occurrences.

RPE – Respiritory Protective Equipment

This type of equipment must be worn over the mouth and nose when working with strong smelling substances, excessive dust and so on.

PPE – Personal Protective Equipment

These might include: hard hats, safety footwear, ear defenders, protective gloves, safety goggles, and so on.

MEWP – Mobile Elevating Working Platform

This is used for working at height when it is not possible to erect a scaffold.

Source: Success for All, Department for Education and Skills

www.successforall.gov.uk

Safety signs

For guidance on safety signs contact the Health and Safety Executive, who will only be too happy to send you details, usually free of charge.

HSE

http://www.hse.gov.co.uk/pubns/indg184.htm

PPE

For more information about PPE why not visit the following website.

HSE

www.hse.gov.uk

Alternatively, product information may be found on the websites of the many commercial companies who produce PPE products.

Site Security

For more information about site security visit the website of an appropriate commercial company.

2 Chapter two

Move and Handle Resources

NVQ Level 1   Unit No. VR 03   Move and Handle Resources

This unit, in the context of brickwork and the construction industry work environment is about:

- following instructions
- adopting safe and healthy working practices
- selecting materials, components and equipment
- handling, moving and storage of materials and components by manual procedures and lifting aids.

There are five sections in this chapter: disposal of waste, information, methods of work, protect work and problems.

This chapter will now cover methods of moving and handling resources.

DISPOSAL OF WASTE   2.1

In this section you will learn about environmental responsibilities, organizational procedures, manufacturers' information, statutory regulations and official guidance.

When you have completed this section you will be able to:

- comply with the given information to prevent damage to the product and surrounding environment.

Know and understand:

- why disposal of waste should be carried out safely and how it is achieved.

Introduction

Waste is all substances that the holder wishes, or is required, to dispose of in solid, liquid or gaseous form.

Over 70 million tonnes of waste is produced in the construction industry each year. This amounts to 24 kg per week for every person in the UK, about four times the rate of household waste production. Government guidance suggests we should follow a prioritizing approach to reduce the amount of waste, and to reuse and recycle what waste is produced.

Whilst the trend is questioning the traditional route of waste disposal in favour of sustainable waste management strategies, the majority of the construction industry has made waste reduction a low priority because of the complexities over reuse and recycling.

Environmental Responsibilities

Every business produces waste of some kind or other, but what waste is and how much is produced will vary greatly across the various industries. With changes in environmental legislation affecting how we handle and dispose of waste, attitudes will have to change or businesses will risk high costs and prosecution.

Behind all this legislation is a drive towards a more sustainable planet through reductions in natural resource use. Minimizing the waste we produce is one way of doing this, as waste is a symptom of inefficient consumption.

But having produced the waste, it all has to be disposed of in a way that inevitably causes some environmental impact and the challenge is to reduce the effect of waste both today and for future generations.

Landfill

Traditionally, the UK has relied on landfill for the bulk of its waste disposal. Over 70 per cent of commercial waste is still landfilled, whilst for household waste, that figure is over 80 per cent. There is plentiful availability of landfill sites so there has been little incentive to find alternatives, but that now has to change as European pressure demands reductions in landfill through targets for reduction, recycling and, possibly even, re-use.

By 2009 the current methods of waste collection will all but disappear. Segregation, treatment and landfill diversion will become the norm as costs rise and legislation bites. Acting now will reduce those costs and improve business.

Recycling

Recycling should not be expensive and should cost no more than general waste disposal. But cost is a function of material type, volume, location and quality together with the savings that can be made on disposal of residual waste. So, for instance, a small office might well find that having an office paper recycling scheme adds to the cost of waste disposal if they simply add it to their existing waste arrangements. But by reducing their residual waste costs by reducing the number of times waste is removed or having a larger container, they might well be able to save overall costs.

The problem is that the UK is starting from a much lower baseline than most of Europe, so we have much more to do. Approximately 60 million tonnes of

---

> *Point to note*

Aluminium cans could be recycled indefinitely saving 95 per cent of the energy needed to make new.

---

key terms

Controlled Waste – means household, commercial and industrial waste. It includes office waste and waste from a house, shop, factory or other business premises. A substance is controlled waste whether it is solid or liquid and even if it is neither hazardous nor toxic.

Special Waste – is the most dangerous (including toxic and hazardous) and difficult commercial and industrial waste. The 1996 Special Waste Regulations define the term special waste. Examples of special waste include oils, lead-acid and nickel cadmium batteries and asbestos from households is also treated as special waste. There are separate controls on radioactive waste.

industrial, commercial and household waste goes to landfill each year in the UK. To meet all the targets, 20 million tonnes of this has to be diverted to alternative uses or simply not produced. But not only will it make a difference to business. It should also cut costs.

Source: Biffa, *Recycling an Overview*.

> Point to note
>
> Composting plant-based, kitchen and garden waste is a growth process for the domestic market, and is collected through various means including Civic Amenity sites and kerbside collection.

Disposal of Waste

There are three important reasons for the disposal of waste:

- Safety
- Health
- Economy

Waste materials left lying around can cause accidents.

Scaffolds and other work areas, doorways and runways must be kept clear.

Waste left lying about makes a breeding ground for vermin.

Materials are expensive; therefore do not waste materials.

Broken bricks, tiles, stone, and so on, can be reused as hardcore beneath concrete slabs for example.

Offcuts of timber can be used as pegs or for making profiles.

✓ Good Practice

When you see a good bricklayer at work the chances are the area in which they are working will be clean and tidy; quality work and a tidy workspace go hand in hand.

Working Area

Keep your work area tidy by stacking the bricks correctly.

Do all your cutting in one place using a cutting mat.

Don't overload the mortar boards.

Keep the tools you are not using in your tool bag.

Leave time at the end of the day to clean the area and leave it ready for the next day.

Sweeping up Debris

On site a brush can be used to sweep fine debris into heaps.

In confined spaces or in the workshop lay the dust by sprinkling water on the area to be swept.

If dust cannot be avoided, always wear a dust mask.

Mortar Bay

The mortar used in colleges is a mixture of lime sand and cement and usually has a shelf life of about 48 hours. On site, mortar is more likely to be a mixture plasticizer and cement. Once the mortar has been used, any surplus should be returned to the mortar bay to be remixed. When returning to the mortar bay, always ensure no particles of brick or block are mixed in with it as this will damage the mixer.

Waste Bins

All brick and block waste should be deposited in waste bins for reuse or recycling.

Materials are expensive do not throw away good bricks and blocks.

> **Point to note**
>
> For recycling, waste office paper is the quality end of the paper market, and the average office worker will generate approximately 35 kg of paper per year.

Good Practice

When you have waste, you have a duty to stop it escaping; store it safely and securely.

If the waste is loose, bag it or cover it.

Keep it in the confines of the container.

Do not pile waste higher than the sides of the container.

Keep lids and doors locked and shut when not in use.

Do not burn waste, it causes damage to the environment.

Prevent unauthorized access to containers by children or vagrants.

DO NOT – enter any container or skip.

DO NOT – pile waste beyond the sides of any container (see Figures 2.1 and 2.2). Waste blowing about the site contravenes the environmental protection act duty of care regulations.

DO NOT – overload containers, it is unsafe to site personnel and dangerous for waste disposal staff to handle the containers.

Fig 2.1 **Container badly filled**

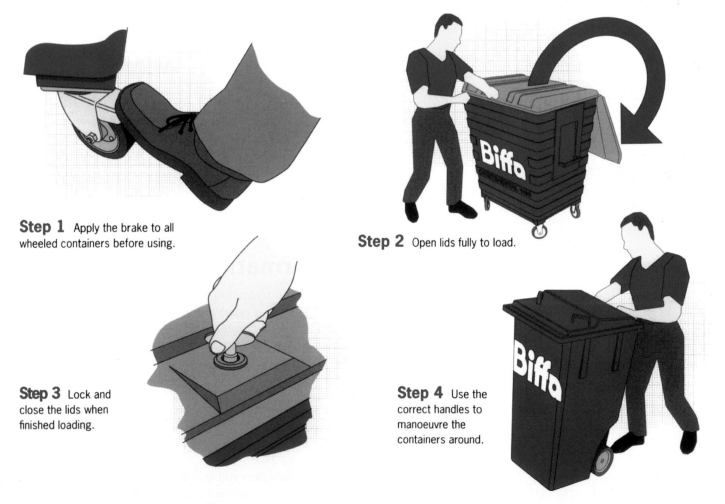

Step 1 Apply the brake to all wheeled containers before using.

Step 2 Open lids fully to load.

Step 3 Lock and close the lids when finished loading.

Step 4 Use the correct handles to manoeuvre the containers around.

Fig. 2.2 Wheeled container waste guidelines

Source: Biffa.

Work-based Evidence Required

■ **Disposal of waste in accordance with legislation. Minimize damage and maintain a clean work space**

To meet this requirement, obtain from your supervisor a witness testimony sheet stating that you have disposed of waste in accordance with legislation to minimize damage and maintained a clean work space. It would also be useful if you could obtain some photographs of yourself carrying out these activities.

When you have received the signed and dated witness testimony sheets from your supervisor, place them in your work-based evidence portfolio when next in college and map and record it against the syllabus.

INFORMATION 2.2

In this section you will learn about technical, product and regulatory information in oral, written and graphical forms.

When you have completed this section you will be able to:

■ comply with the given product information to carry out the work efficiently to the required guidance.

Know and understand:

■ the level of understanding operatives must have of information for relevant, current legislation and official guidance and how it is applied.

Sources of Information

It is not possible to recall all the information required for a particular job or contract. To record this information a variety of systems are installed within the administration of companies. A vital feature of these systems is the need to regularly update information to account for such instances as technical developments, financial alterations and legislative change.

Site managers and supervisors would be well advised to collect suitable quick reference information as soon as possible on the award of a contract. This may then be used to instruct, notify or advise individuals, and determine solutions to problems that may come up.

Throughout your career in construction you will be called upon to make decisions in order to solve a variety of problems, both material and personal, and contribute effectively towards the organization of the companies involved.

To be an effective member of a team of building workers, you will need to be actively researching the sources of information and regulatory publications available to you and the information included in each.

People

One of the best sources of information is other people. As a member of the site team you are part of a large network of people, who for example include:

- members of the site team
- supervisors
- managers
- sub-contractors
- company specialists, e.g. the safety officer.

Any one of these people may be able to help you. All you have to do is ask.

Libraries

Libraries are able to provide a wealth of information material, from books and leaflets on a wide range of subjects, to computers to access the Internet. Most libraries have a reference section that will include dictionaries and directories as well as a host of other information sources. All libraries are part of the inter-library loan scheme, through which it is possible to order books that are not held in the library, provided you know the title, author and publisher. Libraries also hold indexes of periodicals giving details of articles, and most have copies of past newspapers and magazines on file.

College and University Libraries

College and university libraries exist to provide you with facilities and resources to extend your learning and support you in the successful completion of your course.

If you are a student on an NVQ course in brickwork at your local college, then you will automatically be a member of the college library. Most college libraries will have the following resources in printed, audio-visual and electronic formats:

Printed

Books – there are books to support you in your coursework as well as fiction for leisure reading.

Journals – there are subject specific journals such as *Building* magazine and *Construction News* but there are also easy reading magazines.

Audio-Visual

Videos – these are usually available for a one week loan period.

Cassettes – cassettes include audio stories and language learning cassettes.

Electronic

Internet – usually available on all personal computers free of charge.

Intranet – each college usually has its own website that can be accessed from the student Intranet.

Online resources booklet – an in-house guide to electronic sources which can be accessed from the library Intranet.

Facilities

Study areas – both group and individual study areas are usually available.

Drop-in computers – with access to electronic sources and packages to produce your assignments such as, Word, Access, Excel, PowerPoint, Publisher, Photo draw and Front Page.

Laser printing – black and white printing is usually available.

Video viewing – videos can usually be watched on an individual basis.

Photocopying – in colour and black and white is usually available.

Services

All libraries offer a range of services to provide you with access to the resources you need. These will include:

Inter-library loans – they can borrow books from the British Library on your behalf.

Reservations – traps can be placed on items that are checked out so that they will be held for you when they return.

Advanced computer booking – to ensure you have access to a personal computer when you need it.

Information

Libraries have a wide variety of information sources for you to use and you can find the items you require using the following:

Library staff – ask a member of staff to help you locate the items you want.

On-line catalogue – based on a computer this is a database of all resources held in the library. You can search by author, title and subject.

Shelf guides – these labels give an indication of which subject books can be found on which shelves.

Subject guides – there will be a range of guides on different subjects which will outline where you can find book, Internet, journal and CD-ROM sources for your subject area.

If you are not a student but are interested in brickwork do not despair. Most college and university libraries are open to outside users, with the payment of a small fee, or you may simply need to produce a letter from your employer explaining why you need to use the service and for how long.

Quick quiz **Quick quiz** Quick quiz Quick quiz Quick quiz

❶ State three information sources that would provide information on materials required to complete a contract.

❷ State five methods by which information can be communicated on site.

❸ Name three information sources that will provide information on the type and quantity of materials required on a construction project.

❹ Which document will provide information on the correct use of materials.

❺ State one of the best sources of information.

Note: the text does not necessarily include all the answers to these questions, in which case refer to other sources of information for your answers.

METHODS OF WORK   2.3

In this section you will learn about the application of knowledge for safe work practices, procedures, skills and transference of competence for:

- manual handling and storage
- maintenance of lifting aids
- needs of other occupations associated with the resources.

When you have completed this section you will be able to:

- comply with the given product information to carry out the work efficiently to the required standard.

Know and understand:

- How methods of work are carried out, to meet the specification, and problems are reported.

Manual Handling and Storage

Introduction

More than a third of all over-three day injuries reported each year to the Health and Safety Executive (HSE) and local authorities are caused by manual handling, that is, the transporting or supporting of loads by hand or bodily force.

Most of the reported accidents cause back injury, although hands, arms and feet are also vulnerable. In 1995, an estimated average of 11 working days per sufferer was lost through 'musculoskeletal' disorders affecting the back, caused by work. HSE estimated that such conditions cost employers up to £335 million (based on 1995/6 prices).

Many manual handling injuries build up over a period rather than being caused by a single handling incident. These injuries occur wherever people are at work – on building sites, in factories, offices, warehouses and while making deliveries.

Source: HSE.

Legislation

In addition to the responsibilities of the employer and employee as set out in the Health and Safety at Work Act, there are regulations relating to manual handling. The Manual Handling Operations Regulations place a requirement on the employer to deal with risks to the safety and health of employees who have to carry out manual handling at work.

Duties of the Employer

- Avoid the need for hazardous manual handling, as far as reasonably practicable
- Assess the risk of injury from any hazardous manual handling that cannot be avoided
- Reduce the risk of injury from hazardous manual handling, as far as reasonably practicable.

Duties of the Employee

- Follow appropriate systems of work laid down for their safety
- Make proper use of equipment provided for their safety
- Co-operate with their employer on health and safety matters
- Inform the employer if they identify hazardous handling activities
- Take care to ensure that their activities do not put others at risk.

There is no such thing as a completely safe manual handling operation. But working within the guidelines will cut the risk and reduce the need for a more detailed assessment.

Typical Hazards

Care must be taken at all times when handling construction materials and components. Typical hazards are:

- Splinters – wood or metal
- Jagged edges – wood, metal or clay products
- Sharp edges on materials – corner of bricks, metal cladding, cut wall ties
- Falling objects – collapsing stacks, items falling on to hands and feet
- Chemical burns or irritants – cement, lime
- Trapped fingers – lifting or lowering heavy objects

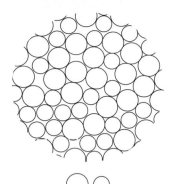

- Muscular strains – lifting or lowering heavy/awkward objects
- Damage to eyes or lungs – dust, powder fumes
- Sharp objects – nails left sticking out of wood, sharp metal offcuts.

Methods of Handling and Storage

Aggregates

Aggregates are granules or particles that are mixed with cement, lime and water to make mortar and concrete. Aggregates should be hard, durable and should not contain any form of plant life, or anything that could be dissolved in water.

Aggregates are classified into two groups:

- Fine aggregates – composed of granules which pass through a 5 mm sieve
- Coarse aggregates – composed of particles which are retained by a 5 mm sieve.

The most commonly used fine aggregate is sand.

Mortar should be mixed using soft or building sand. It should be well graded having an equal quantity of fine, medium and large grains.

Concreting should be carried out using a sharp sand which has more rounded grains as shown in Figure 2.3.

Coarse aggregate should also be used when concreting. The most common coarse aggregate is usually limestone chippings, which are quarried and crushed to graded sizes, usually 10 mm, 20 mm or larger.

Storage of aggregates

Aggregates are normally delivered from lorries and are either tipped, or, more usually, are in 1 tonne bags that are crane handled off the lorry. Aggregates should be stored on a concrete base, with a slope or fall to allow any water to drain away. The different sizes of aggregates should be stored separately to prevent them from getting mixed together as illustrated in Figure 2.4.

Aggregate stores should be sited away from any trees to prevent leaf contamination. Tarpaulin or plastic sheets may be used to cover the aggregates to prevent rainwater and rubbish from affecting the materials.

Notes on handling aggregates

- They are usually delivered by high-sided lorry to prevent spillage
- Always check the quality, grade and quantity to ensure it matches the order form
- Tip into prepared bays or selected areas
- Transfer by grab, mechanical shovel or power-assisted equipment on the weigh batcher
- Transport on site by bucket, hopper, dumper and barrow
- Loss or waste can occur through:
  - indiscriminate handling
  - contamination of any kind
  - using the aggregate as site dressing or to fill site voids.

Poorly graded

Poorly graded

Well graded

Fig. 2.3 **Examples of sand**

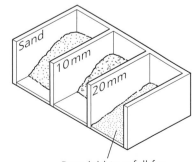

Base laid to a fall for drainage of the aggregates

Fig. 2.4 **Storage bays for aggregates**

Cement and Plaster

Cement

Cement is a material which when water is added to it undergoes a chemical change that causes the cement powder to turn very hard. Cement is made from chalk or limestone and clay, which is crushed into a powder and mixed together and heated in a rotary kiln before being ground into a white powder. It is then bagged and distributed to builders' merchants. There are many different types of cement for various situations.

Plaster

Plaster is applied on internal walls and ceilings to provide a joint free, smooth, easily decorated surface. Plaster is a mixture that hardens after being applied. It is made from gypsum, cement or lime and water, with or without the addition of fine aggregates depending on the background finish.

Gypsum Plaster

This plaster is for internal use only, there are different types and grades available, depending on the background finish. For undercoats, browning plaster is usually used.

Cement and Sand Plaster Rendering

This type of plaster or render is used for external finishes, internal undercoats and waterproof finishing coats.

Lime and Sand Rendering

This type of plaster or rendering is usually used as an undercoat, but may also be used as a finishing coat depending on the specification.

Storage of Cement and Plaster

Both cement and plaster are usually available in 25 kg bags. These bags are made from a multi-wall layer of paper with a polythene liner. Great care should be taken not to puncture the bags before use as this could result in moisture entering the material, which will adversely affect it. Each bag may be off-loaded manually or with a machine and then stored in a well ventilated, waterproof shed or room on a dry floor stacked on wooden pallets, as shown in Figure 2.5.

The bags of cement or plaster should be kept clear of all walls, and be stacked no higher than five bags high. It is important that the bags are used in the same order as they were delivered, this is to minimize the length of time that the bags are in storage. Lengthy storage times may result in the contents setting over the duration of the building project.

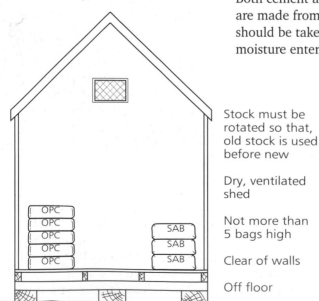

Stock must be rotated so that, old stock is used before new

Dry, ventilated shed

Not more than 5 bags high

Clear of walls

Off floor

Fig. 2.5 **Storage shed for cement or plaster**

Notes on Handling Cement and Plaster

- Delivered in 25 kg paper sacks on timber pallets
- May also be delivered by tanker and pumped into a silo
- Offload by forklift or crane
- Use bagged cement and plaster in order of delivery.

Loss or waste can occur through:

- Humidity causing materials to lump
- Dampness initiating set
- Indiscriminate handling causing bags to burst
- Failure to use deliveries in rotation
- Pilfering
- Leaving stocks unused.

Bricks

Bricks are components that are used for building walls. They are classified by the type of walls that they can be used for and their situation in the building.

Storage of Bricks

Each pack of bricks that arrives on site should contain a sheet of relevant instructions or information for the use of site personnel. This information should include storage, off-loading and site handling advice.

All 'facing' bricks are supplied in strapped packs and normally off-loaded mechanically. This should be carried out as near to the place of work as possible. A standard pack of facing bricks can weigh anything up to 1600 kg and any lifting equipment used for off-loading or transportation on site must be capable of safely handling this weight.

Safe Off-loading

Packs of bricks should never be lifted by their packing straps – the strapping is only designed for safe and convenient transport from the brick manufacturer to the building site. Repeated lifting will loosen the straps and could cause subsequent damage to the bricks.

Caution should also be used when cutting straps. Only wire cutters should be used, with site personnel standing well away from the line of strap to avoid any possible backlash.

When moving and handling bricks on site, it is important that safety helmets and protective gloves be worn. Avoid the use of poles and chains when lifting pallets by crane above head height. Always use an enclosed cage or net as a safeguard should a pack become unstable.

TRY THIS OUT

Your tutor has supplied you with all the necessary materials and components to carry out this activity.

1. Build a stack of 150 bricks, properly dry bonded (see p. 50), on a wooden pallet. Cover the completed stack with a waterproof sheet.

2. Build a stack of 24 aircrete blocks, properly dry bonded onto a wooden pallet. Cover the completed stack with a waterproof sheet.

key terms

Materials – It is generally accepted that material means that from which anything is or may be made. Sand, stone, cement, lime, clay, plaster and wood are obvious examples. Less obvious are items such as adhesives, tiling grout and paint.

Components – The parts or elements from which anything is made up. From this definition, it can be understood that components in a building context are manufactured items such as rainwater goods and fittings, bricks and blocks, lintels, window frames and so on.

Point to note

The difference between the terms 'materials' and 'components', as applied to construction, is vague. As an example, a materials list of items required for a particular activity will not discriminate between materials and components but will include every item needed for that job.

Methods of Storing Bricks

Designated storage areas for bricks should be reasonably accessible to delivery lorries and site handling plant. Bricks should be stored on dry, level ground, or on a well drained level hardstanding, as shown in Figure 2.6, ensuring they are not in contact with soil, sulphate bearing ground or ash.

Bricks should be stored no more than two packs high and protected from the elements, as well as from splashing by passing vehicles, with tarpaulin or polythene sheets.

It is important to protect stored bricks from becoming wet as they may become difficult to lay, due to lack of suction. Wet, dense bricks also tend to float on the mortar bed. Lack of protection during storage may ultimately lead to problems of efflorescence, lime leaching and an increased risk of frost attack in the finished brickwork.

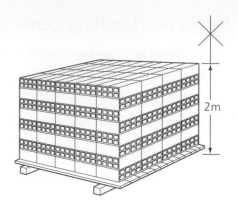

Notes on Handling Bricks

- Delivered in packs or on pallets
- Offload by vehicle-crane, forklift or mobile crane
- Transfer on site by forklift, dumper, crane, hoist or elevator
- Sort all chipped or damaged bricks and set aside
- Do not tip facing bricks
- Cut bands holding packs with proper cutters.

Loss or waste can occur through:

- Using facings for common work or as supports and packing
- Faulty workmanship
- Double handling.

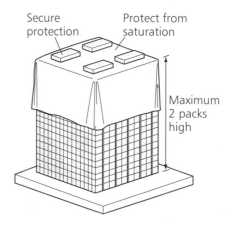

Fig. 2.6 **Storage of bricks**

Blocks

Blocks tend to be of the concrete or aerated type: the former being heavy and dense and the latter being lightweight and less dense.

Storage of Blocks

The storage of blocks is the same as it is for bricks.

Notes on Handling Blocks

- Delivered on pallets or in polythene-covered packs
- Offload by vehicle crane, forklift or mobile crane
- Transfer on site by forklift, crane and so on
- Keep stacks secure: not too high.

Loss or waste can occur through:

- Using blocks as packings
- Excess breakages.

> **Points to note**
>
> Do not stack materials more than 2 metres high.

TRY THIS OUT

Study the list of materials given below and for each write a short guide on:

■ How and where the items should be stored.

■ How you would make sure that old stock was used before new stock (rotation).

List of materials/components:
1. Bags of cement
2. Coarse and fine aggregates
3. Bags of plaster
4. Sheets of plasterboard
5. Facing bricks
6. Concrete blocks
7. Paving slabs
8. Drainage pipes.

Work-based Evidence Required

■ Selection of resources to be moved and/or stored:

■ own work and that of the team
■ materials components and fixings
■ tools and equipment.

To meet these requirements, obtain a witness testimony sheet from your supervisor stating that you selected resources to be moved and stored. For example:

To whom it may concern.

I would like to confirm that between 6 November 2004 and 8 November 2004 Diana Whatmough was working on the contract at St Mary's Gate College. Diana helped with others move a large number of scaffold boards and scaffold clips that were in the way of the building of a boundary wall. They stored the boards and clips in the site compound on the appropriate racks and under cover. Diana then helped load out bricks and mortar for the new walling.

At the end of each working day Diana is responsible for cleaning and storing the cement mixer and other equipment and tools in the site hut which is then locked and secured. Diana always carries out these tasks competently and treats the responsibility in a proper manner.

Yours faithfully

Paul Sysmik (site supervisor)

Place the evidence in your work-based evidence portfolio when next in college and map and record it against the syllabus.

Quick quiz Quick quiz Quick quiz Quick quiz Quick quiz

❶ How should bricks be stacked safely?
❷ Why should care be taken when cutting the banding around pallets of bricks?
❸ Why should bricks and blocks be protected from the weather?
❹ Why are bricks and blocks dry bonded when in stacks?
❺ Why should packs of bricks and blocks not be lifted by their packing straps?

Paving Slabs

Paving slabs are made from concrete, and are available in a variety of sizes, shapes and colours. They are used for pavements and patios, with some slabs being given a textured finish to improve their appearance.

Storage of Paving Slabs

Paving slabs are stored outside and stacked on edge to prevent the lower slabs if stored flat, from being damaged by the weight of the stack. The stack is started by laying about eight to ten slabs flat with the other slabs leaning against them as illustrated in Figure 2.7.

It is good practice to put an intermediate flat stack of slabs in long rows of slabs to prevent them from toppling. Slabs should be stored on firm, level ground with timber bearers below to prevent the edges from being damaged. To provide protection from rain and frost, it is advisable to keep the slabs under cover, by placing tarpaulin or polythene sheet over them.

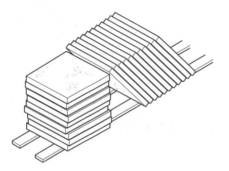

Fig. 2.7 Storage of paving slabs

Kerbs

Kerbs are concrete components laid at the edge of a road. The size of a normal kerb is 150 mm wide, 300 mm high and 1 m long.

Pre-Cast Concrete Lintels

Lintels are components placed above openings in brick and block walls to bridge the opening and support the brick and blockwork above. Lintels made from concrete have a steel reinforcement placed on the bottom, which is why pre-cast concrete lintels will have a T or top etched into their top surface. Pre-cast concrete lintels come in a variety of sizes to suit the opening width.

Storage of Pre-Cast Concrete Lintels and Kerbs

Kerbs and lintels should be stacked flat on timber bearers. This will assist in lifting and lowering these components by providing a space for hands or lifting slings if machine lifting is to be used.

When stacking kerbs on top of each other, the stack must not be more than three kerbs high. To protect the kerbs and lintels from the rain and frost, it is

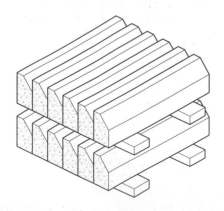

Fig. 2.8 Storage of kerbs

advisable to cover them with a tarpaulin or polythene sheet as illustrated in Figure 2.8.

Notes on Handling

🔧 Offload and transport with care using correct equipment and any lifting points provided in the casting

🔧 Protect edges where slings or cables are used for lifting

🔧 Lifting equipment should be fully capable of raising the load.

Loss or waste can occur through:

🔧 Damaged or broken units: these will be expensive to replace; repeated orders cost money

🔧 Duplication of items: leftover components means waste

🔧 Shortage of pre-cast items: repeat ordering can cause delays.

Drainage Pipes

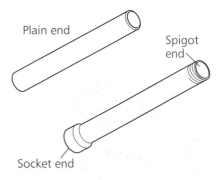

Fig. 2.9 **Drainage pipe**

Made from vitrified clay or plastic, drainage pipes may have a socket and spigot end or be plain as shown in Figure 2.9.

Clay pipes are easily broken if misused, so care must be taken when handling these items.

Storage of Drainage Pipes and Fittings

Pipes should be stored on a firm, level base and prevented from rolling by placing wedges or stakes on either side of the stack as shown in Figure 2.10.

Clay pipes with socket and spigot ends, should be stored by alternating the ends on each row, they should also be stacked on shaped timber cross-bearers to prevent them from rolling as illustrated in Figure 2.11.

Do not stack pipes any higher than 1.5 m and taper the stack towards the top.

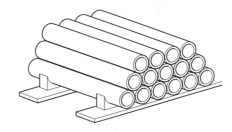

Fig. 2.10 **Correct method of stacking pipes**

Fittings and special shaped pipes, like bends, should be stored separately and, if possible, in a wooden crate until required.

Notes on Handling

🔧 Fix as work proceeds to avoid damage to structure

🔧 Check angles, offsets and bends for any damage.

Loss or waste can occur through:

🔧 Pilfering

🔧 Damage by site traffic

🔧 Vandalism

🔧 Failure to collect surplus lengths and fittings

🔧 The effects of low temperatures which make plastic materials brittle.

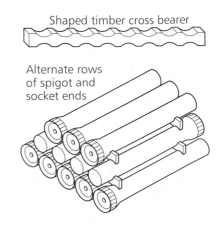

Fig. 2.11 **Storage of pipes with socket and spigot ends**

Storage of Pipes and Cylindrical Materials

Pipes and other types of cylindrical items are often brought to a site for immediate use. These materials can be stored on the floor. Use a wedge or some other blocking device to prevent the stacked pipes from moving or rolling during stacking or removal as shown in Figure 2.12.

Remove large diameter pipes from a stack by pulling them out from the ends as shown in Figure 2.13 Do not remove by lifting from the sides.

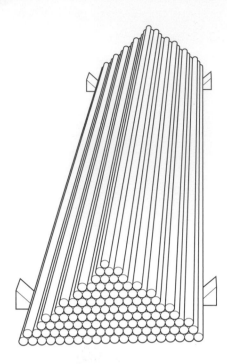

Fig. 2.12 **Storage of pipes**

> **Points to note**

To avoid accidents, do not stand or walk on stacked pipes when placing or removing pieces.

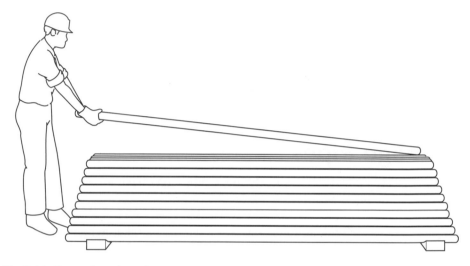

Fig. 2.13 **Removing pipes from a stack**

Reinforcing and Structural Steel

Reinforcing steel should be stored and grouped by diameter in order to facilitate identification and handling as shown in Figure 2.14.

Notes on Handling

- Offload as close to fixing point as possible
- Lay on timber skids to keep steel above ground

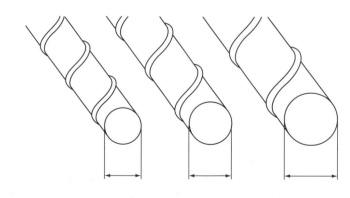

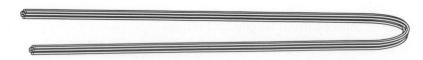

Fig. 2.14 Grouping of steel items

- Check type and quantity delivered
- Cut with proper tools
- Hoist bundles of bars or sheet reinforcement with care.

Loss or waste can occur through:

- Careless handling
- Leaving bars behind in fixing areas
- Failing to fix steel as specified
- Cutting bars incorrectly.

Flexible Damp Proof Course

Damp proof course (DPC) may be made from polythene, bitumen or lead and is supplied in rolls of various widths for different uses.

Storage of Rolled Materials

Rolled materials, whether damp proof course or roofing felt should be stored in a shed or room on a level, dry surface. Narrow rolls may be best stored on shelves, but in all cases they should be stacked on end to prevent them from rolling, and to reduce the possibility of damage being caused by compression as layers of bitumen meld together when under pressure (see Figure 2.15).

Notes on Handling

- Unroll quantity to be used only
- Replace surplus amounts in safe storage
- Use proper knife for cutting to length
- Use correct widths as specified.

Loss or waste can occur through:

- Leaving unused rolls lying around
- Using incorrect widths or cutting unnecessarily.

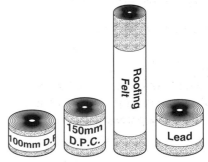

Rolled materials stored on end

Fig. 2.15 **Rolled material stored correctly**

Sheet Materials

Flat sheets, such as plywood, plasterboard, hardboard and chipboard, are called sheet materials. They are obtained in packs or individually. Sizes vary but a common size is 2440 mm × 1220 mm, thickness also varies.

Plywood and Plasterboard

Plywood consists of an odd number of thin layers of timber glued together with their grains alternating in direction, used for flooring, formwork and stud partition walling.

Plasterboard is made from a gypsum plaster centre sandwiched between two sheets of heavy paper, used for ceilings and stud partition walling.

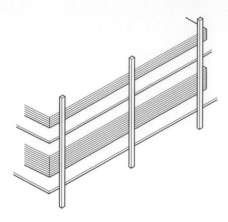

Fig. 2.16 Plasterboard stacked on racks

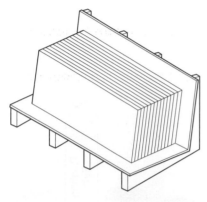

Fig. 2.17 Where space is limited, plasterboard can be stacked on a specially made rack

Storage of Sheet Materials

Plywood and plasterboard is best stored flat on racks in a warm dry place as illustrated in Figure 2.16. Plasterboards with a foil backed surface should be stacked in pairs with their foil surfaces together.

Where space is limited sheet materials can be stored on edge in a specially made rack which allows the outer board to be supported on the previous board and keep its shape as shown in Figure 2.17.

Once off-loaded, it is the building contractor's responsibility to move all materials to a safe and secure place until needed.

Notes on Handling

- Delivered by supplier
- Off-loaded by forklift; requires platform to support the boards
- Manual handling and stacking requires two men to each board
- Plastic or foil-backed boards should be handled with reverse face to face.

Loss or waste can occur through:
- Using wrong sized boards causing excess cutting
- Poor stacking
- Indiscriminate handling
- Lack of protection from weather.

Work-based Evidence Required

■ **Handle and store occupational resources to meet product information and/or organizational requirements relating to:**

- ■ sheet material
- ■ loose material
- ■ bagged or wrapped material
- ■ fragile material
- ■ components
- ■ liquid material

To meet these requirements, ask your supervisor to fill out a witness testimony sheet stating that you have handled and stored occupational resources to meet product information and organizational requirements related to the above. It would be also useful if you could obtain photographs of yourself carrying out some of these activities.

When you have received the signed and dated witness testimony sheets from your supervisor, place them in your work-based evidence portfolio when next in college and map and record them against the syllabus.

Quick quiz Quick quiz Quick quiz Quick quiz Quick quiz

❶ Define the word component.
❷ What is the difference between materials and components?
❸ What source would you use to identify and select materials and components?
❹ List ten materials and components used in brickwork.
❺ List five companies that supply materials and components to the construction industry.

Manual Handling Techniques

Lifting heavy or awkward objects, such as bags of cement and plaster, can cause injury if not performed correctly. Incorrect lifting techniques can put stress on the lower back and after years of bad lifting, the discs between the various vertebrae in the backbone become disjointed and are prone to 'slipping'. By using the kinetic method of manual handling, injuries to the back can be avoided.

Kinetic Method

The kinetic method is based on two principles:

1. Fully employing the strong leg muscles for lifting, rather than the weaker muscles of the back
2. Using the momentum of the weight of the body to begin horizontal movement.

These two motions are combined in smooth continuous movements by correct positioning of the feet, maintaining a straight back and flexing and extending the knees.

In practice, this requires: correct positioning of the feet, a straight back, arms close to the body when lifting or carrying, the correct hold, keeping the chin tucked in and using the body weight (see Figure 2.18).

Safe Handling

The Health and Safety Executive outline important handling points, using a basic lifting operation as an example.

Fig. 2.18 **Correct lifting techniques**

Stop and Think

Plan the lift. Where is the load to be placed? Use appropriate handling aids if possible. Do you need help with the load? Remove obstructions such as discarded wrapping materials. For a long lift, such as floor to shoulder height, consider resting the load mid-way on a table or bench to change grip (see Figure 2.19).

Position the Feet

Place your feet apart, giving a balanced and stable base for lifting. Place the leading leg as far forward as is comfortable and if possible, pointing in the direction you intend to go (see Figure 2.20).

Adopt a Good Posture

When lifting from low level, bend the knees. But do not kneel or over-flex the knees. Keep the back straight, maintaining its natural curve. Lean forwards a little over the load if necessary to get a good grip. Keep the shoulders level and facing in the same direction as the hips (see Figure 2.21).

Get a Firm Grip

Try to keep the arms within the boundary formed by the legs. The best position and type of grip depends on the circumstances and individual preference, but will be secure. A hook grip is less tiring than keeping the fingers straight. If you need to vary the grip as the lift proceeds, do it as smoothly as possible (see Figure 2.22).

Keep Close to the Load

Keep the load close to the body for as long as possible. Keep the heaviest side of the load next to the body. If a close approach to the load is not possible, slide it towards you before trying to lift.

Do Not Jerk

Lift smoothly, raising the chin as the lift begins, keeping control of the load.

Move the Feet

Do not twist your body when turning to the side.

Put Down, Then Adjust

If precise positioning of the load is necessary, put it down first, then slide it into the desired position (see Figure 2.23).

> Points to note

Wear protective gloves to avoid cuts, abrasions and splinters.

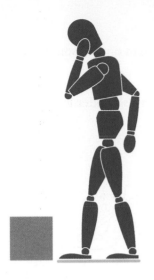

Fig. 2.19 **Stop and think: planning safe lifting**

Fig. 2.20 **Positioning the feet for safe lifting**

Fig. 2.21 **Adopt a good posture for safe lifting**

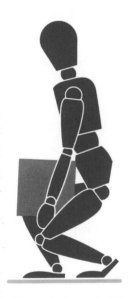

Fig. 2.22 **Firm grip for safe lifting**

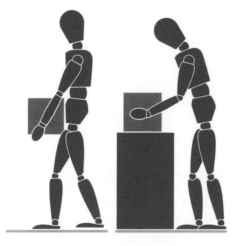

Fig. 2.23 **Put down then adjust**

> **Points to note**
>
> It is recommended that the feet are placed about 50 cm apart. This distance is suitable for a person having a height of about 175 cm.
>
> Do not attempt to lift or carry any load exceeding 25 kg alone.

Lifting a Load From a Bench

Keep your back straight, extend your arms in front of you and bend your knees slightly, until you can grasp the load firmly (see Figure 2.24).

Pull the load towards you, straighten up and lean back slightly (see Figure 2.25).

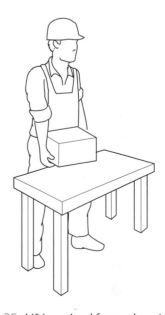

Fig. 2.24 **Lifting a load from a bench (1)**   Fig. 2.25 **Lifting a load from a bench (2)**

Lifting and Carrying Long Loads

In general, a load longer than 6 metres requires more than one person to lift and carry it (see Figure 2.26).

When being lifted by one person, one end is raised above shoulder level (see Figure 2.27).

Fig. 2.26 **Carrying long loads** (one end raised above shoulder level)

Fig. 2.27 **One person carrying a long load**

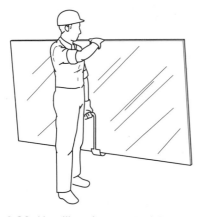

Fig. 2.28 **Handling sheet materials**

The operative then walks forward, moving his hands along the length until the point of balance is reached. The load is then balanced.

Handling Sheet Materials

Large sheets of material are awkward shapes to pick up. By using an easily made hook, with a long handle, a large sheet of material can be lifted and carried quite easily, as shown in Figure 2.28.

Alternatively, sheet materials and other large items can be moved by a walking process. This is done by lifting one side and swivelling the item on the opposite corner. Care should be taken to avoid damaging corners when walking items.

Quick quiz Quick quiz Quick quiz Quick quiz Quick quiz

❶ What two principles is the kinetic lifting method based upon?

❷ What is the maximum weight that you are allowed to lift or carry on your own?

❸ Explain the term 'safe lifting techniques'.

❹ Why should risks be assessed before handling items?

❺ List five important handling techniques.

Work-based Evidence Required

■ Safe Lifting Techniques

Work skills to:

■ move, position, secure and use lifting aids and kinetic lifting techniques.

To meet these requirements, obtain a witness testimony sheet from your supervisor stating that you have moved, positioned and used lifting aids employing kinetic lifting techniques. Place the evidence in your work-based portfolio when next in college and map and record it against the syllabus.

Team Lifting

If an object has been assessed as being too heavy or awkward for one person to lift, then a colleague should help you. When team lifting, those lifting should be approximately the same height and build as each other. The effort should be the same for each person, and only one person should be responsible for giving instructions.

These instructions should be clearly given, using a recognized call such as, 'lift after three: one, two, three, lift'. Prior to lifting, any objects that are in the immediate area should be removed. It is important that you wear suitable protective clothing such as boots, gloves and overalls, as illustrated in Figure 2.29.

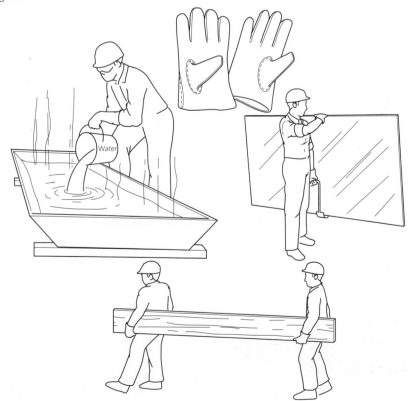

Fig. 2.29 Person wearing PPE when lifting (safety boots, gloves and overalls, etc.)

Examining Loads

Always examine the load in order to ascertain whether you can lift it. If you feel that this is not possible, then obtain help. Always check the route you are to take for any obstructions and that the area where the object is to be placed is clear.

Bagged Materials

The carrying of bagged materials such as cement and plaster can be very tiring, as the bags are awkward to lift. The easiest way is to place the bag on your shoulder. This is made easier if your shoulder is supported. It may make it easier still if you support your shoulder by putting your hand on your hip, holding the bag with your other hand.

Loose Materials

Loose materials such as aggregates, bricks, blocks and bags of cement may be moved by using a wheelbarrow or trolley. Building sites can form rough terrain, and it may be hard work pushing loaded barrows over such rough ground. In these circumstances barrow runs may be used, these are boards laid down over the ground. If the board run is to be over trenches always ensure that the boards are thick enough to carry the weight imposed on them. Always load the barrow evenly with most of the weight above the wheel as shown in Figure 2.30.

Do not throw bricks into a wheelbarrow: place them in neatly. When unloading bricks from a barrow it is important that they are taken out by hand and not tipped, this saves any damage to the bricks. Care must be taken not to damage any material or its packaging when moving it.

Trolleys are best used for moving items on hard surfaces such as in warehouses or workshops since the relatively small wheels will sink into soft surfaces. It is better to take several smaller loads than risk injury by overloading wheelbarrows or trolleys.

Fig. 2.30 **Correct method of using a wheelbarrow**

Delivery of Materials

It is the manufacturer's responsibility to ensure that the products conform with the established standards and are brought to the customer safely and efficiently. Products should arrive at the point of delivery in a satisfactory condition for use.

Work-based Evidence Required

■ Safe use and storage of lifting aids and equipment

To meet this requirement: obtain a witness testimony sheet from your supervisor stating that you have safely used and stored lifting aids and equipment. Place the evidence in your work based evidence portfolio when next in college and map and record it against the syllabus.

❶ Before a delivery of materials is received on site, state the actions that should be taken.

❷ State the regulations that control the handling and storing of materials on site.

❸ State the actions you would take if you identify unsafe storage conditions.

❹ Give four factors that need to be considered when requesting a delivery of materials.

❺ What is meant by the term 'just in time delivery'?

❻ What is the maximum height at which cement bags should be stacked?

❼ Describe the storage requirements for cement and plaster.

❽ Give the storage conditions for materials that contain noxious fumes.

❾ What are the storage conditions for aggregates?

❿ Describe the procedure for stacking long tubes?

PROTECT WORK   2.4

In this section you will learn about protecting work against damage from general workplace activities, other occupations and adverse weather conditions.

When you have completed this section you will be able to:

■ comply with organizational procedures to minimize the risk of damage to the work and surrounding area.

Know and understand:

■ how to protect work from damage and the purpose of protection.

Effects of Weather Conditions on Walling Construction

Exposure of Brickwork

Water affects the performance of bricks and blocks. Good design aims to minimize water penetration, as excessive wetting can lead to frost or sulphate attack and staining or corrosion of non-stainless steel wall ties or reinforcement. Use of the appropriate damp proof course materials in the correct positions will also significantly reduce the possibility of the walls becoming wet.

The exposure of the site and of different parts of the building will have a bearing on the choice of both bricks and the mortar mix. The degree of exposure of the site is classified either in terms of the local 'dry/wet spell indices', or in calculations referring to the British Standards as shown in Figure 2.31.

Source: Hanson.

Brickwork

Areas of severe exposure

Areas of the United Kingdom where the meteorological criteria for severe exposure apply are indicated in the map below. These areas are identified in Table 1 by their postcode districts, although in only a few instances does a whole postcode district lie within an area of severe exposure.

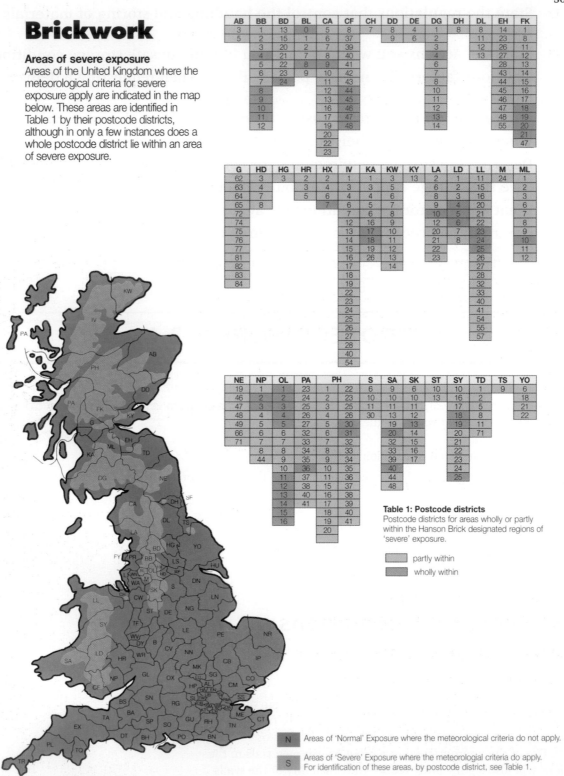

AB	BB	BD	BL	CA	CF	CH	DD	DE	DG	DH	DL	EH	FK
3	1	13	0	5	8	7	8	4	1	8	8	14	1
5	2	15	1	6	37		9	6	2		11	23	8
	3	20	2	7	39				3		12	26	11
	4	21	7	8	40				4		13	27	12
	5	22	8	9	41				6			28	13
	6	23	9	10	42				7			43	14
	7	24		11	43				8			44	15
	8			12	44				10			45	16
	9			13	45				11			46	17
	10			16	46				12			47	18
	11			17	47				13			48	19
	12			19	48				14			55	20
				20									21
				22									47
				23									

G	HD	HG	HR	HX	IV	KA	KW	KY	LA	LD	LL	M	ML
62	3	3	2	2	1	1	9	13	2	1	11	24	1
63	4	3	4	3	5	5		6	2	15			2
64	7	5	6	4	4	6		8	3	16			3
65	8		7	6	5	7		9	4	20			6
72				7	6	8		10	5	21			7
74				12	16	9		12	6	22			8
75				13	17	10		20	7	23			9
76				14	18	11		21	8	24			10
77				15	19	13		22		25			11
81				16	26	14		23		26			12
82				17						27			
83				18						28			
84				19						32			
				22						33			
				23						40			
				24						41			
				25						54			
				26						55			
				27						57			
				28									
				40									
				54									

NE	NP	OL	PA	PH		S	SA	SK	ST	SY	TD	TS	YO
19	1	1	23	1	22	6	9	6	10	1	9	9	6
46	2	2	24	2	23	10	10	10	13	2	18		18
47	3	3	25	3	25	11	11	11		17	5		21
48	4	4	26	4	26	30	13	12		18	8		22
49	5	5	27	5	30		19	13		19	11		
66	6	6	32	6	31		20	14		20	71		
71	7	7	33	7	32		32	15		21			
	44	8	34	8	33		33	16		22			
		9	35	9	34		39	17		23			
		10	36	10	35		40			24			
		11	37	11	36		44			25			
		12	38	15	37		48						
		13	40	16	38								
		14	41	17	39								
		15		18	40								
		16		19	41								
				20									

Table 1: Postcode districts
Postcode districts for areas wholly or partly within the Hanson Brick designated regions of 'severe' exposure.

- partly within
- wholly within

N Areas of 'Normal' Exposure where the meteorological criteria do not apply.

S Areas of 'Severe' Exposure where the meteorological criteria do apply. For identification of these areas, by postcode district, see Table 1.

Fig. 2.31 Factors showing degrees of exposure

Protection of Brick and Blockwork

All newly built brick and blockwork under construction must be protected adequately from rain, snow and frost. In most cases this is achieved by covering the top of the wall as shown in Figure 2.32 with a water resistant material.

However, problems can arise in some situations, for example in brickwork facing to concrete construction, where rain may frequently run off the concrete in quantity and penetrate behind the facing brickwork.

In this situation, a water resisting material is usually fixed to the vertical surface of the concrete and draped over, and clear of, the brickwork, the material being lifted as work proceeds.

Every opportunity must be made to allow the brick and blockwork to dry out when conditions permit. To encourage drying out, the covering material should be supported clear of the face of the wall, either by laying it over a wooden frame or over projecting bricks, so that ventilation can take place beneath the cover.

Hessian is frequently used as an insulating layer in sunny weather, but it is useless if it becomes wet. Apart from losing its insulation value, hessian, which is wet, will frequently cause serious staining and efflorescence of the brickwork. It must therefore, be covered with plastic or other waterproof materials in adverse conditions. Mortar splashing and staining of brickwork will also occur in wet weather unless the inner scaffold board is turned back when work is left for the day.

Where site traffic is to pass close to buildings, protection should be provided to avoid damage through splashing and impact. The internal face of door frames should also be protected to prevent damage from wheelbarrows as they pass through, as illustrated in Figure 2.33.

Source: CITB-ConstructionSkills, *Training Workbook*, **1994.**

Exposure of Brick and Blockwork

Certain parts of the country have been designated areas of severe exposure. The meteorological criteria for these areas are defined below.

Meteorological criteria:

- Average annual frost incidence more than 60 days
- Average annual rainfall more than 1000 mm
- Elevation of the site more than 90 m above sea level.

Exposure Within Brick and Blockwork Construction

The exposure category of tall buildings and those located on high ground should be classified as one grade more severe than would appear to be required. Figures 2.34 and 2.35 illustrate certain parts of a building that may need a more severe grading. For example, parapet walling, chimneys, tops of walls not protected by roof overhangs, freestanding walls and areas of walls below damp proof courses adjacent to ground level.

Source: Ibstock Brick Ltd.

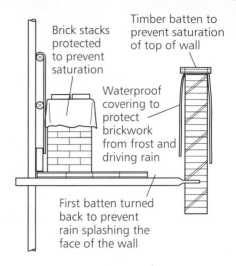

Fig. 2.32 **Protection of a wall from adverse weather conditions**

Fig. 2.33 **Protection of frames: e.g. door frames from damage by wheelbarrows**

key terms

Hessian – A rough textured sacking type material, much used in brickwork for the covering of walls.

Efflorescence – A white powdery deposit on the face of brickwork due to the drying out of soluble salts washed from the bricks following excessive wetting.

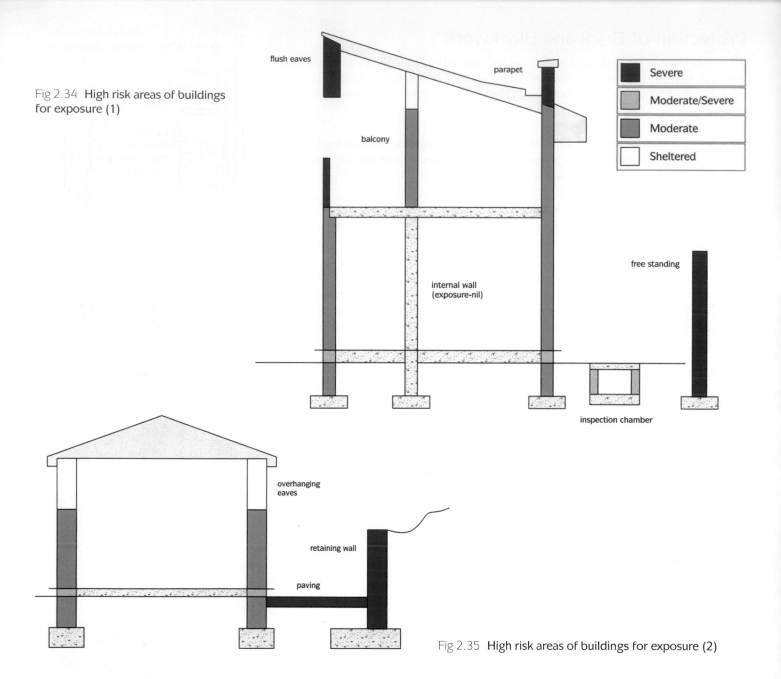

Fig 2.34 High risk areas of buildings for exposure (1)

Fig 2.35 High risk areas of buildings for exposure (2)

Water Penetration

Some water will inevitably penetrate the outer leaf of brickwork when there are long periods of wind-driven rain. The degree of penetration depends largely on the intensity and duration of the wind and rain.

During periods of light wind-driven rain, as illustrated in Figure 2.36, damp patches usually appear first at the joints on the cavity face of the brickwork. When the rain stops they will dry out.

After longer or more intense periods of wind-driven rain, the entire face of the wall may become wet and eventually water may run freely down the inner face of the wall, as illustrated in Figure 2.37.

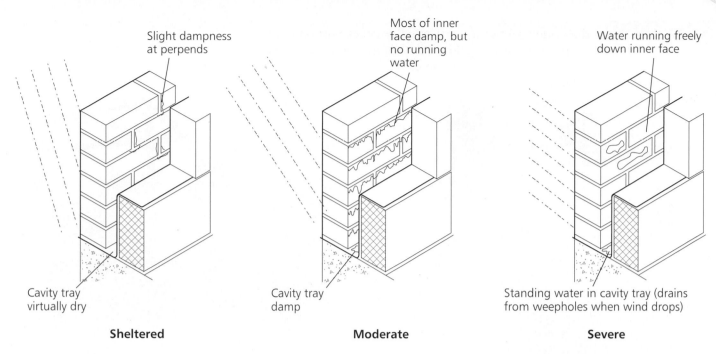

Fig. 2.36 **Light rain on a wall**

Fig. 2.37 **Heavy rain on a wall**

Exclusion of Water

Good design contributes greatly in reducing the risk of water penetration. The wetting of walls can be reduced by ensuring that water is thrown clear of the wall by the use of adequate overhangs and drips and by providing drainage to take water away from brick and blockwork. Large areas of glazing can produce large amounts of surface run-off, which can cause excessive wetting and the possibility of water penetrating the masonry below.

Where walls are to remain wet for long periods, consideration should be given to the use of stronger mortar mixes or sulphate resisting cement.

Work-based Evidence Required

■ Protection of the product and its surrounding area from damage

To meet this requirement, obtain photographs of the construction site where you are working, showing the security fencing or hoarding erected around the perimeter. For evidence of protecting brickwork you could have a photograph, taken at the end of the day showing walling sheeted over to protect it from the weather. Similarly materials such as bricks could be shown placed on pallets sheeted up from the rain. For equipment it could be a photograph of setting out levels and tripods being placed in a secure site hut.

When the photographs have been developed place them on a photographic evidence sheet, and get your supervisor to authenticate them by signing and dating them. Place the evidence in your work-based evidence portfolio, when next in college and map and record it against the syllabus. Figures 2.38 and 2.39 show examples of the type of evidence required.

Fig. 2.38 Site showing security fencing

Fig. 2.39 Protective sheeting on site

Quick quiz Quick quiz Quick quiz Quick quiz Quick quiz

❶ What do we use hessian for?
❷ What are weep holes?
❸ What can happen if bricks become saturated?
❹ What is efflorescence?

PROBLEMS   2.5

In this section you will learn about problems arising from information, resources and methods of work that include:

■ own authority to rectify

■ organizational reporting procedures.

When you have completed this section you will be able to:

■ comply with the given product information to carry out the work efficiently to the required guidance.

Know and understand:

■ how the resources should be handled and how any problems associated with the resources are reported

■ how methods of work, to meet the specification, are carried out and problems are reported.

Defining Problems

We come up against problems every day and in many different ways. It is therefore important for this section to decide on a definition that relates closely to the information, resources and methods of work you employ.

Problems at work could include:

➤ Site personnel absent

➤ Bad weather conditions preventing work from being carried out

➤ Breakdowns of machinery and equipment

➤ Injuries or accidents on site

➤ Shortages of labour and or materials.

The examples above would be described by most people as problems. Problems can be defined as:

➤ Difficult situations

➤ Occurrences causing work to stop

➤ Situations where decisions need to be made

➤ A situation preventing site personnel from getting the job done.

However, for the purposes of this section, the last idea is probably closest to the definition we require, which is:

➤ A problem is a situation that causes a deviation from a known plan.

This definition assumes that we have a plan: in other words, we know what is supposed to happen. No building project would get very far without a plan, even if it is in note form; a situation more common for a small company.

Of course, the planning of events makes us take decisions and decisions are closely allied to problems. This is because we solve them by deciding between different possible scenarios. Therefore, a suitable definition of a decision would be the following:

➤ A decision is a choice between alternatives, where we choose the one that best meets our objectives.

Therefore, one of the benefits of having a plan is that we can sometimes predict a problem occurring. This is called a potential problem.

The problem has not occurred yet, but our planning suggests it might. We therefore take action to prevent this happening, like wearing personal protective equipment on site. Or we have a contingency plan ready for it, like following the drill precautions in the event of a fire alarm sounding.

So we can say that this section is about three ideas:

- Problems and how we effectively deal with them
- Making effective decisions
- Dealing with potential problems.

Solving Problems

The ability to solve a problem involves planning because when you are trying to solve a problem, planning helps you work through it. If you follow the plan you will know the logical actions to take to arrive at a suitable solution.

Following the plan should enable you to use your time more effectively. It should also reduce the risk of making a decision that may turn out to be the wrong one. Not that making decisions is wrong, it just sometimes happens that you will make the wrong one. If this happens, what reasons could you give for making a wrong decision? What about the following:

- The problem was not thought through adequately
- The situation demanded that I act to prevent further losses
- Because of pressure of work I did not have time to look at the alternatives
- I lost sight of what the company was trying to achieve
- More information was required, but I did not know how to go about finding it
- I should have asked more questions.

The list above gives some of the reasons for failing to solve problems during the decision making process. You may have noticed that reasons two and three often occur at work, and that is something you may have to take into account. A building contract is unlikely to run as smoothly as it might or as it was planned. Always remember you will rarely have enough time to think things through properly: that is the nature of the industry.

However, if you have a plan to follow, then your problem solving will improve, as long as you follow each stage of the plan as thoroughly as possible.

Planning

The activity of solving problems falls into three areas:

Understanding the problem

- Thinking of solutions and using the best one
- Putting the solution into effect and then evaluating it.

In other words:

- This is what I think is wrong
- This decision should fix it
- Did the solution work?

Remember every activity has several important stages that make up the whole problem-solving plan.

The plan is a means to understand the problem. So what might be the structure of the plan? The answers lie in the plan itself, the plan must be problem-solving and include the following ideas:

Understanding the Problem

Recognize the problem

Define the problem.

Identify its Causes

Creating and choosing solutions:

Think of possible solutions

Decide on the best solution.

Implement and Evaluate:

Implement the chosen solution

Monitor the outcome and evaluate the results.

Remember decision making is an important part of solving problems.

Source: CITB-Construction Skills, *Problems and Decisions*, **1994.**

Materials, Waste Disposal and Recycling

The following bodies provide official guidance and useful information on materials, general recycling and waste disposal issues.

Environment and Energy Helpline. Tel. 0800 585 794

Free telephone advice on waste minimization and management.

Environmental Technology Best Practice Programme
www.etbpp.gov.uk

Provides impartial authoritative information on best practice and managing resource use. Their publications are disseminated through many channels including trade associations, Business Links and the Environment Agency. These include:

Finding Hidden Profit – 200 Tips for Reducing Waste.

Green Efficiency: Running a Cost Effective, Environmentally Aware Office.

Saving Money Through Waste Minimization: Teams and Champions.

The British Standards Institute
www.bsi.org.uk

ISO 14001 is the international standard which specifies the requirements for an environmental management system. ISO 14001 is a management tool which organizations of any type can use to help them control the impact on the environment of their activities, products and services in a structured and systematic way.

Sources of Information

The British Standards Institute (BSI)

www.bsi-global.com

British Standards is the national standards body of the UK, responsible for facilitating, publishing and marketing British Standards and other guidelines.

BSI provides:

■ The development of private, national and international standards
■ Information on standards and international trade
■ Independent certification of management systems and products
■ Product testing services
■ Training and seminars
■ Commodity inspection services

With collaborative ventures and a strong national and international profile, British Standards are at the heart of the world of standardization.

The Building Research Establishment (BRE)

www.bre.co.uk

The BRE provides impartial information on all aspects of the built environment.

For information, or technical advice, on building and construction, and the prevention and control of fire, consult the website
www.bre.co.uk

Details of BRE publications are available from the BRE bookshop
www.brebookshop.com

Manual Handling

For more information about manual handling and storage of materials why not visit the following website.

Health and Safety Executive

www.hse.gov.uk

The HSE website contains information about the objectives of HSE, how to contact HSE, how to complain, recent press releases and research and current initiatives. Information about risks at work and information about different workplaces is also available.

The Effects of Weather

For further information about the effects of the weather on walling construction, why not visit the websites of the better known manufacturers and suppliers.

Problem Solving

For more information about problem solving why not visit the following websites.

CITB-Construction Skills

www.citb-constructionskills.co.uk.co.org

CITB-ConstructionSkills have an excellent series of learning modules entitled Supervisor Development in the Construction Industry that cover in detail problems and decisions. They are highly recommended as a learning resource.

3

Chapter three

Prepare and Mix Concrete and Mortars

NVQ Level 1   Unit No. VR 36   Prepare and Mix Concrete and Mortars

This unit, in the context of brickwork and the construction industry work environment, is about:

- interpreting instructions
- adopting safe and healthy working practices
- selecting materials, components and equipment
- preparing and mixing, by hand and mechanically, concrete and mortars.

There are four sections in this chapter: maintenance, methods of work, programme and resources.

This chapter will now cover preparing and mixing concrete and mortars.

MAINTENANCE   3.1

In this section you will learn about maintenance and the responsibility of an operative for the care of hand tools, mixers and ancillary equipment.

When you have completed this section you will be able to:

- comply with the given contract instructions to carry out the work efficiently to the required specification.

Know and understand:

- how maintenance of tools and equipment is carried out.

Hand Tools

Tools of any description deserve careful treatment. The reward to the owner is a prolongation of their life and greater efficiency and ease when working. Because of the nature of the work, concreting tools can easily spoil through rusting or, in the case of timber tools, through constant changes of climatic conditions. It should, therefore, become a habit to thoroughly clean and dry all tools after each day's work, with the steel floating and finishing trowels greatly benefiting from a periodic application of linseed oil.

Power Tools

Powered hand tools should be cleaned regularly. This is especially important with cutting and abrasive tools because the dust produced can easily pass into and damage the motor. Clean every tool regularly before dust accumulates to a harmful extent. This may mean a daily clean for tools in constant use.

Information for cleaning and maintaining power tools can be found in the instruction manual for each machine.

Mixers

Daily Maintenance

Powered mixers are very expensive and must be cleaned and serviced daily in order to:

- increase the working life of the mixer
- maintain the ease of operation of the mixer
- maintain the productivity of the mixer by reducing breakdowns.

Normally the operator of the mixer will carry out the daily maintenance of the mixer, which involves cleaning and lubricating correctly.

Lubrication

Ask your supervisor or tutor to identify and locate the lubricating points on your mixer and demonstrate the use of a grease gun.

Cleaning

For cleaning the mixer you will require:

- water and a stiff brush for washing and cleaning cement from the drum, chassis and motor cover.

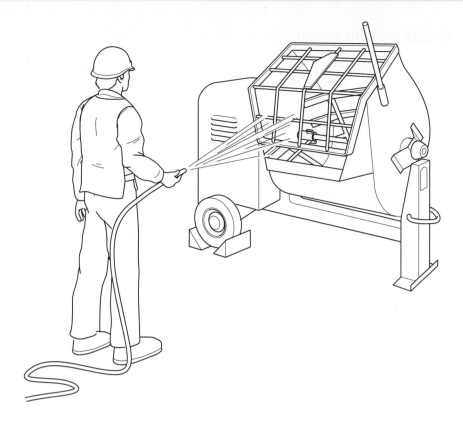

Fig. 3.1 **Operative cleaning mixer**

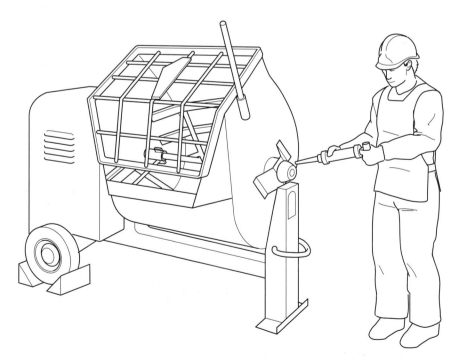

Fig. 3.2 **Operative cleaning and lubricating mixer**

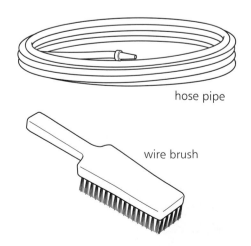

hose pipe

wire brush

Fig. 3.3 **The mixing and cleaning tools**

Avoid wetting the engine as moisture can prevent the engine from starting.

Point to note

The information in this section of the book is to be used only as a guide for studying the manual you will be using.

Point to note

Remove oil drain plug and drain oil while the engine is still warm.

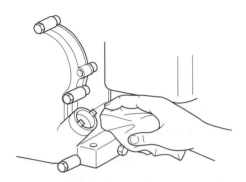

Fig 3.6 Cleaning around oil fill

Checking Oil Level

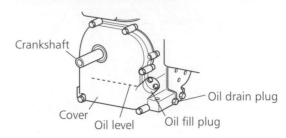

Crankshaft

Oil drain plug

Cover   Oil fill plug

Oil level

Fig. 3.4 **Checking oil level (1)**

Check oil level regularly – after each five hours of operation.

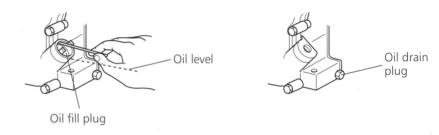

Oil level

Oil drain plug

Oil fill plug

Fig. 3.5 **Checking oil level (2)**

Ensure Oil Level Is Maintained ▰▰▰

Change Oil

Change oil after five hours of operation. Thereafter change every 25 hours of operation.

To Fill Crankcase with Oil

Place the engine on level surface. Clean area around oil fill before removing oil fill plug, oilminder or dipstick.

Oil Fill Plug

Remove oil fill plug, oilminder or cap and dipstick and refill with new oil of proper grade.

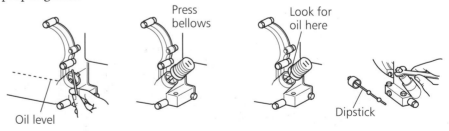

Press bellows

Look for oil here

Oil level

Dipstick

Fig. 3.7 **Removing oil fill plug**

Using a Funnel

Fill crankcase to point of overflowing.

POUR SLOWLY.

Replace oil fill plug, oilminder or dipstick.

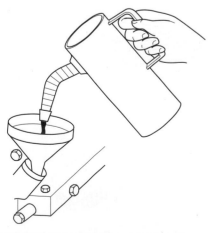

Fig. 3.8 **Using a funnel**

Servicing a Single Element Air Cleaner

Clean and re-oil foam element at three month intervals or every 25 hours, whichever occurs first.

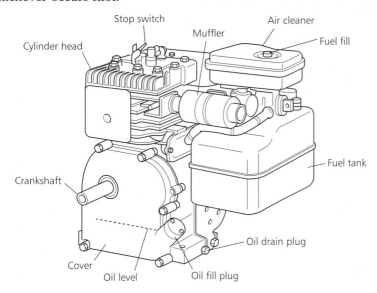

Stop switch
Air cleaner
Cylinder head
Muffler
Fuel fill
Fuel tank
Crankshaft
Oil drain plug
Cover
Oil fill plug
Oil level

Fig. 3.9 **Example of an air cleaner**

Clean Cooling System

Dust or dirt may clog the rotating screen and the air cooling system, especially after prolonged service.

Clean yearly or every 100 hours, whichever occurs first, remove the blower housing and clean the areas shown to avoid overspending, overheating and engine damage.

Clean more often if necessary.

> Point to note

Service air cleaner more often under dusty conditions.

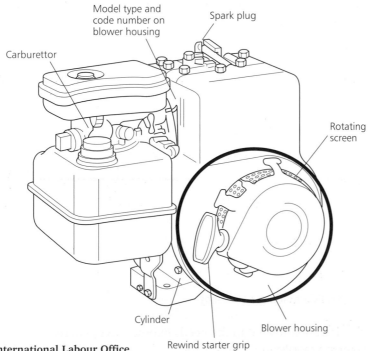

Model type and code number on blower housing
Spark plug
Carburettor
Rotating screen
Cylinder
Blower housing
Rewind starter grip

Source: International Labour Office

Fig. 3.10 **Cleaning cooling system**

Ancillary Equipment

Work-based Evidence Required

■ Use and Maintain:

■ hand tools

■ mixing plant and equipment

■ ancillary equipment

To meet these requirements, ask your supervisor to fill out a witness testimony sheet for you stating that you have used and maintained hand tools, mixing plant and equipment and ancillary equipment.

When you have received the signed and dated witness testimony sheet, place it in your work-based evidence portfolio, when next in college and map and record it against the syllabus.

Quick quiz Quick quiz Quick quiz Quick quiz Quick quiz

❶ How might tools spoil?
❷ What can easily damage power tools?
❸ Why should mixers be cleaned and serviced?
❹ What do you require for cleaning a mixer?
❺ How often should you service a single element air cleaner?

METHODS OF WORK 3.2

In this section you will learn about the application of knowledge for safe work practices, procedures, skills and transference of competence, relating to the area of work and material used to:

■ gauge and mix concrete and mortars by hand and mixer
■ use hand tools, mixing plant and equipment
■ work with crane handled or mechanically handled loads.

You will also learn about teamwork and communication related to the needs of other occupations associated with preparing and mixing concrete and mortars.

When you have completed this section you will be able to:

■ comply with the given contract instructions to carry out the work efficiently to the required specification.

Know and understand:

■ how methods of work are carried out and problems reported.

Gauging Concrete

Concrete is a mixture of sand, gravel, cement and water that sets and hardens.

There are two common methods of gauging or proportioning materials in the mixing of concrete:

➤ using volumes or ratios such as 1 : 2 : 4. this method is based on prescribed specifications, which show the volume relationship between each ingredient

➤ weighing the aggregate in relationship to the weight of 1 cubic metre of concrete.

> **Definition**
>
> The accurate proportioning of concrete materials to produce a specified concrete mix.

> **Point to note**
>
> Weight gauging is the most accurate of the two methods.

Mixing by Volume

Concrete mixes are designated by three numbers, for example 1 : 2 : 4. This describes the quantity relationship or ratio, which is determined by the architect or engineer.

The first number (1) refers to cement – one part or one bag.

The second number (2) refers to the fine aggregate or sand – therefore, two parts of sand.

The third number (4) refers to the coarse aggregate or stone – therefore, four parts of stone.

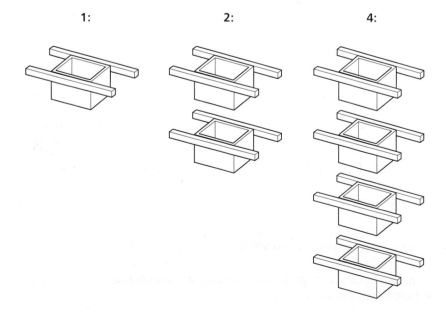

Fig. 3.11 Concrete mixing: mixing by volume

Fig. 3.12 Cement – example of one part – one part or one bag

Fig. 3.13 Two parts – see text

Fig. 3.14 Four parts – see text

Therefore the ratio 1 : 2 : 4 is defined as:

1 part cement

2 parts sand

4 parts stone.

The strength requirements of the concrete determines the mixing proportions.

Mixing by Weight

Figure 3.15 shows the amounts of materials (by weight) needed to produce 1 cubic metre of concrete.

Strength in kg/cm²	Water/ Cement Ratio	Cement kg	Fine Aggregate (Sand)	Coarse Aggregate (Stone)	Water Litres *
350	0.52	355	880	950	185
300	0.58	320	910	950	186
250	0.66	280	940	950	185
200	0.74	245	970	950	182
150	0.86	210	1000	950	181

Point to note

The table gives the total amount of water required. However, if the sand and stone are wet then the amount of water required will have to be reduced.

* The table gives the total amount of water needed. However, if the sand and stone are very wet then the amount of water required will have to be reduced.

Fig. 3.15 Mixing by weight. Table showing amount of materials by weight needed to produce 1 cubic metre of concrete

The table is used as follows:

➤ The architect or engineer will specify the concrete strength required.

The specification calls for a concrete strength of 350 kg/cm². This means that the concrete must support a load of 350 kg per square centimetre.

Now read across the table from left to right on the appropriate line.

➤ The number 350 represents the predictable ultimate strength of the concrete

➤ The number 0.52 represents the water/cement ratio

➤ The number 355 represents the weight of cement required

➤ The number 880 represents the amount of sand required

➤ The number 185 represents the amount of water required.

Strength in kg/cm²	Water/ Cement Ratio	Cement kg	Fine Aggregate (Sand)	Coarse Aggregate (Stone)	Water Litres *
➤ 350	0.52	355	880	950	185
300	0.58	320	910	950	186
250	0.66	280	940	950	185
200	0.74	245	970	950	182
150	0.86	210	1000	950	181

Fig. 3.16 Table with arrow indicating appropriate line

Gauging Mortar

Mortar is a mixture of sand and cement or lime, or all three, that hardens as it dries and is used for jointing brickwork or as a render. Normally the mortar design specification is determined by the requirements of the structure to be built. Once the required mortar design specification is known, gauging has to strictly follow these instructions.

The most commonly used binding materials in mortar preparation are lime and cement, used separately or in combination.

Gauging Mortar – The accurate proportioning of mortar materials to produce a specified mortar mix.

Gauging and Mixing

Accurate proportioning and consistent mixing times and conditions are essential if uniform mortar mixes are to be produced. The two biggest sources of error in mortar mixing are the use of the shovel as a gauge of quantity, and the bulking of wet sand. Proportioning by weight gives the closest control but, if materials are to be proportioned by volume, gauge boxes or buckets should be used, carefully filled to capacity and struck off level. On balance, the proper gauging of ready-mixed lime-sand mixes with cement results in a better proportioned mix than do separate dry ingredients.

Proportions and Ratios

Mortar as stated is proportioned by volume using the ratios specified. The ratio is always accompanied by the description of the mortar type, for example:

- Cement/Lime Mortar 1 : 1 : 6
- Cement Mortar 1 : 6
- Lime Mortar 1 : 6.

Volume ratios express the quantitative relationship between ingredients. For example, the cement/lime mortar ratio 1 : 1 : 6 means that there are three ingredients.

In the order written, each is:

- One (1) part cement
- One (1) part lime
- Six (6) parts sand.

Point to note

The capacity of the gauge box should be equivalent to exactly one bag of cement.

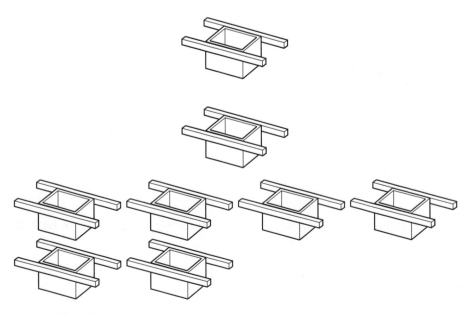

Fig. 3.17 **Mix ratio**

The most common types of mortar are:

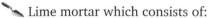 Cement mortar which consists of:

– cement

– sand

– water

Fig. 3.18 Cement mortar – example of mix ratio

Lime mortar which consists of:

– lime

– sand

– water

Fig. 3.19 Lime mortar – example of mix ratio

Cement/Lime mortar which consists of:

– cement

– lime

– sand

– water

Fig. 3.20 Cement/lime mortar – example of mix ratio

Fig. 3.21 Bag of cement

Fig. 3.22 Bag of lime

Factory prepared mortar which consists of:

– factory proportioned and bagged cement and lime

– sand

– water.

For example in a cement/lime mortar (1 : 1 : 6):

the first number in this ratio 1 : 1 : 6 is always the cement

the second number in this ratio (1 : 1 : 6) is always the lime

the third number in this ratio (1 : 1 : 6) is always the aggregate or sand.

If the ratio is given in two numbers, for example (cement/mortar 1 : 6):

it means that 1 is the proportion of cement

6 is the proportion of aggregate (sand).

If the ratio is given as a lime mortar 1 : 6:

the first number 1 is the proportion of lime

the second number 6 is the proportion of aggregate.

Fig. 3.23 Aggregate or sand

Source: International Labour Office

Mixing Concrete by Hand and Mixer ▬

Hand Mixing Concrete

Figure 3.24 shows a typical set-up for hand mixing concrete.

Fig. 3.24 Illustration of hand mixing concrete

You have been provided with the basic material required for mixing concrete. These materials have been measured by volume to produce a 1 : 2 : 4 ratio mix.

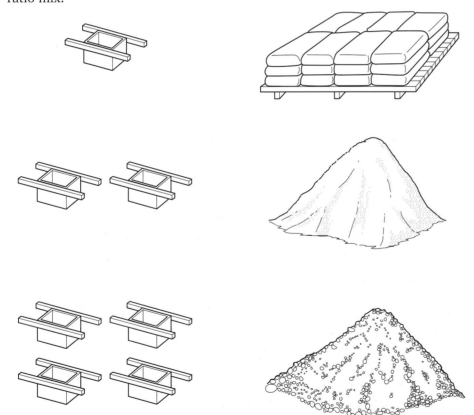

Fig. 3.25 Materials for the mix

Using as a guide the instructions listed in this section of the book, make a batch of concrete using proportions of 1 : 2 : 4.

Method

Place one half of the sand onto the mixing base.

Place one half of the stone on top of the sand.

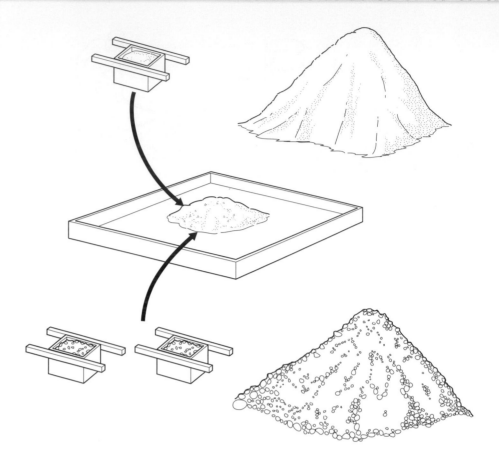

Fig. 3.26 **Mixing the sand and stone**

Now place approximately half of the cement on top of this pile.

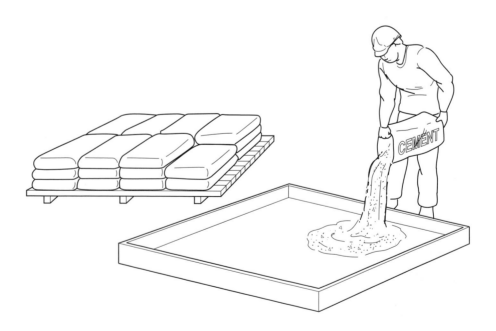

Fig. 3.27 **Placing the cement**

Repeat the procedure for the remainder of the materials.

Dry mix the aggregate and cement. Proceed as follows:

Using a shovel turn the material over bottom to top as shown in
Figure 3.28.

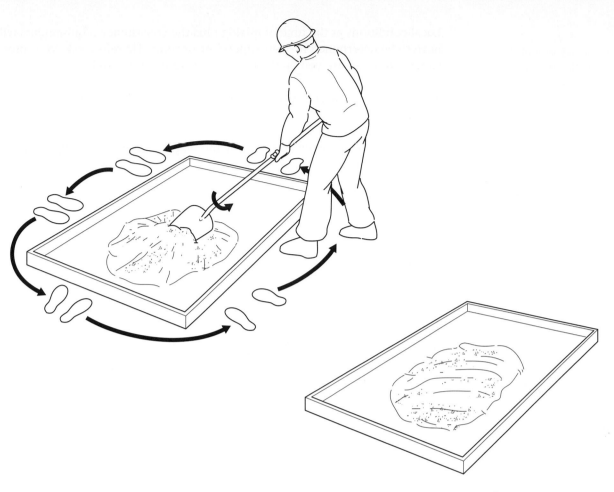

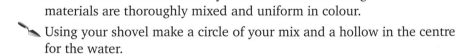

Fig. 3.28 **Turning over concrete**

![shovel] Move around the material as you mix. Continue mixing until all the materials are thoroughly mixed and uniform in colour.

![shovel] Using your shovel make a circle of your mix and a hollow in the centre for the water.

Fig. 3.29 **Making a hollow for water**

> **Point to note**

Normally the quantity of water required for this ratio mix would be 32 litres. The water content of the aggregate will determine whether less water will be required for mixing.

Local conditions at the time of mixing plus the consistency requirements will have to be determined by your supervisor or tutor. Therefore ask your tutor or supervisor to advise you on the quantity of water to be used.

Now fill the hollow with water, using your shovel to turn the mix outside to centre.

Once the water has been absorbed by the material, use a chopping motion to mix the materials.

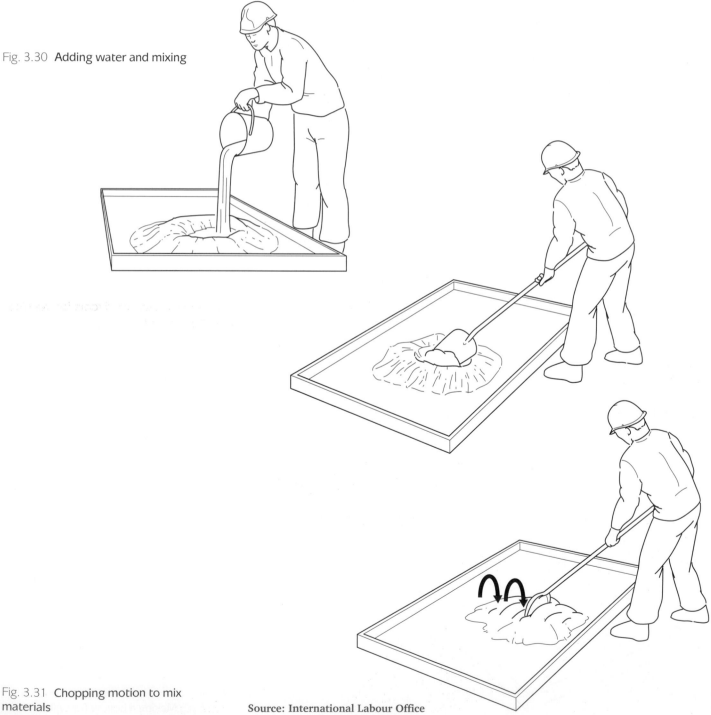

Fig. 3.30 Adding water and mixing

Fig. 3.31 Chopping motion to mix materials

Source: International Labour Office

Ask your tutor or supervisor to check your mix to see if it is acceptable.

Clean your tools and equipment before storing them away.

Machine Mixing Concrete

You have been provided with all the materials and equipment illustrated below.

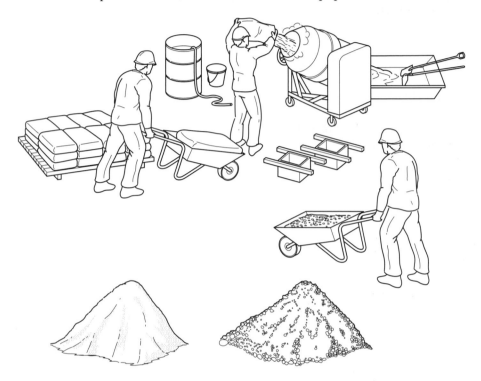

Fig. 3.32 **Materials and tools for machine mixing concrete**

Place your mixing materials as close as possible to where you are working to allow for speedy placement of concrete.

Position the mixing equipment close to the mixing materials.

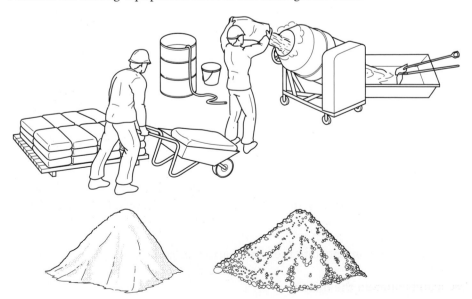

Fig. 3.33 **Mixing equipment (next to materials)**

Now you will mix a batch of concrete proceeding as follows:

Position your mixer safely – that is, level, and chock wheels to prevent movement once you have started the motor.

To avoid overloading the mixer, check its drum capacity.

Ask your supervisor or tutor for the mix specification.

Start the mixer. With the safety cover in place add about half of the water.

Using the gauge box add all the sand.

Add all the cement.

Add a little water to the mix. This will loosen the mix and relieve the strain on the engine or motor.

Fig. 3.34 Adding water to the concrete mix

Fig. 3.35 Adding sand to the concrete mix

Fig. 3.36 Adding cement to the concrete mix

Fig. 3.37 Adding more water to the mix

Point to note

Be careful not to add too much water. Excess water lowers the strength of the concrete.

Using the gauge box add all the coarse aggregate to the drum.
Pour in more water.

Remember that the water–cement ratio varies according to the moisture content of the sand.

dry

wet

normal.

Allow 5 to 6 minutes mixing time after all the materials have been loaded in the drum.

Empty the drum contents into the wheelbarrow or containers.

Clean and maintain the mixer.

Source: International Labour Office

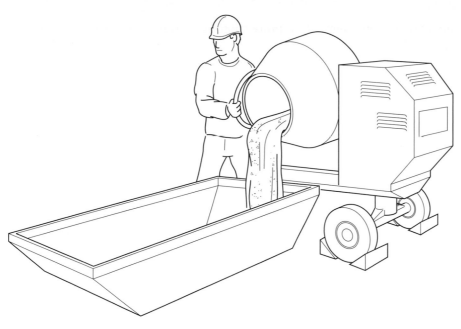

Fig. 3.38 **Emptying the contents of the mixer**

Mixing Mortar by Hand and Mixer ▬▬

Hand Mixing Mortars

Mortar as stated is a mixture of sand and cement or lime, or all three, that hardens as it dries and is used for jointing brickwork or as a render.

Figure 3.39 shows a typical set-up for hand mixing mortar.

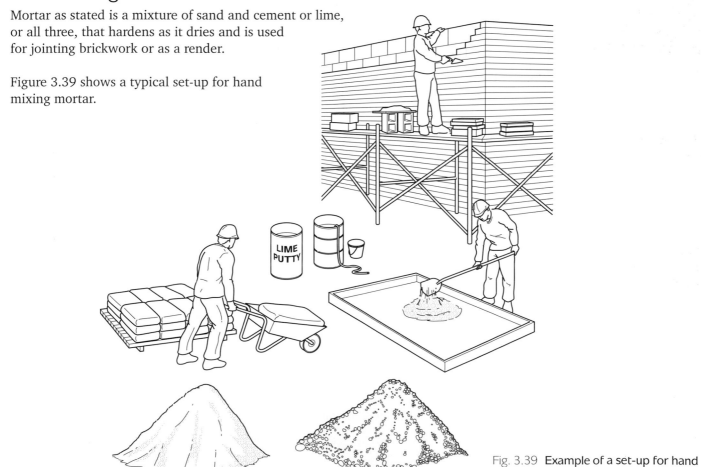

Fig. 3.39 **Example of a set-up for hand mixing mortar**

Fig. 3.40 1 part cement

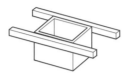

Fig. 3.41 1 part lime

> *Point to note*

Gauge boxes are built to hold exactly the same volume, regardless of the material being measured.

The most common method for proportioning mortars mixes is by ratio, for example 1 : 1 : 6.

The first number (1) always refers to cement – therefore one part cement.

The second number (2) always refers to hydrated lime – therefore one part hydrated lime.

The third and last number of the ratio (6) refers to sand – therefore six parts sand.

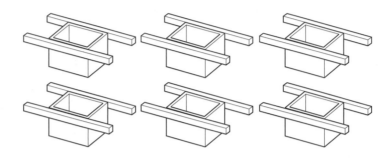

Fig 3.42 6 parts sand

The most common types of mortar are:

- factory prepared mortar
- lime mortar
- cement mortar
- cement/lime mortar (gauged mortar).

Factory prepared mortar requires only the addition of water to the mix.

> *Point to note*

The quality of the sand may vary from place to place. This means that the proportion of sand in a mortar mix may vary accordingly.

Fig 3.43 Examples of mortar

Lime mortar consists of lime, sand and water.

Fig. 3.44 **Lime mortar**

To make a lime mortar you should proceed as follows:

According to the instructions or specifications you have been given, measure out the materials with the gauge box.

Place one half of the sand on the mixing platform.

Wet the sand.

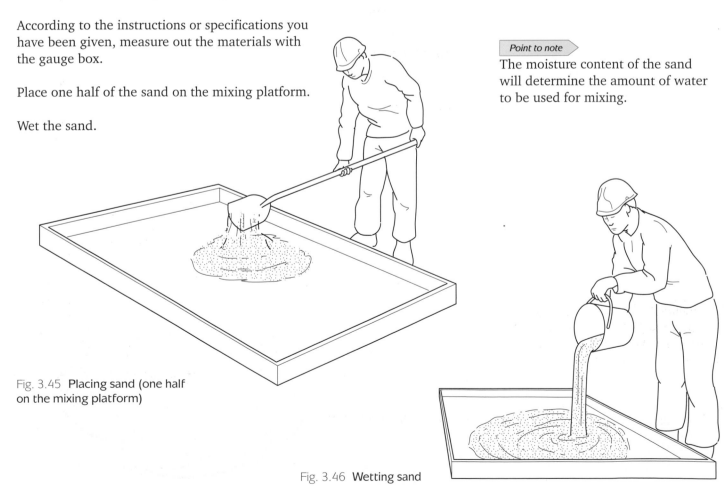

Fig. 3.45 **Placing sand (one half on the mixing platform)**

Fig. 3.46 **Wetting sand**

Now spread it out with your shovel.

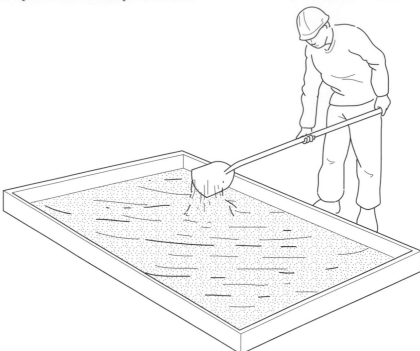

Fig. 3.47 Spreading the sand out using a shovel

Place one half of the lime on top and spread it out. Now place the rest of the sand and the lime on the mix.

Turn the material over with your shovel from bottom to top as shown in Figure 3.48.

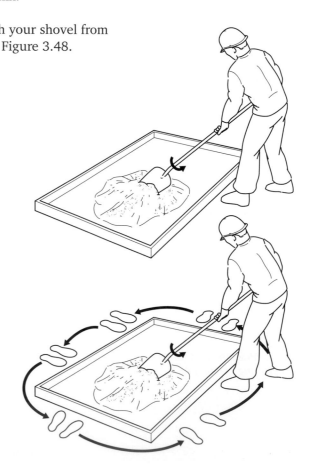

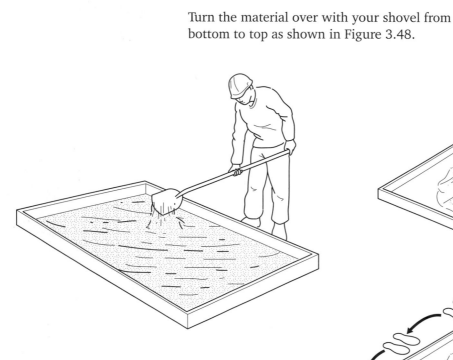

Fig. 3.48 Turning mortar over using a shovel

Move around the material as you mix. Continue mixing until all the materials are blended well and uniform in colour.

The mix may require more water but before you add water ask your supervisor or tutor to check.

Then, when the water has been absorbed by the material, use a chopping motion to mix the materials. Lime mortar can be used as soon as it is mixed.

To produce a cement mortar, the same technique is used except that you do not add the water until you have dry mixed the sand and cement.

Say, for example, that the specification you have received calls for a 1 : 4 cement mortar. This means one part cement to four parts sand.

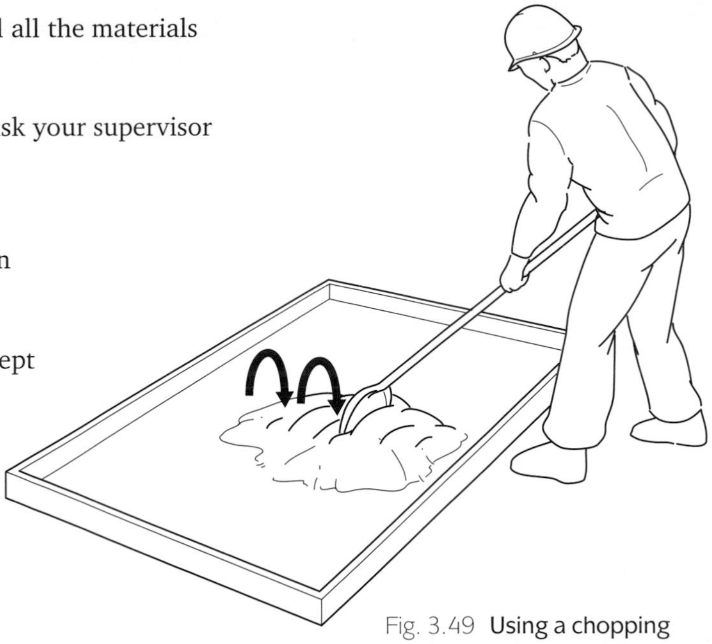

Place half of the sand on the mixing platform.

Spread half of the cement on top of this.

Fig. 3.49 **Using a chopping motion to mix materials**

Fig. 3.50 **Placing the sand and cement on the mixing platform**

Now repeat this operation exactly putting first the remainder of the sand and then the remainder of the cement on the mix. This is called a sandwich mix.

Dry mix the materials by turning the material over with your shovel from bottom to top until the colour of the mix is uniform.

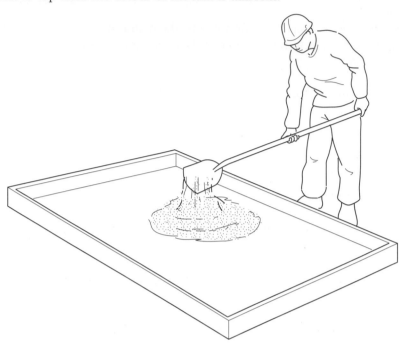

Fig. 3.51 Dry mixing the materials

Now add water and mix again, keeping in mind that the water content of the sand will determine the exact amount of water for mixing.

Fig. 3.52 Adding water to the dry mix

> **Point to note**

When mixing mortars always wear safety glasses and the appropriate personal protective equipment.

Source: International Labour Office

In order to produce a cement/lime mortar (gauged mortar), you only have to add the specified amount (measured by ratio) of cement to the measured quantity of lime mortar. A 1 : 1 : 6 is a good gauge mix ratio.

Clean your tools and equipment before storing them away.

Machine Mixing Mortars

You have been provided with all the materials and equipment listed below:

- Mixer – petrol/diesel or electric
- Gauge box
- Wheelbarrow
- Shovels
- Cement – Portland variety
- Sand
- Water
- Buckets
- Fuel – compatible with mixer
- Electrical outlet and cable for connecting
- Lime – hydrated.

Locate your mortar mixing equipment as close as possible to where you are working in order to provide quick access to the materials.

Study carefully the placement of equipment and materials illustrated in Figure 3.53.

Place the mixing equipment close to the mixing materials.

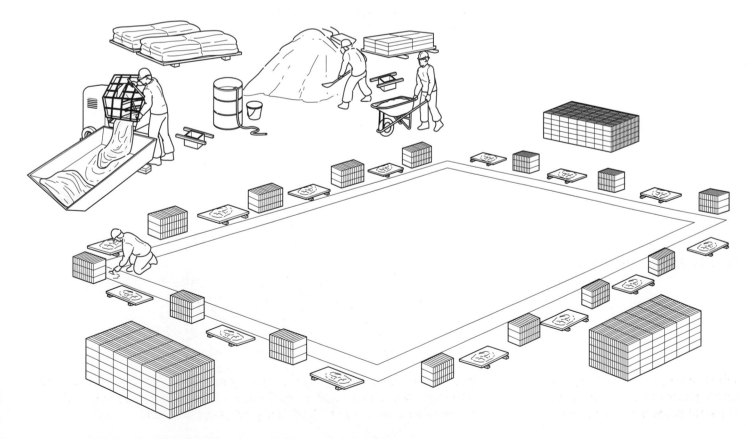

Fig. 3.53 **Placement of materials and equipment for machine mixing mortars**

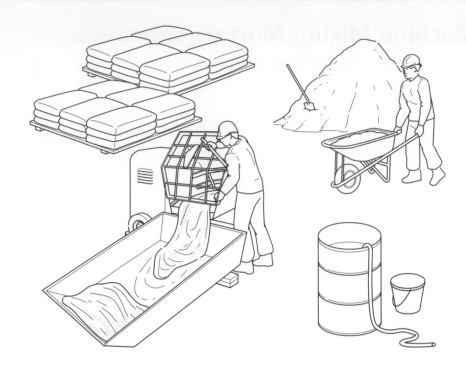

Fig. 3.54 **Place the mixing equipment next to the materials**

Now you will mix a batch of mortar, proceeding as follows:

Position the mixer safely – that is, level, and chock wheels to prevent movement once you have started the motor. To avoid overloading the mixer, check its drum capacity.

Point to note

Overloading can cause accidents. If there are no manufacturer's specifications ask your supervisor or tutor for this information.

Ask your tutor or supervisor for the mixing specifications.

- Type of mortar
- Ratio.

Start the mixer. With the drum safety cover in place add about 50 per cent of the water.

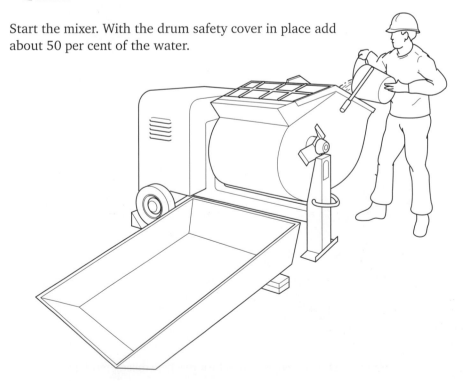

Fig. 3.55 **Adding water to the mixer**

Using the gauge box add all the sand.

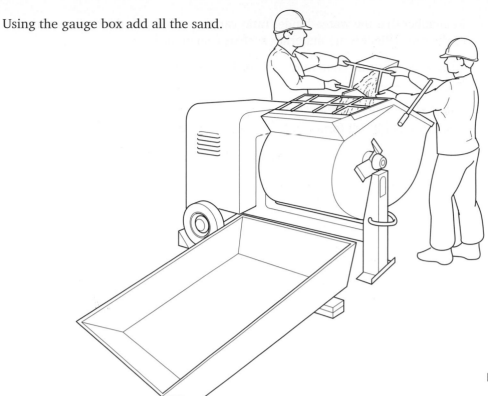

Fig. 3.56 **Adding sand using the gauge box**

If you are mixing cement mortar, add the cement. If you are mixing a gauged mortar, add the lime requirements. If you are mixing a factory mixed mortar then place it in the mixer.

If the mixer motor seems to be straining, add a little water to the mix. This will loosen the mix and relieve the strain on the engine or motor.

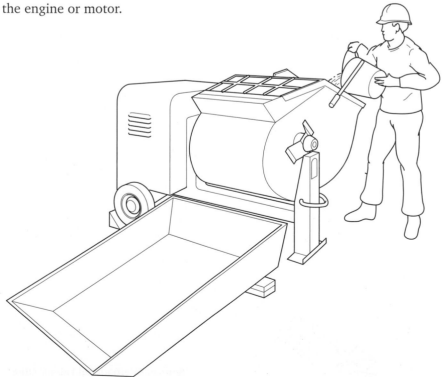

> **Point to note**
>
> Since this is a trial batch of mortar ask your tutor or supervisor to check the consistency of the mix as the quality of the mortar should relate to the type of material to be laid, i.e. porous or non-porous building components.

Fig. 3.57 **Adding water to the mix**

Remember that the water–binder ratio varies according to the moisture content of the sand. Binders are materials such as cement or lime.

To test the moisture content of sand pick up a handful and squeeze into a ball.

- If dry it will crumble
- If wet it will drip water
- If normal it will form a ball and retain its shape.

Allow 5 to 6 minutes mixing time after all the materials are in the drum.

Empty the drum contents into the wheelbarrows or containers.

Clean and maintain your mixing tools and equipment after the mixing has been completed.

Do not allow the materials to harden on your tools and equipment.

> **Caution**
>
> Do not operate mixers without your tutor's or supervisor's permission.

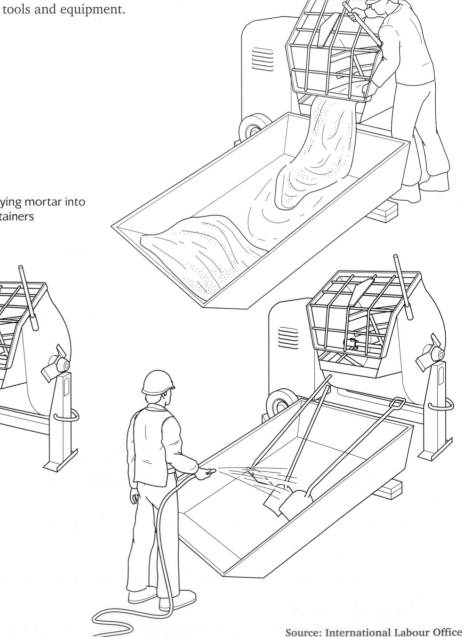

Fig. 3.58 **Emptying mortar into barrows or containers**

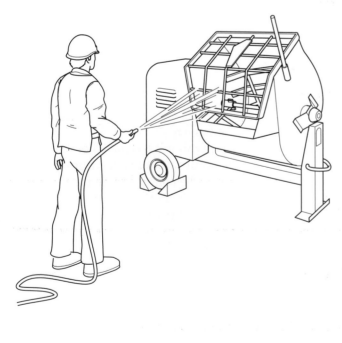

Fig. 3.59 **Cleaning the machine**

Source: International Labour Office

Work-based Evidence Required

■ Work skills to:

■ gauge and mix

■ Gauge and mix to contractors' working instructions:

■ mortars and/or concrete

To meet these requirements, ask your supervisor to fill out a witness testimony sheet for you describing your work skills in gauging and mixing mortar and concrete to your employer's working instructions.

When you have received the signed and dated witness testimony sheet, place it in your work-based evidence portfolio when next in college and map and record it against the syllabus.

Quick quiz Quick quiz Quick quiz Quick quiz Quick quiz

❶ What does the term gauged mortar mean?
❷ Define the term 'measured by ratio'.
❸ What are the ingredients of a lime mortar?
❹ What does the term turning over concrete mean?
❺ Give an example of a mix ratio for a cement mortar.

PROGRAMME 3.3

In this section you will learn about agreed starting and finishing times.

When you have completed this section you will be able to:
■ complete the work within the allocated time, in accordance with the programme of work.

Know and understand:
■ what the programme is for the work to be carried out and why deadlines should be kept.

Programmes

Programmes of Work

The programme of work is the key document containing the time to be taken, or duration, and order, or sequence, of operations for the completion of the building. It covers three critical areas.

The master programme shows start and finish dates, duration, sequencing and relationships for the whole contract.

The stage programme covers a precise stage of the contract, or the overall programme for a one to two month period in much greater detail.

The weekly programme functions at the level where the work takes place; it requires frequent up-dating and reviews.

Monitoring and Control of Operations

It requires a great deal of information to be able to monitor and control work progress. Programmes of work do this for us. They let us know:

- What resources (workers, machinery, tools) have been allocated
- The planned output to achieve the programme
- The productivity rates used in the tender or contract plan
- The key control operations.

When we have this information we can monitor and control work progress. Information for the work programme comes from various sources. For example, the tender and contract programme will be based on calculations of the resources needed and the planned output to achieve the programme.
There will usually be stage programmes that list the resources and output for different parts of the contract.

In order to measure progress we need to compare the actual output against the planned output. So, we measure against what was planned.

There are a number of factors, some outside the control of management, which can lead to a programme's modification. These include:

- Bad weather
- Labour shortages
- Industrial action
- Contract variations
- Bad planning.

Recording Progress

There are a number of methods of recording progress, for example:

- Bar charts
- Annotated plans
- Numerical schedules
- Histograms
- Graphs and other similar methods.

The type of programme adopted for small and medium sized contracts is usually based on the Gantt chart, which provides a graphic description of each operation, as illustrated in Figure 3.60. Because Gantt charts are presented as a series of horizontal bars, they are generally referred to as bar charts.

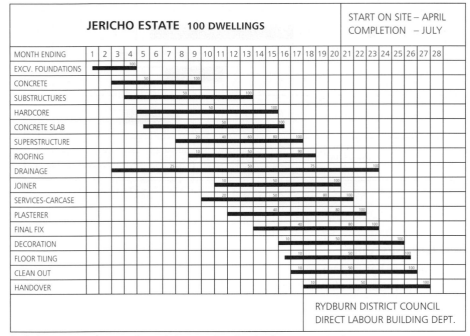

Typical programme for rate of completion on a housing development contract

Fig. 3.60 **A Gantt chart**

Operations are shown separately with the length of each bar depending on the duration of the activity. These bars have a limited dependency upon each other, and this is one of the shortcomings of the system because some operations can be in advance of others that may have fallen behind. The results can be interpreted in different ways, which means that agreement is not always unanimous when assessing progress at meetings.

Schedules and Charts

Bar charts are the most common form of monitoring progress on a construction site. The main advantage of bar charts is that they relate to the programme of work. A bar chart lists all the jobs that need to be carried out, bearing in mind that certain tasks have to be completed before others can begin. A bar chart shows the expected start and finish dates for each of the tasks that need to be carried out.

Monitoring Progress

There are several ways of monitoring progress, using a bar chart.

Single Bar System

This chart involves a single bar indicating the activity. As work progresses, the bar is filled to indicate the amount of work completed, as shown in Figure 3.61.

REMEMBER

Most bar charts are based on a five-day working week.

The single bar system is very simple and probably the least informative of bar chart systems.

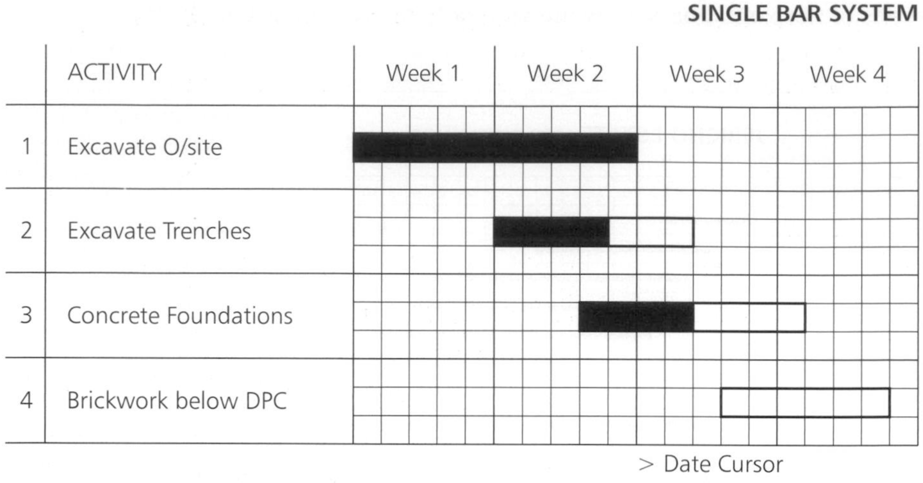

SINGLE BAR SYSTEM

	ACTIVITY	Week 1	Week 2	Week 3	Week 4
1	Excavate O/site				
2	Excavate Trenches				
3	Concrete Foundations				
4	Brickwork below DPC				

> Date Cursor

Fig. 3.61 **A single bar system**

Two Bar Systems

Using the two bar system you can tell how much has been completed for each week of operation as shown in Figure 3.62.

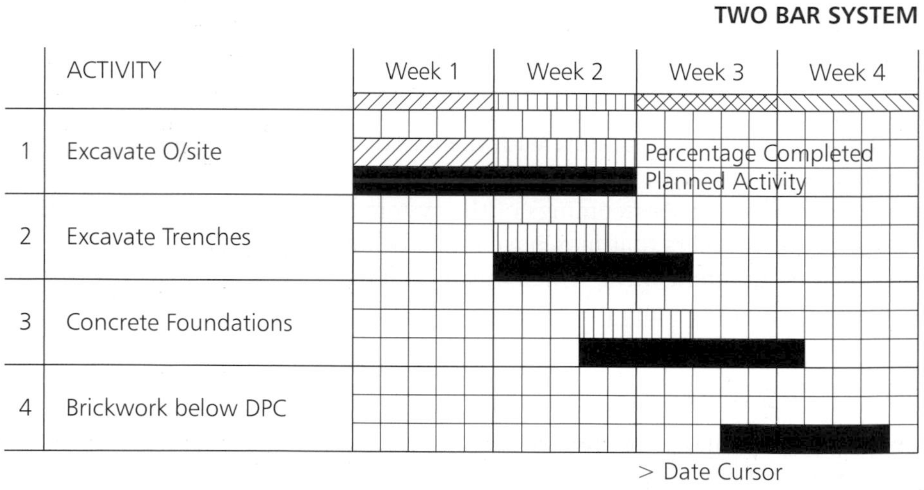

TWO BAR SYSTEM

	ACTIVITY	Week 1	Week 2	Week 3	Week 4
1	Excavate O/site			Percentage Completed	
				Planned Activity	
2	Excavate Trenches				
3	Concrete Foundations				
4	Brickwork below DPC				

> Date Cursor

Fig. 3.62 **A two bar system**

Blocks of colour are used to show when jobs are planned to start and finish. The number of coloured blocks tells you the number of days the job is planned for.

We can see from the chart that the following activities have been carried out:

Item one: It is clear that 50 per cent of the work has been completed in week one, leaving 50 per cent to be completed in week two.

Item Two: This task is behind schedule, only just above half of the excavation has been carried out, whereas it has been planned for some 70 per cent to have been done.

Item Three: On the programme it was planned to have some 25 per cent of the work completed by the end of week two, whereas 50 per cent has been carried out. So the two bar system tells us that the contract is 100 per cent ahead of schedule.

Three Bar Systems

Three bar systems are basically the same as two bar systems but with the addition of a bar which indicates how many days have been worked on each activity. The system shows the percentage of tasks completed, the planned duration of the activity, and the number of days worked. Study the example shown in Figure 3.63 to better understand how the three bar system works.

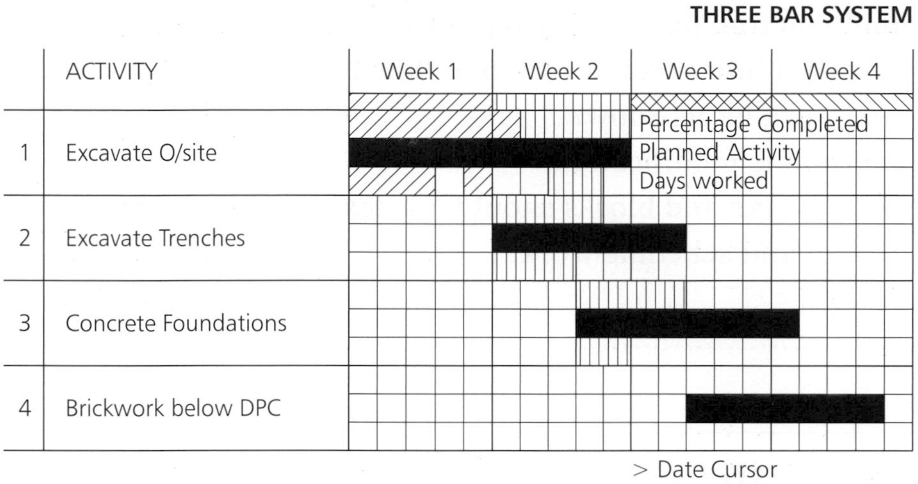

THREE BAR SYSTEM

	ACTIVITY	Week 1	Week 2	Week 3	Week 4
1	Excavate O/site			Percentage Completed / Planned Activity / Days worked	
2	Excavate Trenches				
3	Concrete Foundations				
4	Brickwork below DPC				

> Date Cursor

Fig. 3.63 **Example of a three bar system**

The chart tells us a number of things! We can see that the date cursor is set early on the Monday of week number three. You can see by looking at activity number one that all of the excavation of the over-site has been completed. The chart also tells us that some 60 per cent of the work was completed in week number one, only four days being spent on the activity. The remaining 40 per cent was finished in week number two, with only Wednesday and Thursday needed to complete the job.

The three-bar method gives more information than the earlier bar charts. However, one thing it does not inform us of, is what resources were used on each activity.

Source: CITB-Construction Skills.

> REMEMBER

Each week on the chart represents five working days.

Work-based Evidence Required

■ Completion of own work within the time allowed

To meet this requirement, ask your supervisor to fill out a witness testimony sheet stating that you completed work given to you in the time allowed.

When you have received the signed and dated witness testimony sheet from your supervisor, place them in your work-based evidence portfolio when next in college and map and record it against the syllabus.

Quick quiz Quick quiz Quick quiz Quick quiz Quick quiz

① Why is it important to produce a programme of work?
② Name three types of bar chart.
③ What are the main differences between a single and a two bar chart?
④ What information would you find on the horizontal rows of a bar chart?
⑤ What should always be taken into account on a bar chart?
⑥ What do programmes of work let us know?
⑦ What can lead to a programme modification?
⑧ Approximately how many bricks and blocks should a bricklayer lay per hour?
⑨ Why is it important to plan and schedule work?
⑩ Define the term estimation.

RESOURCES 3.4

In this section you will learn about materials, components and equipment relating to types, quantity, quality and sizes of standard and/or specialist:

- aggregate, sand, lime, cement, water, additives
- hand tools and mixing plant and equipment
- methods of calculating quantity, length, area and wastage associated with the method/procedures to prepare and mix concrete and mortars.

When you have completed this section you will be able to:

- select the required quantity and quality of resources for the methods of work.

Know and understand:

- the characteristics, quality, uses, limitations and defects associated with the resources
- how the resources should be used.

> **Definition**
> Crushed stone, gravel or other material added to cement to make concrete and mortar.

Aggregates

Concrete

Concrete as a high quality building material will consist of the following:

- Fine aggregates – fine grains which will pass through a 5 mm sieve known to us as sand.
- Coarse aggregates – particles larger than 5 mm known as gravel or shingle.
- Cement – used as a matrix (adhesive) binding each particle together.

Mortar

Mortar is composed of a matrix and an aggregate which, when mixed with a certain quantity of water, becomes sufficiently plastic to be spread in thin layers. The aggregate is the inert material forming the body of the mortar; sand being normally used for this purpose.

Fine Aggregate

Fine aggregates can be obtained from river beds or sandpits. Sea shore sand should never be used because of the high salt content.

The size and shape of the grains of sand can greatly influence the strength of a sample of concrete.

If the grain size is small it will increase the total surface area. As each grain of sand has to be coated with cement this increased surface area may result in particles being missed, causing a weakness in the finished mix.

Clay particles (silt) will also break down the bond of cement on the individual particles. Note – every load delivered to site should be tested for cleanliness.

Sand should not contain more than 8 per cent silt.

Sand used in mortar for brickwork should be free from all earthy and organic matter and not too fine. While it should generally be fairly sharp, an addition of soft sand will make the mortar easier to manipulate.

Well Graded Sands

The size of grains in a good sample of sand will vary from 5 mm down. This provides a well graded mix with the smaller grains filling the voids left by the larger grains – see Figure 3.64.

If the grains are all one size then the sample is said to be uniform. A uniform sample will produce a weak porous mix with very poor workability.

Workability is the term used to describe the ease with which a concrete can be placed and compacted.

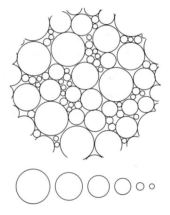

Fig. 3.64 **A well graded sample of sand**

Bulking of Sand

Dry sand and saturated sand have about the same volume, but a sample of damp sand will show a marked increase in volume. This is known as bulking. The increase can be as great as 30 per cent in samples of fine sand.

This can have an adverse effect on mixes if they are being gauged by volume. The amount of bulking should be worked out and the gauge box enlarged to compensate for the shortfall in sand.

Coarse Aggregate

Coarse aggregate can be in the form of gravel or crushed rock. The size of coarse aggregate will vary according to the job it is to be used for. Its particle size will range from 5 mm to 38 mm.

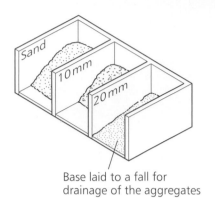

Base laid to a fall for drainage of the aggregates

Fig. 3.65 **Storage bays for aggregates**

As with fine aggregates, the sample should be well graded containing a full range of sizes. Check the size of aggregates before tipping and leave for 24 hours before use, to enable moisture to drain out of them.

Storage of Fine and Coarse Aggregates

The method of storage will depend upon the size of the site and the duration of the contract. But for large or small sites the objectives are the same:

- to keep aggregates clean, not contaminated by soils or site debris
- to allow moisture to drain away from stockpiles
- to prevent different types of aggregates from mixing in the stockpiles.

On small sites this can be achieved by using steel sheets and timber battens.

On a large site a concrete base and partition walls may be used.

Lime

This is produced by the burning of calcium carbonate in the form of chalk, limestone, or marble, the resultant being calcium oxide or quicklime.

For building purposes, quicklime requires slaking. Slaking is brought about by adding water to the quicklime, which becomes hot, swells and breaks down into small particles. As more water is added a putty like substance is eventually produced. This is slaked lime in a saturated condition. In this state it is added to the sand to form a lime mortar.

Lime manufacturers now supply lime as a hydrated lime in the form of a dry powder. This hydrated lime is ordinary quicklime which has been slaked by the combination of just sufficient water to break it down from the lump to a dry powder, without any excess. If properly stored, it remains dry and is ready for immediate use by mixing with water.

Lime Mortar

This usually consists of one part lime to three parts of sand by volume, but may vary in its proportions according to the type for which it is intended. If slaked quicklime is used, the method of preparation will differ from that required for powdered hydrated lime. When hydrated lime is used it is more convenient to mix the lime with the sand before any water is added.

Cement

For bedding brickwork, Portland cement is used largely as a matrix in preparing mortar.

It is made by an artificial process by combining about 75 per cent of limestone with 25 per cent of clay. During manufacture these are mixed together and formed into a slurry with the addition of water. In this state the slurry is fed into a furnace which it leaves in the form of a clinker. The clinker is then ground to the required degree of fineness and in this state is ready to use.

Types of Cement

Ordinary Portland cement is the most commonly used binder in bricklaying mortars.

Masonry cement consists of ordinary Portland cement to which has been added a fine mineral powder and an 'air-entraining agent' so that when mixed with sand and water the mortar will have a good workability and cohesion without the need for added lime.

Sulphate Resisting Cement as its name suggests is resistant to attack by sulphates that can be found in some types of soils and groundwater, which would cause deterioration of mortar made from ordinary Portland cement.

Rapid hardening cement – the term rapid hardening should not be confused with quick setting cement. Rapid hardening cement sets roughly the same as Ordinary Portland cement. It is only after the initial set that it gains strength more rapidly.

Good Practice

Cement is manufactured by several companies. All will achieve the same end result but the one big difference is that they influence the colour of the mortar.

Do not change brands part way through construction.

Never get masonry cement mixed with ordinary Portland cement if you are making concrete, it only contains 75 per cent of cement.

Storage

Rules for storage are as follows:

- store in a ventilated waterproof shed
- stack off the floor
- stack to no more than five bags high
- use in the sequence in which they are delivered, that is, first in first out, never stack new bags on old
- limit the storage to 4 to 6 weeks.

For small jobs cement is usually purchased in bags, but for larger jobs, cement can be stored in large silos with storage capacities for 10 to 50 tonnes.

Water

All water use in the mixing of concrete and mortar should be clean and free from organic or mineral impurities.

Sufficient water only should be added to the dry materials to make them completely plastic or workable, easily placed in position, and in the case of concrete, capable of being rammed where necessary to increase the density.

Water Cement Ratio

The quantity of water required for a mix is expressed as a decimal fraction of the weight of cement.

Example 1

For a water–cement ratio of 0.50 for every 50 kg of cement, 0.25 kg of water will be required, that is, 25 litres.

Example 2

For a water–cement ratio of 0.60 for every 50 kg of cement, 0.30 kg of water will be required, that is, 30 litres.

The water–cement ratio will determine the type of compaction required to provide a dense concrete.

With a 0.50 water–cement ratio, hand compaction becomes difficult and mechanical methods should be used.

Hand Tools and Mixing Plant and Equipment

Compacting Equipment

Compaction of concrete means removing all the air bubbles from the mix so allowing the individual particles to come into contact, giving maximum density.

Manual Compaction

For over-site concrete or pathways this will mean tamping.

This involves slightly overfilling the shutters and compacting by tamping: tapping down with a tamp board. For large spans the tamp board may be fitted with handles.

This action has two effects:

- It removes the trapped air from the concrete mix creating a dense mix
- It brings a mixture of fine aggregate cement and water known as 'laitance' to the surface. This enables the surface to be treated.

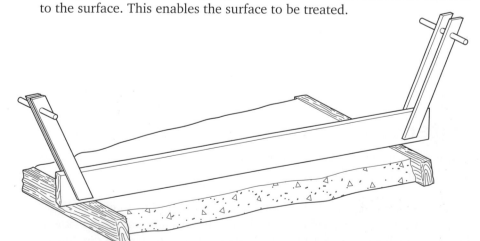

Fig. 3.66 **A tamp board**

Compressive Strength

Your role on site as a bricklayer will not involve you in the design of concrete mixes for specific jobs. The design of a mix will have been determined by a structural engineer taking into account the loads it is to carry and the stresses placed upon it. The structural engineer will, at regular intervals during a contract, need to check the quality of the concrete.

One of these tests will be for compressive strength which may involve you in making cubes that will be crushed at 7 days and 28 days to ensure design strength is being maintained.

Your role is vital in achieving the designed strength of concrete on site when you consider the following:

- Every 1 per cent loss of compaction could result in a 6 per cent loss of strength
- Ten per cent of 28 day strength can be lost if early curing procedures are not followed.

Curing is the retention of water in a mix of concrete.

Mechanical Compaction

This can be placed under three headings:

- surface vibrators
- internal vibrators
- external vibrators.

Surface Vibrators

The hand tamp illustrated previously can be turned into a surface vibrator by bolting on a petrol driven vibrating unit.

The tamp is laid on top of the screeds with the vibrating unit motor running and is moved slowly along the concrete slab.

This will have a greater compaction than if the tamp is used as a hand tamp.

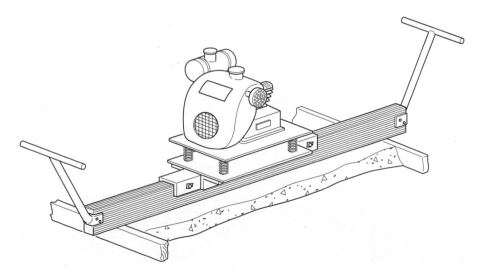

Fig. 3.67 **A surface vibrator**

Vibrating Beam

Vibrating beams manufactured from steel channels or box sections are widely used.

The principal is the same as the bolt on vibrating unit but consists of two beams: the forward beam having greater vibration than the rear beam.

The finish left by this type of vibrating unit is ideal if the concrete slab is to be finished later with a steel float or with a power rotary float.

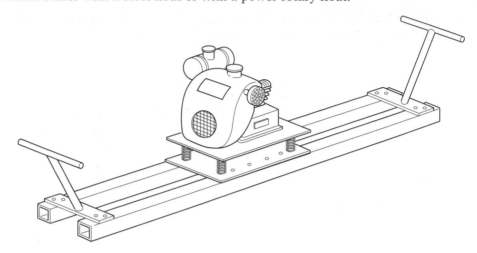

Fig. 3.68 **A vibrating beam**

Rotary Float

The edges of the revolving float blades are turned up on the edges to prevent them digging into the concrete slab.

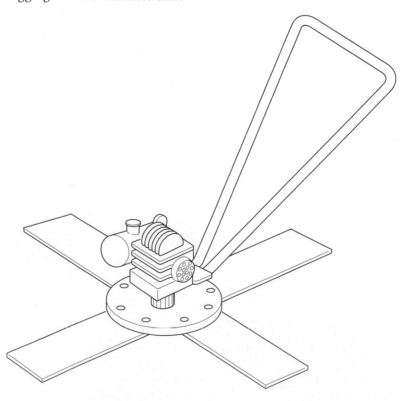

Fig. 3.69 **A rotary float**

Placing Reinforcement

The position of reinforcing within a floor slab or foundation will be specified. As with all reinforcing it must be provided with cover. This protects the reinforcement from fire and atmospheric conditions which could cause corrosion.

Simple floor slabs will be constructed with reinforcing mats which will be placed in position on spacers prior to concreting commencing.

Make sure all reinforcement is free from mill scale, loose rust, grease or mud before placing in shuttering as illustrated in Figure 3.70.

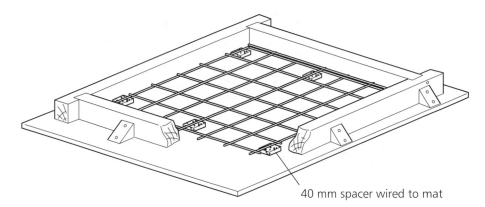

40 mm spacer wired to mat

Fig. 3.70 **Reinforcement placed in shuttering**

Shuttering

Timber Shuttering

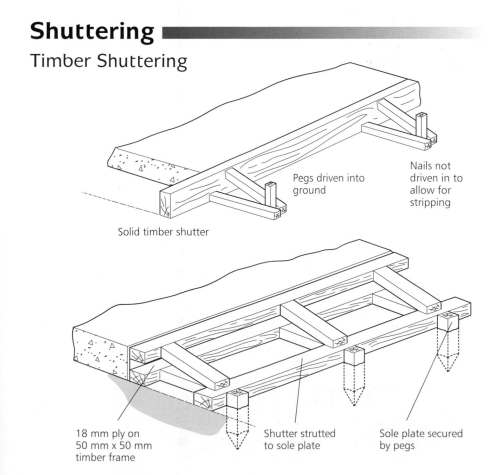

Pegs driven into ground

Nails not driven in to allow for stripping

Solid timber shutter

18 mm ply on 50 mm x 50 mm timber frame

Shutter strutted to sole plate

Sole plate secured by pegs

Fig. 3.71 **Annotated illustration of timber shuttering**

Road Formers

Steel road formers are often used for paths and driveways

Screed Rails

Where large spans of concrete are to be laid in one go it may be necessary to lay screed rails for intermediate support to split large bays into two.

On completion of the two sections, the screed rail should be removed and the recess filled with concrete. This should be carried out before the initial set takes place.

The degree of finish required will be dependent upon the final surface finish required on the concrete.

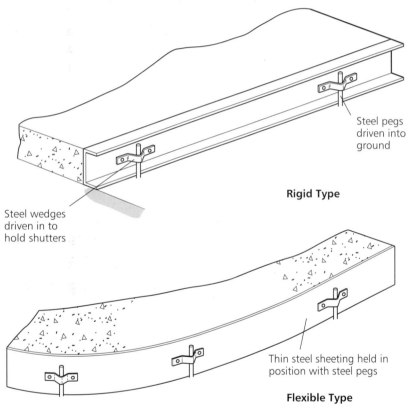

Steel pegs driven into ground

Rigid Type

Steel wedges driven in to hold shutters

Thin steel sheeting held in position with steel pegs

Flexible Type

Fig. 3.72 **Annotated illustration of road formers**

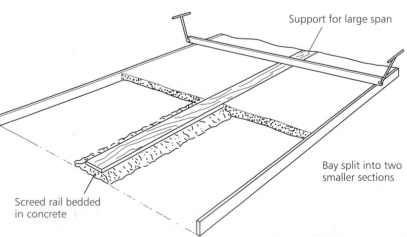

Support for large span

Bay split into two smaller sections

Screed rail bedded in concrete

Fig. 3.73 **Screed rails**

Work-based Evidence Required

■ **Selection of resources associated with own work:**

■ materials and components

■ tools and equipment

To meet these requirements, ask your supervisor to fill out a witness testimony sheet stating that you have selected materials and components associated with brickwork as well as tools and equipment.

When you have received the signed and dated witness testimony sheet from your supervisor, place it in your work-based evidence portfolio when next in college and map and record it against the syllabus.

Quick quiz Quick quiz Quick quiz Quick quiz Quick quiz

❶ What is meant by curing concrete?
❷ What is the purpose of the slump test?
❸ What are road formers often used for?
❹ List three types of mechanical compaction.
❺ List four different types of cement.

Hand Tools

For further information about bricklaying and other tools, why not visit the websites of the better known manufacturers and suppliers?

Power Tools

For further information about power tools, why not contact the websites of the better known manufacturers and suppliers?

Mortar Mixing Machines

For further information about mortar mixing machines, why not visit the websites of the better known manufacturers and suppliers?

Mortars, Cements and Limes

For further information about mortars, cements and limes, why not visit the websites of the better known manufacturers and suppliers? Or the Mortar Industry Association
www.mortar.org.uk

Programmes

For more information about programmes used on site, why not visit the following website.
www.citb-constructionskills.co.uk

The CITB have an excellent series of learning modules entitled Open Learning for Supervising managers in the Construction Industry which cover in depth the monitoring, controlling and programming of work progress. They are highly recommended as a learning resource.

Mortars, Cements, Limes and Aggregates

For further information about mortars, cements, limes and aggregates, why not visit the websites of the better known manufacturers and suppliers?

Mixing Plant and Equipment

For further information about mixing plant and equipment, why not visit the websites of the better known manufacturers and suppliers?

Chapter four

Lay Bricks and Blocks to Line

NVQ Level 1   Unit No. VR 37   Lay Bricks and Blocks to Line

This unit, in the context of brickwork and the construction industry work environment is about:

- interpreting instructions
- adopting safe and healthy working practices
- selecting materials, components and equipment
- laying bricks and blocks to line and forming a joint finish.

There are two sections in this chapter: methods of work and resources.

This chapter will now cover laying bricks and blocks to line.

METHODS OF WORK   4.1

In this section you will learn about the application of knowledge for safe work practices, procedures, skills and transference of competence, relating to the area of work and material used to:

- bond brickwork
- lay to line common and facing bricks, traditional and thin joint blocks
- lay damp proof membranes
- form a joint finish
- use hand tools and equipment
- work at height
- use access equipment.

You will also learn about team work and communication relating to the needs of other occupations associated with brick and blockwork.

When you have completed this section you will be able to:

- select and name correct tools and equipment for laying bricks and blocks to line
- work out the required number of bricks and blocks

- lay bricks and blocks to line and gauge
- check that levels, face deviation and perpends are within allowable tolerances
- point up joints on facework
- comply with the given contract instructions to carry out the work efficiently to the required specification.

Know and understand:

- how methods of work are carried out and problems are reported.

Lay to Line Common and Facing Bricks, Traditional and Thin Joint Blocks

key terms

Bonding of Brickwork – The arrangement of bricks to form a wall is known as bonding.

Bonding of Brickwork

When building with bricks it is necessary to lay the bricks to some pattern or bond as illustrated in Figure 4.1.

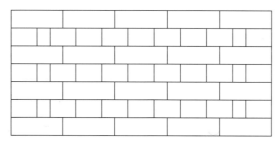

A bonded wall face with no vertical straight joints

Fig. 4.1 **A bonded wall**

All the various bonds are designed so that no vertical joint in any course is directly above a vertical joint in the previous course. The bonds are planned to give the largest possible lap to all the bricks in the wall, which should never be less than a quarter of a brick in length.

Purposes of Bonding Brickwork

1. To strengthen the wall by spreading any load over the wall

2. To give stability and resistance to side thrust

3. To give a pleasing appearance.

Rules of Bonding

1. When working out the bond the bricklayer applies some basic rules. These rules should be taken as a guide when solving a problem, but there

may be more than one solution to the problem, so that the bricklayer's knowledge and experience will be used to work out the bond in that particular circumstance.

The bond is set out dry along the face of the wall starting from each end, to the centre with the end bricks on each course being the same. If the length is such that a piece or cut is required then we have what is known as broken bond. It follows therefore that any broken bond (necessitating a cut brick, or 'bat') will be in the centre of the wall as illustrated in Figure 4.2.

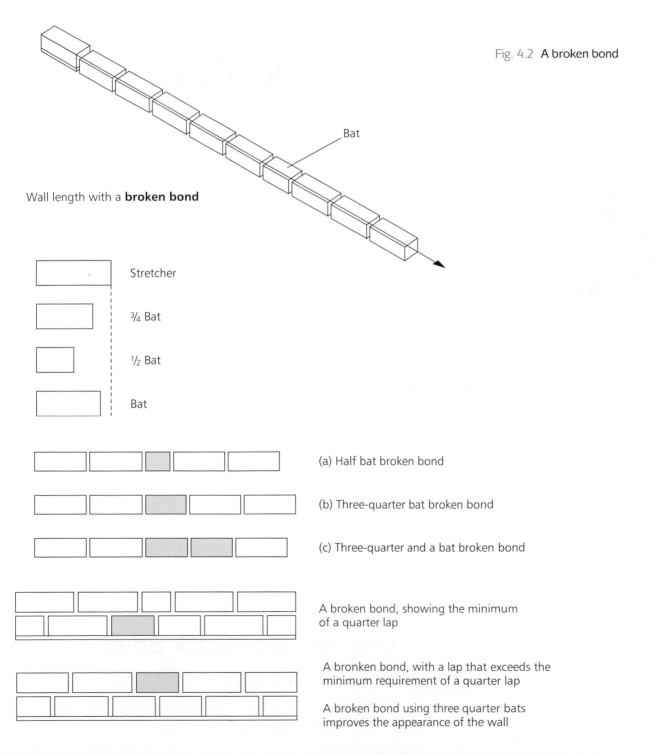

Fig. 4.2 **A broken bond**

Bat

Wall length with a **broken bond**

Stretcher

¾ Bat

½ Bat

Bat

(a) Half bat broken bond

(b) Three-quarter bat broken bond

(c) Three-quarter and a bat broken bond

A broken bond, showing the minimum of a quarter lap

A bronken bond, with a lap that exceeds the minimum requirement of a quarter lap

A broken bond using three quarter bats improves the appearance of the wall

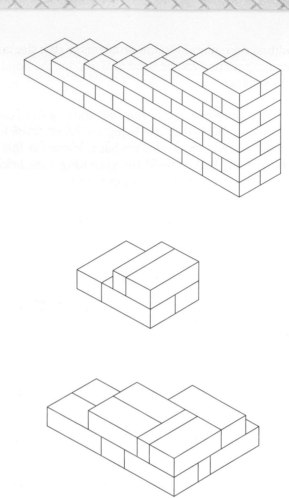

Fig. 4.3 **The use of queen closures**

When a quarter bond is used, a closer is placed next to the header at the quoin or stopped end, as shown in Figure 4.3.

Building a Corner

Corners serve a very important function in brick, block, stone and other similar types of masonry construction.

Return corners when built correctly:

- establish wall ends
- establish wall angles
- establish wall bond patterns
- establish wall and course heights
- establish wall and course heights.

Identifying Types of Brick Bond

The word bond, when used in reference to brickwork, may have three meanings:

1. Structural Bond

This is the method by which individual bricks are interlocked or tied together to cause the masonry to act as a single structural unit.

2. Pattern Bond

This is the pattern formed by the bricks and the mortar joints on the face of a wall. The pattern may result from the type of structural bond used or may be purely decorative, unrelated to the structural bonding.

3. Mortar Bond

The adhesion of mortar to the bricks or to reinforcing steel.

Terminology

Each horizontal layer of bricks in a wall is called a course. Two common types of brick courses are frequently used in brick walling:

Header courses

Stretcher courses.

A header is a brick laid flat with its end face showing in the wall. A header course contains only headers.

A stretcher is a brick laid flat with its long face parallel to the wall. A stretcher course contains only stretchers.

The arrangement of stretchers and headers in courses determine the bond or pattern. Sometimes special types of courses are used for structural or decorative purposes.

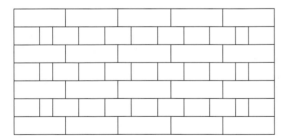

A bonded wall face with no vertical straight joints

Bonded bricks lap over another brick in two ways:

Half lap

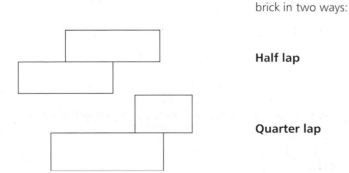

Quarter lap

Fig. 4.4 **Header and stretcher courses**

The most frequently used bonds are as follows:
- Stretcher bond
- English bond
- Flemish bond.

To avoid a great deal of cutting, the bond is arranged as shown in Figure 4.5. That is, two half bricks and a stretcher placed alternately. If uncut bricks are used, wide cross joints would appear on the face.

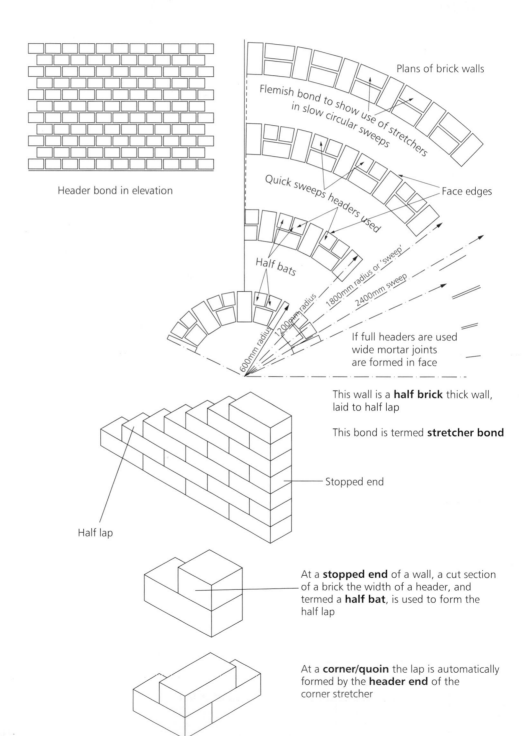

Header bond in elevation

Plans of brick walls

Flemish bond to show use of stretchers in slow circular sweeps

Quick sweeps headers used

Face edges

Half bats

600mm radius

1200mm radius

1800mm radius or 'sweep'

2400mm sweep

If full headers are used wide mortar joints are formed in face

Fig. 4.5 **A header course**

This wall is a **half brick** thick wall, laid to half lap

This bond is termed **stretcher bond**

Stopped end

Half lap

At a **stopped end** of a wall, a cut section of a brick the width of a header, and termed a **half bat**, is used to form the half lap

At a **corner/quoin** the lap is automatically formed by the **header end** of the corner stretcher

Fig. 4.6 **A stretcher bond wall**

Stretcher Bond

A basic bond used in half brick or cavity wall construction where a stretcher is used throughout, lapped centrally over each face below, as illustrated in Figure 4.7.

English Bond

This type of bonding consists of alternate courses of headers and stretchers as illustrated in Figure 4.8. English bond is mainly used in the construction of solid brick walls of various thicknesses, i.e. one brick, one and a half brick and two brick walls.

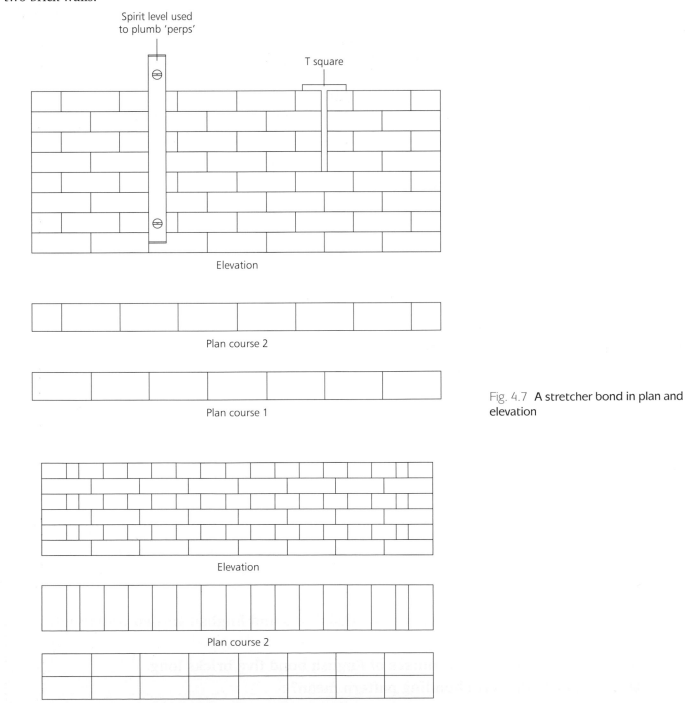

Spirit level used to plumb 'perps'

T square

Elevation

Plan course 2

Plan course 1

Fig. 4.7 **A stretcher bond in plan and elevation**

Elevation

Plan course 2

Plan course 1

Fig. 4.8 **English bond in plan and elevation**

Flemish Bond

This type of bonding consists of headers and stretchers alternately on the same course. It is used mainly because of its attractive appearance as illustrated in Figure 4.9.

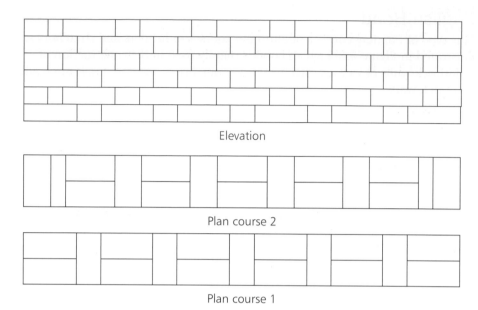

Elevation

Plan course 2

Plan course 1

Fig. 4.9 Flemish bond in plan and elevation

English Garden Wall Bond

Considered to be more economical than true English bond, frequency of header courses may vary.

Mortar

Mortar is the material with which bricks are laid. Mortar is an essential ingredient of brickwork and is subject to the same exposure as the brick; unfortunately it is not given the same degree of consideration as the brick.

In a completed wall, the mortar is seen as narrow bands about 10 mm wide. In terms of surface area, the mortar is a surprisingly large proportion of what you can see, varying from around 17 per cent to 25 per cent, depending on the way the bricks are arranged.

Quick quiz Quick quiz Quick quiz Quick quiz Quick quiz

❶ Describe stretcher bond.
❷ What is the difference between English bond and English garden wall bond?
❸ What is mortar?
❹ Draw in elevation two courses of English bond five bricks long.
❺ What does the term bonding pattern mean?

TRY THIS OUT

Bonding Arrangements

Objectives

When you have completed this activity, you will be able to:

- Carry out bonding arrangements for return corners in Flemish and English bond.

Resources

- Pencils
- Ruler
- Set square
- Graph paper.

Carry out the bonding arrangements for the first and second courses of a one brick return corner in Flemish bond and English bond using the scale 1 to 10.

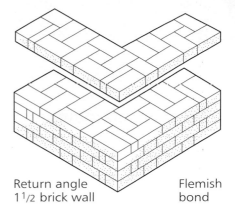

Return angle
1 1/2 brick wall   Flemish bond

Fig. 4.10 **Outline of Flemish bond return corners**

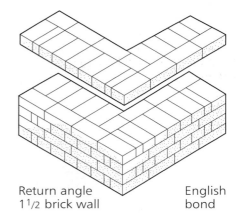

Return angle
1 1/2 brick wall   English bond

Fig. 4.11 **Outline of English bond return corners**

TRY THIS OUT

1. Draw to a scale of 1 : 10, the front elevation of a garden wall, 4 m long by 1 m high in stretcher bond. The wall is built off a level concrete slab.

2. Write down the type of mortar required and the ratios of the various materials.

3. Look through building merchants' catalogues and choose a rustic facing brick for building the garden wall. Find out how much the facing bricks cost, delivered to site five miles away from the merchants.

4. Calculate how many bricks will be needed to build the wall allowing 5 per cent for cutting and waste. Calculate the total cost of the bricks, delivered to the site.

5. List the tools and equipment you would need to build the wall.

6. List the PPE you would need to carry out the work.

Work-based Evidence Required

■ Work skills to:

■ measure, mark out and lay

■ Use and maintain:

■ hand tools

■ Laid to contractors working instructions:

■ brickwork (to line only and joint finished as required)

■ traditional and/or thin bed blocks (to line only and joint finished as required)

> Point to note
>
> This last item may be simulated if required.

To meet these requirements obtain photographs of yourself measuring, marking out and laying bricks and blocks, traditional and thin joint, to the line and applying a joint finish. It will also be necessary to obtain evidence of tools being maintained, this could be a photograph of you cleaning and drying your tools at the end of the day and then locking them away safely.

When the photographs have been developed place them on a photographic evidence sheet, and get your supervisor to authenticate them by signing and dating them. Place the evidence in your work based evidence portfolio when next in college and map and record it against the syllabus.

Quick quiz Quick quiz Quick quiz Quick quiz Quick quiz

1. Define the term bonding.
2. List three reasons for bonding brickwork.
3. List three rules of bonding.
4. Describe broken bond.
5. What do all brick bonds have in common?
6. Define the term pattern bond.
7. What is the usual term for a horizontal layer of bricks in a wall?
8. Name three frequently used bonds.
9. What bond consists of headers and stretchers, alternately on the same course.
10. What is a stretcher and what is a header?

Lay Damp Proof Membrane

Frost rarely penetrates more than a few millimetres below the finished ground level, so neither bricks nor mortar are at risk from frost action below ground level.

The courses of the outer leaf of brickwork immediately above and below finished ground level are subject to more demanding conditions. If surface water is drained away from the brickwork in these conditions, then the majority of the facing bricks can be used with confidence.

The Building Regulations state that no wall or pier shall permit the passage of moisture from the ground to the inner surface of the building that would be harmfully affected by such moisture.

At ground level this can be achieved by building in a non-absorbent layer of material. This is called a damp proof course (DPC) and consists of a damp proof 'membrane' made of polymer material.

The horizontal damp proof course (DPC) must be built in a full 150 mm above finished ground level. This is to prevent the surrounding ground building up and allowing the earth's moisture to bypass the DPC. Any damp proof membrane under adjoining floor slabs should be built into the horizontal DPC. Where the DPC has to be joined on the length of the wall and at a junction, a minimum lap of 100 mm should be provided.

When it is not possible to drain surface water away from brickwork, it is advisable to use a frost-resistant brick in the two courses above and the one below, finished ground level. This is necessary for the outer leaf only.

On sloping sites, the brickwork between ground level and the damp proof course may act as a retaining wall. To prevent water migrating into the brickwork, it is essential to apply water-proofing treatment to the face of the brickwork which comes into contact with the retained material.

The range of facing and common bricks produced by the majority of brick manufacturers can be used below the damp proof course and in foundations, with the exception of the instances just described. The bricks are not attacked by sulphates which may exist in the ground water or subsoil, so their durability under these conditions is not an issue.

Mortars, however, can be attacked by sulphates. When they are known, or thought, to occur in the groundwater or subsoil, it is best not to use ordinary Portland cement. Instead it is good practice to use sulphate resisting cement in a mortar not weaker than those shown in the section dealing with mortar mix proportions (chapter 3).

Damp proof courses and their location within certain features of a building are shown in Figures 4.12 and 4.13.

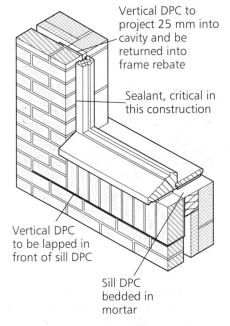

Vertical DPC to project 25 mm into cavity and be returned into frame rebate

Sealant, critical in this construction

Vertical DPC to be lapped in front of sill DPC

Sill DPC bedded in mortar

Fig. 4.12 **Window opening with flush jambs**

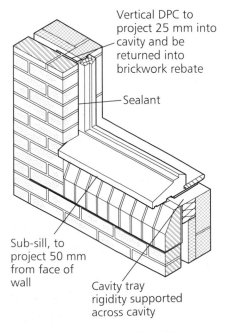

Vertical DPC to project 25 mm into cavity and be returned into brickwork rebate

Sealant

Sub-sill, to project 50 mm from face of wall

Cavity tray rigidity supported across cavity

Fig. 4.13 **Window with rebated jambs**

Placing Damp Proof Barriers

- Bed flexible damp proof barriers on fresh, smooth mortar
- Always lap damp proof barriers by a minimum of 100 mm
- Do not cover the exposed edge of damp proof barriers to project into cavities
- Always use the correct type of damp proof barrier for the type of job undertaken.

Bedding Damp Proof Courses

Care must be taken to ensure flexible damp proof courses do not get damaged during the building in process and when the load of the wall is placed on them.

Using Hand Tools and Equipment

Bricklaying Skills

Traditionally the bricklaying trade has demanded high standards of quality and skill. Training of apprentices took several years and those learning the trade did so largely through choice rather than necessity. Historically, almost all bricklayers would have had the opportunity to become involved in creative brickwork, since the vast majority of domestic dwellings included ornate details and special shaped units. Although there has been a welcome revival in the use of 'specials', they are nowadays only used in volume for commercial and prestigious buildings.

Lay Out of Bricks and Mortar Boards

The positioning of material prior to laying bricks is usually called loading out. The materials must be placed to ensure economy of movement for the bricklayer with everything within easy reach.

First, a rough calculation of the bricks or blocks required should be carried out and the total number of bricks or blocks spread evenly along the length of the wall in neatly bonded stacks.

The stacks should be 600 mm from the face of the wall to give adequate working space as illustrated in Figure 4.14.

Before mortar boards are loaded out with mortar they should be dampened to ensure they do not absorb water from the mortar mix. This weakens it and spoils the workability of the mortar.

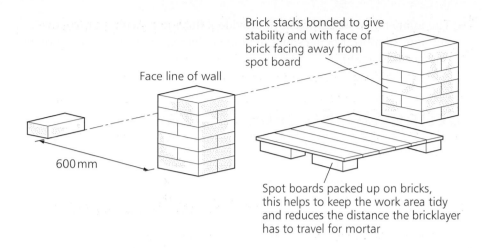

Brick stacks bonded to give stability and with face of brick facing away from spot board

Face line of wall

600 mm

Spot boards packed up on bricks, this helps to keep the work area tidy and reduces the distance the bricklayer has to travel for mortar

Fig. 4.14 **Layout of bricks and mortar boards**

Rolling Mortar for Bed Joints

Picking up the mortar from the board is a technique only developed by repeated practice, but the success of this first step depends on the ease and simplicity with which later operations may be carried out.

Method

From the mortar heap on the board and using the trowel knife fashion, a portion of the mortar is cut away and drawn towards the front of the board in the form of a roll about 220 mm long. The amount cut away will depend on the nature of the work but, for the student, it is advisable only to cut away sufficient mortar to lay one brick. Figure 4.15 shows the position of the mortar on the trowel before lifting, the mortar being brought into this position by a sharp drive of the trowel. Then with the blade almost flat against the board its point is kept behind the roll from the beginning to the end of the movement.

Fig. 4.15 **Mortar on trowel before lifting**

Placing Mortar on the Wall

The mortar from this position is placed about 25 to 50 mm back from the face of the wall and is followed by a pushing movement with the back of the trowel which spreads the mortar out in a layer approximately 15 mm thick, as shown in Figure 4.16.

By subsequently drawing the point of the trowel through the centre of the layer, a mortar bed suitable to receive the brick is formed. A brick laid on mortar prepared in this manner will first rest on the two outer edges of the mortar and when rubbed down to its correct level will not only squeeze mortar from the front and back of the brick but will also squeeze it into the hollow left in the centre of the mortar bed.

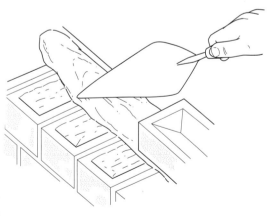

Fig. 4.16 **Spreading mortar on a wall**

A well spread bed joint should achieve the following:

- It should be sufficient to lay two to three bricks

- It should allow the bricks to be laid by using hand pressure to position them, avoiding the need for hammering down with the trowel

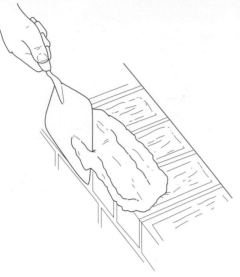

Fig. 4.17 Cutting off surplus mortar

The joint should be sufficient to provide a flush joint without excessive amounts of mortar being squeezed out, so increasing the risk of smudging the face of the wall.

Cutting Off Surplus Mortar

Before and after laying a brick, a certain amount of mortar will project beyond the face of the wall, and this must be removed. Figure 4.17 shows the position of the trowel for these operations, during which care must be taken to prevent any contact between the mortar and the face of the brick.

Cross Joints and Bed Joints

Brickwork joints come under two headings:

Horizontal joints are known as bed joints and play a major role in the structural strength of the brickwork

Vertical joints are known as cross joints or perps, an abbreviation of perpendicular.

It is important to apply full cross joints to the end of each brick. This is required to resist the penetration of driving rain. Surplus mortar, if kept

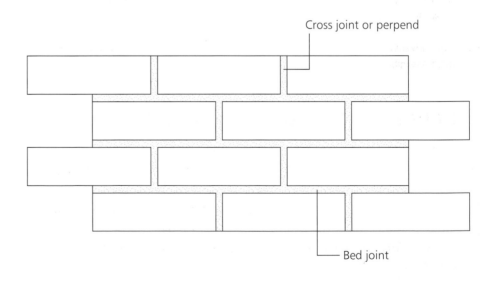

Fig. 4.18 Bed and cross-joints

on the trowel, is usually enough to form a cross joint which can be placed on the brick that is going to be laid next, as illustrated in Figure 4.19 or directly on to the brick that has already been placed on the wall, as illustrated in Figure 4.20.

Fig. 4.19 **Placing a cross-joint while holding a brick**

Fig. 4.20 **Placing a cross-joint while brick is on wall**

With either method, a wedge shaped joint filling, with its thicker part at the front of the brick, must be formed to ensure a solid cross-joint on the face of the wall between the bricks.

Tip jointing, caused by wiping joints on to the two faces of the brick only, is poor workmanship. It is a very bad habit to get into.

Further Uses of the Brick Trowel

Other operations carried out with the brick trowel are:

- tapping the brick down into position, a practice that should be avoided, it being better to rub the brick down to the correct level
- smoothing or ironing of face joints as the work is built, this is dealt with in further detail in chapter 6 on pointing and jointing
- filling or flushing up the internal vertical joints when a course is completed.

Gauging Brickwork

Gauge is the name given to the combined depth of a brick plus the bed joint. If a 10 mm joint is used with a 65 mm brick the gauge would be 65 mm + 10 mm = 75 mm.

This would give you the standard gauge of four courses to 300 mm.

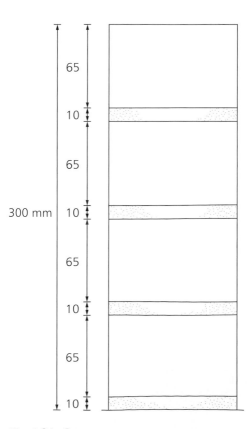

Fig. 4.21 **Gauge**

Gauge Rods

The gauge is maintained throughout the height of the wall by the use of a gauge rod. This is made from a length of timber approximately 50 mm × 35 mm in cross section. The depth of each course (brick depth plus bed joint) is marked on the gauge rod with a pencil, but it is good practice to convert the pencil marks into shallow saw cuts. Over a period of time the weather would remove the pencil marks.

Fig. 4.22 **A gauge rod**

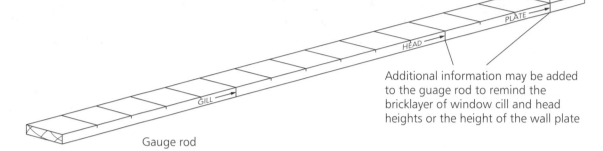

Gauge rod

GILL

HEAD

PLATE

Additional information may be added to the guage rod to remind the bricklayer of window cill and head heights or the height of the wall plate

Any variation in the size of individual bricks will be taken up in the size of the joint.

Levelling a Corner

When a corner brick is laid it should initially be checked for height or gauge. The top of each course must be kept level with the marks on the gauge rod. The brick should then be checked for level, and finally to see that it is vertically over the bricks below it. This procedure is known as plumbing. For the purpose of levelling, a 1 m level may be used, although, for one brick, it is usually more convenient to use the shorter boat level.

Plumbing a Corner

For plumbing purposes the level is kept tightly against the bottom brick with the foot as shown in Figure 4.23 and held firmly with the left hand, leaving the right hand free to tap the bricks with the trowel into the correct position.

This last task may be reduced to a minimum if, when first laying a corner brick, it is placed as nearly as possible to its correct position by sighting vertically down the corner.

In order to plumb a corner after the full height of the spirit level has been reached, the level should only be raised enough to reach each subsequent course. This leaves the greater part of the level against the wall, which reduces the degree of error to a minimum. It is also important to note that the position of the level should be approximately 50 mm back from the corner of the wall, with the level being held as plumb as possible.

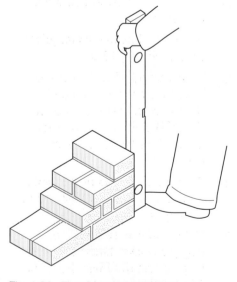

Fig. 4.23 Plumbing up a corner

Running in Facework

Assuming that a corner has been built at each end of the wall, the bricks between them may be tested for alignment along the top and face of the wall, with a straight edge as shown in Figure 4.24 or, where the distance is too great for a straight edge, with line and pins.

In this method a line would be stretched from the top of one brick to the top of the brick at the other end of the wall, the line being held in position by inserting the pins into a suitable perpend. The bricks are now laid so that their top edges just coincide with the inside of the line as shown in Figure 4.25.

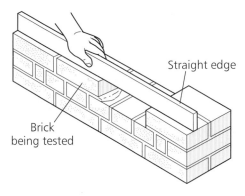

Fig. 4.24 **Testing the wall for alignment with a straight edge**

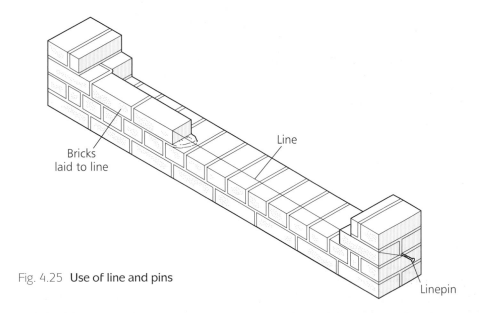

Fig. 4.25 **Use of line and pins**

Tips for Maintaining the Quality of Workmanship

The quality of workmanship on site can have an overriding effect on the weather resistance of brickwork.

Cutting Bricks

Where cut bricks occur, ensure they have been cut cleanly and accurately. Masonry saws will give the best results and minimize wastage, although cutting with a hammer and sharp bolster is normally satisfactory. On face brickwork, avoid cutting bricks with a trowel or brick hammer.

Cavity Walling

When constructing cavity walls, ensure that the cavities are kept clean. Do not allow mortar to drop down the cavity and accumulate on wall ties, cavity trays, lintels and so on. The use of a cavity draw batten is strongly recommended. Whilst there is a great reluctance to use them, they are an effective means of

> **Point to note**

- Cuts used in blockwork can be smaller than one half of a full block
- Bricks should be laid on a full bed of mortar
- All cross joints and collar joints should be fully filled
- Immediately after the brick is laid, excess mortar should be struck off the external face of the work and off the internal faces of the leaves of cavity walls
- Care should be taken to ensure that mortar is not scraped on to the exposed face of the brick
- Unless otherwise specified, frogged bricks should be laid frog up and the frogs should be filled with mortar completely.

keeping the cavity clean and help to avoid expensive remedial work at a later date. Ensure that all ancillary components, such as wall ties, damp-proof courses, cavity trays, movement joints and so on, are of the specified type and incorporated into the brickwork in accordance with design specifications and the manufacturers' instructions.

Quick quiz Quick quiz Quick quiz Quick quiz Quick quiz

❶ What is a gauge rod used for?
❷ Explain the purposes of a damp proof membrane.
❸ What should a well spread bed joint achieve?
❹ Give two examples of testing for wall alignment.
❺ What is a cavity draw batten used for?

Use Access Equipment

Working Platforms Relating to Brickwork

When you have worked through this section, you will be able to:

➤ Differentiate between the various types of working platforms relating to brickwork.

Types of Access Equipment Materials and Components

A working platform or form of access is essential to a great deal of construction activities particularly bricklaying. There are a number of systems available, some of which are described below.

There are four main types of access equipment used in relation to brickwork:

➤ mobile and static towers

➤ trestle scaffolds

➤ independent scaffolds

➤ putlog scaffolds.

Mobile and Static Towers

Mobile and static towers are quickly assembled staging, usually with wheels for ease of movement.

Trestle Scaffolds

A trestle scaffold is usually a basic working platform supported on A frames, bandstands or similar type folding supports.

Trestles are only intended for work of a short duration. A more substantial scaffold would be required if work is to go on for any length of time.

Independent Scaffolds

Independent scaffolds usually provide a working platform around an existing building.

They require bracing and ties for stability.

The erection sequence requires two rows of standards.

Putlog Scaffolds

A putlog scaffold, or bricklayer's scaffold, is normally used on the construction of new brickwork.

A putlog scaffold is built into walls as brickwork progresses.

The scaffold is dependent upon the building for support and stability.

TRY THIS OUT

1. Using the library, internet, builders' merchants, manufacturers' technical literature and so on as sources, carry out research into the following components and equipment associated with access platforms.

- Ladders and stepladders
- Trestles
- Scaffold boards
- Staging
- Mobile towers.

2. Describe each component or piece of equipment and annotate all major parts. Your descriptions should include the following information:

- sizes available
- types available
- materials they are made from
- intended purpose
- trade usage.

Defects Found in Access Materials and Components

The main tasks of a scaffolder, or any other person erecting a working platform, includes the following:

- erection of the access platform
- inspection of the access platform
- maintenance of the access platform
- dismantling of the access platform.

Checking Components

One of the key roles in any scaffolding operation is that of checking the components for defects. A working platform has to withstand many differing weather conditions and hard usage and has to be of sufficient strength to remain in a safe condition.

Checks should be made on a weekly basis to ascertain whether any defects have occurred in the components that make up scaffolds, access towers and associated equipment.

Defects

Typical defects are generally those that are stress related or impact created within metal framed products, or natural defects found in timber-based ladders and trestles.

The majority of defects can be rectified simply if found at an early stage which is a safe and cost effective way of maintaining equipment. Ignoring signs of defects and choosing not to recognize safe working practices is both foolish and expensive in the long term.

Many of the defects found in scaffold components are caused by rough handling and poor working practices. These practices are unnecessary and should be seen as such by supervisory staff.

Always remember that there is no excuse for lack of personal safety, therefore all reasonable care, effort and time should be taken for safety and the maintenance of access equipment.

Ladders and Stepladders

Point to note

Always be aware of the safety requirements in erecting ladders and stepladders.

When you have worked through this section, you will be able to:

- erect ladders and stepladders in a safe and competent manner.

Ladders

Pole Ladders

Pole ladders are single length ladders, the stiles of which are manufactured from one single length of timber. They are made this way to ensure that each stile has an even strength and flexibility, the rungs have reinforcing bars spaced at regular intervals for the same reason.

Pole ladders are usually used to gain access to tubular scaffolding and must extend at least 1 m above the working platform to assist safe mounting and dismounting of the scaffold.

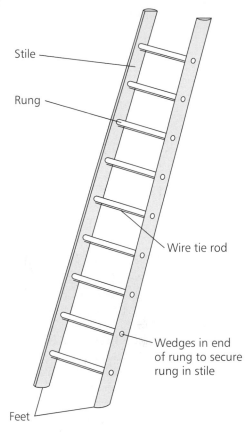

Storage Considerations

Pole ladders must be stored undercover and be evenly supported along their length to prevent warping.

Inspection

Ladders should be inspected frequently with the following checked.

- **The stile** – Check for splits or cracks, splintering or warping
- **The rungs** – Check for signs of undue wear, ensure that there are no rungs missing
- **The wedges and tie rods** – Check for tightness
- **The Feet** – Check for splitting or fraying.

If after inspection, defects in a ladder are found, report these to your supervisor, clearly marking the ladder as defective and remove from site.

Fig. 4.26 **A pole ladder**

Extension Ladders

Extension ladders are usually manufactured from wood, aluminium or glass fibre.

> **Point to note**
>
> If a ladder is beyond repair then it must not be used.

Wooden Extension Ladders

Wooden extension ladders are excellent to work with as they are not noisy and are frequently lightweight in use. This type of ladder requires correct storage to avoid rapid deterioration.

Advantages

- Their weight provides a solid feel and gives the user a sense of security
- They are very durable if not mistreated
- They are available in a range of different sizes
- They are quiet to use; they don't produce 'noise fatigue'
- Minor repairs can be carried out by a competent person.

Disadvantages

- They are expensive, particularly if manufactured to the British Standard and Kite marked.

They may become damaged by incorrect storage; the timber tends to shrink when stored in a heated environment and the components can become loose

The timbers will degrade if left for long periods in wet conditions.

Aluminium Extension Ladders

Aluminium extension ladders are the most popular type used in the construction industry. They come in a variety of sizes the most common being the double or triple extension format.

Advantages

They are strong and lightweight

They are not sensitive to adverse weather conditions and can therefore be stored outside

They are available in a wide range of formats

They are equipped with safety features such as non-slip feet and rungs.

Disadvantages

They are noisy in use, resulting in noise fatigue

They can easily be blown over or dislodged if left unattended

Kite mark versions are very expensive.

Storage Considerations

Metal ladders should be stored in a dry, well ventilated area laid flat on racking along their full length.

Inspection

The following checks should be made with metal ladders.

Check for cracks or corrosion at welded joints

Check all brackets and hooks for condition and anchorage

Check rubber feet for firmness and condition.

British Standards Institute (BSI)
The BSI is the UK national standards body. It sets standards which products much reach (the BS standard), as well as testing products to see that they conform to that standard, as a result of which the product may be given the BSI Kite Mark.

TRY THIS OUT

Using the resources available to you, library, internet, manufacturers' technical literature and so on, research the defects likely to be found in the following types of access equipment.

Ladders, Stepladders and Trestles

■ Think of each piece of equipment in terms of the components that make it up and then think of the many ways the equipment could fail.

■ Make a list of all component parts for each piece of equipment and then describe the likely defects.

If you experience difficulties in carrying out this assignment speak to your tutor who will help you.

Stepladders

When you have worked through this section, you will be able to:

 safely erect a stepladder and be aware of the safety measures to adopt when using one for work activities.

Stepladders are one of the most common forms of access used within the construction industry. They are often taken for granted and not as frequently checked for faults as they should be. Figure 4.27 illustrates some important points that should be checked before using a stepladder and some of a stepladder's built-in safety features.

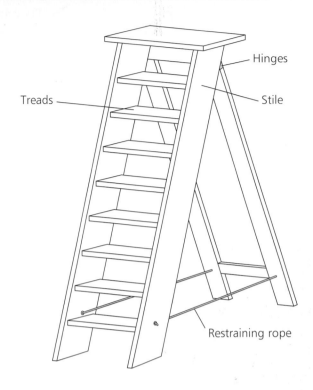

Hinges

Treads

Stile

Restraining rope

Fig. 4.27 **A stepladder**

Good Practice

When using stepladders always observe the following procedures:

- Never use stepladders on a working platform, for example a tower scaffold

- Never work off the top rung of a stepladder and always keep your knees below the top step

- Never use a stepladder in the closed position like you would a ladder

- Never paint a stepladder as this could hide any potential defects

- Always store under cover after use.

Wooden Stepladders

Wooden stepladders are perhaps the most common type of stepladder used within the construction industry.

Advantages

 Their weight provides a solid feel and gives the user a sense of security

 They are easy to carry about a job, the ropes allowing the back frame to fold with ease

 They are very durable if not mistreated

- They are available in a range of different sizes
- They are quiet to use, there being no noise fatigue
- Minor repairs can be carried out by a competent person.

Disadvantages

- They are expensive, particularly if manufactured to the British Standard and Kite mark
- They may become damaged by incorrect storage; the timber tends to shrink when stored in a heated environment and the components can become loose
- The timber components will degrade if left for long periods in wet conditions
- Large stepladders can become tiring to use, particularly if the work involves frequent changes in job location around the site.

Those stepladders manufactured to the British Standard and which display the Kite mark are the most preferable to use.

Aluminium Stepladders

Aluminium stepladders are available in a range of different sizes and formats from ordinary stepladders to multi-function stepladders.

Advantages

- They are very strong
- They are lightweight
- They are extremely versatile, certain types can be adjusted for use on staircases and can convert to form relatively long ladders, as well as other functions
- Certain types are manufactured with a small working platform
- They are easily stored.

Disadvantages

- They can be noisy to work from, thus creating noise fatigue
- If they are damaged they cannot easily be repaired
- They conduct electricity
- Certain types require folding when moving from one location to another.

Those stepladders manufactured to the British Standard and which display the Kite mark are the most preferable to use.

Fibreglass Stepladders

Stepladders made from glass reinforced plastic are growing in popularity particularly amongst electricians. They are preferred on sites where a strict health and safety regime exists, such as oil rigs and refineries.

They range from ordinary stepladders to multi-function access platforms.

Advantages

- Their weight provides a solid feel and gives the user a sense of security
- They are versatile
- They are very durable if not abused
- They are available in a range of different sizes
- They are quiet to use as there is no noise fatigue
- They do not conduct electricity.

Disadvantages

- They are expensive to buy
- If damaged they cannot be repaired
- They require folding when moving from one job to another.

Those stepladders manufactured to the British Standard and which display the Kite mark are the most preferable to use.

TRY THIS OUT

Prepare checklists on the access equipment and components listed below.

- scaffold boards
- proprietary staging
- proprietary towers
- putlog scaffolds
- independent scaffolds.

Carry out research into each piece of equipment and components in respect of the following:

- use of the component
- limitations of the component
- safety regulations.

In order to create a more complete piece of work include illustrations of regulatory information in your text; as well as information from manufacturers' technical literature which is available on the web and from builders' merchants.

① What does the term 'footing the ladder' mean?

② What action would you take if you discovered that a ladder had a broken rung?

③ What is the reason for metal ladders never being used near electricity cables?

④ Where should a ladder be fixed in position, on the stiles or the rungs?

Ladderwork

The use of ladders to gain access to certain tasks can be the most economical option available, for works of short duration, the task can be prepared and completed before a tower scaffold can be erected or moved into position.

The use of a ladder may be an economic solution to an access problem but they may not be the safest or the most suitable.

> Points to note

If the work cannot be carried out with one hand while the other hand is holding the ladder, an alternative means of access should be found.

If it is decided after a risk assessment of the task has been carried out that a ladder would be suitable, then the equipment must be checked over thoroughly to ensure that it is safe to use.

Ladder Safety Checks

All Ladders

- general condition must be clean and sound
- no loose, bent or missing rungs
- no damaged stiles
- foot pads must be in good order.

Wooden Ladders

The same checks apply, with the addition of:

- no warped stiles
- no evidence of wood worm or timber decay
- ladders should not be painted as this could hide defects.

Sequence of Erecting Ladders

To erect a single ladder, follow the procedures illustrated below.

1. Ensure that the ground is firm and level.
2. Place the ladder against a wall.
3. Lift the ladder and move down the ladder, rung by rung until the ladder is upright.
4. Rest the ladder in the desired position, ensuring that the base is one measure out from the wall to four measures up.

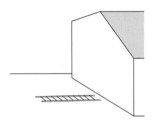 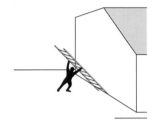 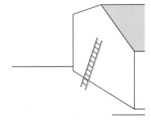

Fig. 4.28 Base of ladder against a wall   Fig. 4.29 Lifting the ladder   Fig. 4.30 Resting the ladder

To raise an extension ladder, follow the procedures illustrated below.

1. Raise both sections.
2. Insert the top section into the lower section.
3. Slide the top section up the wall and place the rung lock on the third rung from the bottom.
4. If the ladder is too heavy get someone to assist you. Extend the ladder to the desired position ensuring a minimum overlap of four rungs.
5. Always make sure that the ladder is secure at the base by getting someone to foot the ladder or use a ladder stabilizer.

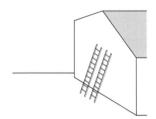 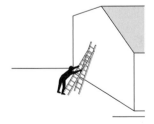 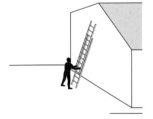

Fig. 4.31 Raising both sections   Fig. 4.32 Inserting the top section into the lower section   Fig. 4.33 Sliding the top section up the wall

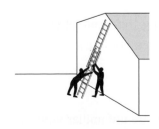 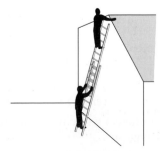

Fig. 4.34 Getting someone to assist you if the ladder is too heavy   Fig. 4.35 Making the ladder secure at the base

Safe Use of Ladders

Never stand on any of the top three rungs, even if you think you can hold on to part of a structure. A very slight movement at the base of the ladder could send you falling.

Never rest a ladder on to plastic guttering, because it may break, if a breakage occurred as you were working at height the sudden shock could send you falling. Always use a ladder 'stand off'.

Never over-reach. This can easily upset the balance of the ladder, sending you falling. This action is one of the most common causes of ladderwork accident.

Always ensure that there is sufficient overlap of rungs. Leaving four rungs overlap is a good factor of safety.

A ladder must have an angle of 75 degrees. This is achieved by ensuring the base is one measurement out at the bottom to four measurements up to the top of the ladder.

Certain types of aluminium ladders have a safety sticker on the side of the stile featuring a red stripe. When the red stripe is in a vertical position then the ladder is at the correct angle.

Slipping of Ladders

One of the main difficulties with using ladders is that they are prone to slipping sideways at the top and away from the wall at the bottom.
To prevent this occurring, ladders should be tied at the top or footed at the bottom.

Ladder Stabilizers

The ladder stabilizer is the modern method of securing a ladder without the need to tie at the top of the ladder or foot it at the base.

Advantages

- The stabilizer is a permanent fitting
- It is approved by the relevant safety authorities
- It can be fitted to most ladders
- It provides a safe, stable and effective alternative to footing of ladders
- It stores neatly along the stiles of the ladder when not in use.

Disadvantages

- Additional training is required
- It can take a while to set up, particularly if you are unfamiliar with the equipment
- It increases the time it takes to move the ladder from job to job.

Storage of Ladders

To avoid undermining site security, always remove ladders from the site if at all possible and place them in a secure compound.

Wooden ladders are best stored outside but under cover. They should be placed ideally flat on racks and supported along their length. Alternatively they can be hung from their stiles on wall brackets.

Never store a ladder by suspending it vertically from a rung.

If ladders are stored vertically they must be strapped to the wall to prevent them from falling.

Always store ladders safely out of reach of children.

If ladders are stored incorrectly they are easily damaged, wooden ladders warp and aluminium ladders twist.

TRY THIS OUT

This assignment asks you to carry out a check on the amount of scaffolding and access equipment available on your site and then to prepare a report on them for health and safety purposes.

The checks will require you to examine the following:

- the condition of stored scaffold boards
- the condition of stored trestles
- the condition of stored ladders
- the number of items of scaffolding in stock
- the condition of stored components.

It is important that you visit as many different trades and areas as possible in order to get a proper picture of the condition of scaffolding and components on the site.

You will then need to prepare a stock list of all the items that you have inspected, noting those components and equipment that may not be to the required standard.

Quick quiz Quick quiz Quick quiz Quick quiz Quick quiz

1. List three defects that you could come across when working with ladders.
2. What is the name of the ladder most commonly used on scaffolding on a construction site?
3. Name four components you would find on a step ladder.
4. At what ratio of angle should a ladder be erected?
5. How often should access equipment be inspected?
6. Why should wooden ladders not be painted?

Trestles

When you have worked through this section, you will be able to:

➤ recognize the different types of trestle available

➤ safely erect and dismantle the different types of trestles and be aware of the safety requirements in their use.

Trestle Scaffolds

A trestle scaffold is made up of a working platform of either scaffold boards or lightweight staging suspended between two or more trestles.

The safe spacing of trestles depends upon the thickness of the boards used and the necessity to avoid a dangerous trap end.

Scaffold boards should extend a distance of no greater than four times the thickness of the board or staging.

The height of the working platform should be no greater than 2 m unless suitable toe boards and hand rails are provided.

It is good practice to include a further trestle for additional support on long spans.

Advantages

➤ They are quick and easy to erect

➤ They are relatively inexpensive

➤ It gives good access length to face work.

Disadvantages

➤ They are only suitable for working platforms of up to 2 m in height

➤ They are not suitable on uneven or sloping ground

➤ They are not very manoeuvrable.

Trestle Scaffolds or Painters' Trestles

Trestles like the type illustrated in Figure 4.36 can be manufactured from steel and aluminium. Trestles are similar in appearance, made from the same materials and have similar characteristics to stepladders.

Trestles should never be used as a substitute for a pair of stepladders because the rungs are not designed for a person to work from.

Fig. 4.36 **A painter's trestle**

Adjustable Steel Trestles (Bandstands)

Trestles are used in place of the more expensive scaffolding. They come in various types and sizes but all scaffolding regulations still apply. However, as a general rule trestles should only be used for light work and where there is little risk of injury.

Adjustable steel trestles or bandstands, as shown in Figure 4.37 are preferred by bricklayers for small works for the following reasons:

They can take four scaffold boards to form a suitable working platform.

They are stronger than other types of trestle and can therefore take loads such as bricks and blocks.

Ground preparation is essential if these types of trestle are to be used on rough or uneven ground. Trestles should always be placed on flat scaffold boards once the ground has been levelled and compacted.

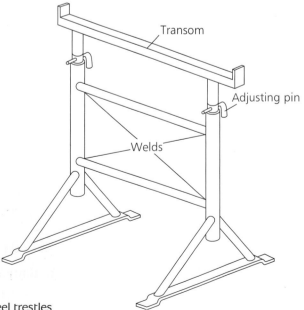

Fig. 4.37 **Adjustable steel trestles**

Good Practice

Trestles should only be ever used on firm level ground.

If used above 2 m in height, toe boards and guard rails must be used.

Always use the correct trestle pins when adjusting the trestles for height and never use nails or screws as these could shear and break.

Always stack materials above the trestle arm the same as you would over the standards of a scaffold. Remember to spread all loads for maximum safety.

TRY THIS OUT

Carry out a report into the items of essential safety equipment used when constructing scaffolding and access platforms. Use manufacturers'
- technical literature
- websites
- builders merchants
- the library

as resources for your research.

Quick quiz Quick quiz Quick quiz Quick quiz Quick quiz

1. What is the minimum width of a working platform used for bricklaying operations?
2. What is the purpose of the metal band at the end of a scaffold board and what information would you find on it?
3. Name the component that should be placed under the base of an adjustable trestle in order to spread the load on it?
4. What document will give you information on the correct erecting method for the assembly of working platforms?
5. Give the name of the regulations that govern the use of working platforms.

Scaffold Boards

Boards

Definition – A softwood board combined with other boards to form access, working platforms and generally used for protective components such as toe-boards on a scaffold.

Scaffold boards are made from straight grained, good quality soft wood, and should comply with British Standard 2482 Specification of timber scaffolding boards, as shown in Figure 4.38; they should be free from:

- excessive knots
- splits and warps.

The thickness of the scaffold board determines the distance between supports:

- 32 mm boards can span 1 m
- 38 mm boards can span 1.5 m
- 50 mm boards can span 2.5 m.

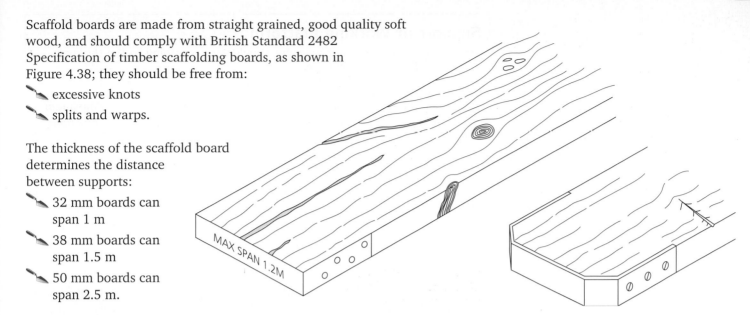

Boards are various lengths but widths are usually 225 mm but not less than 200 mm. They should not be painted or treated in any way so as to hide any defects. The ends of each board should be banded with a metal hoop. Boards must be capable of supporting loads of 670 kg/m² or 350 bricks when supported at 1.2 m centres.

Fig. 4.38 **A scaffold board**

Board Identification

Every board can be identified by the following information, which is usually marked on the band or nail plate.

- British Standard number BS 2482
- the identification mark of the supplier
- the letter M or V which denotes whether a board has been machine or visually graded
- the word support followed by the maximum span in metres over which the board has to be supported.

This band provides the end of the board with protection as shown in Figure 4.39.

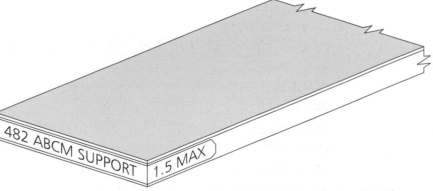

Fig. 4.39 **End projection to a board**

Rules for the Use of Boards

Maximum overhang is equal to four times the thickness of the board.

Never exceed this overhang rule as a trap is caused which could lead to falls.

Maximum span is 1.5 m between supports. However, in practice all 38 mm thick boards are supported at approximately 1.2 m centres.

Support of Working Platform

The spacing of putlogs and transoms should vary according to the thickness and length of boards being used.

Maximum spacing for boards 3.90 m long.

Nominal thickness of boards	Maximum span between supports	Minimum overhang	Maximum overhang
mm	m	mm	mm
38	1.5	50	150
50	2.8	50	200
63	3.25	50	250

Fig. 4.40 Chart diagram of board spacings

Support between boards is very important, not enough support and the boards can bend or break. Look at the Figure 4.40 to see if you are using the correct spacings.

Storage of Boards

All boards should be stacked no more than 20 high, bonded together with short timber battens and placed on level timbers, off the ground for protection from surface water. Scaffold boards should be protected from adverse weather and have a free circulation of air as shown in Figure 4.41.

Timber spacers to allow air to circulate

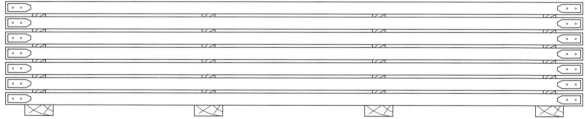

Timber bearers to provide a firm level base and keep boards off the ground

Fig. 4.41 **Storage of boards**

Inspection of Boards

Great care must be taken of boards in use. On no account should boards be over-stressed by overloading them.

Boards should never be used as ramps or platforms over spans longer than their design capabilities.

Boards that show evidence of any damage should be taken out of use and replaced.

Boards should be kept clean and any loose or missing identification plates secured or replaced.

Scaffold boards should never be painted.

Common faults in boards, could be: cracked, split ends, worn and cut, excessive knots and warping.

TRY THIƧ OUT

- Prepare safety checklists for site personnel who are working on the various types of scaffolding and access equipment on your site.
- Make a note of five safe working practices that should be carried out for each piece of equipment. For example:

Ladders

Safe Working Practice

1. 1 : 4 ratio
2. Lashed top and bottom
3. Inspected before use
4. Stored safely after use
5. If damaged supervisor informed.

Your checklist should include the following types of access systems and equipment:

Stepladders, Trestles, Scaffold Boards, Proprietary Staging, Tower Scaffolds, Putlog Scaffolds and Independent Scaffolds.

If you experience any difficulties in carrying out this assignment, speak to your tutor who will help you with it.

Quick quiz **Quick quiz** Quick quiz Quick quiz Quick quiz

❶ **Why should scaffold boards be cleaned and turned at the end of a working day?**

❷ **What are the differences between a lightweight staging and a scaffold board?**

❸ **What is the permissible overhang for a scaffold board that is 38 mm in thickness?**

❹ **Why should scaffold boards not be placed on the treads of stepladders?**

❺ **Give the correct storage procedures for scaffold boards.**

Proprietary Staging

When you have worked through this section, you will be able to:

🔧 recognize the different types of proprietary staging available and its uses.

🔧 safely erect and dismantle proprietary staging.

Proprietary staging is designed to span greater distances than scaffold boards and is particularly useful.

Trestle Scaffolds

These are for suspending between components of a structure such as factory roof trusses.

This type of working platform is sometimes called a cat walk. It provides a 600 mm wide platform in various sizes up to 7 m in length. Proprietary staging is usually constructed from timber or aluminium and is able to:

🔧 support the weight of three operatives

🔧 take an additional load of up to 275 kg as long as it is evenly distributed

🔧 span distances without additional intermediate supports.

Youngman Staging

Youngman staging boards are made from timber and reinforced with steel wire as shown in Figure 4.42 and are made in various lengths up to 6 m. They are designed to provide access for operatives using lightweight materials such as painters and electricians.

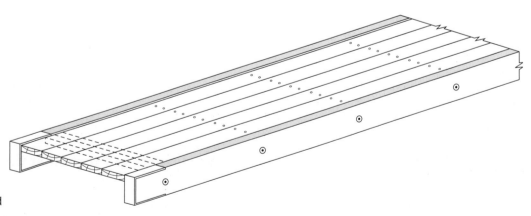

Fig. 4.42 **Youngman staging board**

Storage Requirements

Boards and staging must be cleaned and stored under cover, and supported throughout their length if placed on racks.

Step Ups and Hop Ups

Step ups or hop ups can be a convenient method of reaching low level work of short duration.

They require a working platform of 600 mm × 600 mm and must be solidly constructed, as shown in Figure 4.43 this means they can be rather heavy and cumbersome to move about.

Hop ups

'Hop ups' are small platforms that enable an operative to reach work that is just out of reach from the floor

They can be permanently constructed from timber having a maximum height of 600 mm

They should have a working platform of at least 500 mm square

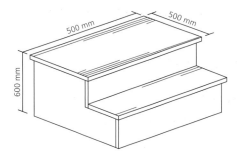

> Point to note
>
> Items such as bottle crates and chairs should never be used to gain access to surfaces.

An intermediate step provides safe access

On a more temporary basis 'hop ups' can be constructed from joinery trestles and planks

Care must be taken to ensure the trestles are on a level base

Material should not be stored on this type of platform

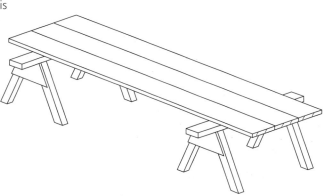

Fig. 4.43 **Hop ups**

A hop up can also be a bracket to attach, usually to the inside of a scaffold in order to enable boards to be placed between the scaffold and the building.

Splithead Scaffolding

Splitheads are adjustable metal stands which take timber bearers, over which a close boarded platform can be constructed as illustrated in Figure 4.44.

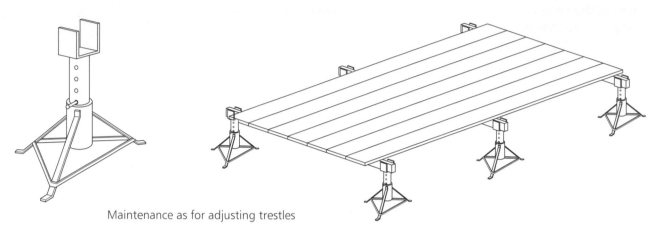

Maintenance as for adjusting trestles

Fig. 4.44 **A splithead (splithead scaffolding)**

TRY THIS OUT

In securing ladders to scaffolds or access platforms we need to use various types of knots and hitches.

There are four in common use – name and describe them in a report for your supervisor.

This type of scaffold can be particularly suitable for gaining access to the whole of a ceiling for operations such as plastering.

The Safe Use of Splithead Scaffolding

Splitheads must be well oiled and in good working order.

The boarded platform must be as close to the walls of the room as possible.

To prevent the bearers from rocking they must be wedged with timber.

Quick quiz Quick quiz Quick quiz Quick quiz Quick quiz

❶ With the aid of an illustration, describe a split head scaffold.
❷ Why are outriggers sometimes used on tower scaffolds?
❸ What should be placed on a scaffold under construction?
❹ What is the permitted overhang for timber scaffold boards?
❺ What would the correct storage procedures be for scaffold fittings?

Proprietary Towers, Static and Mobile

Mobile Towers

Mobile tower scaffolds are used extensively throughout the construction industry, they can be constructed from scaffold tubes and couplers or more usually a proprietary system of purpose made interlocking components.

Proprietary system mobile towers are the type usually found on construction sites and are usually made from the following materials:

➤ Steel

➤ Aluminium

➤ Glass Fibre.

Steel Towers

Mobile towers constructed of steel gate sections as illustrated in Figure 4.45 are now becoming obsolete as they tend not to meet current requirements for guard rails. However, there are still many examples in use.

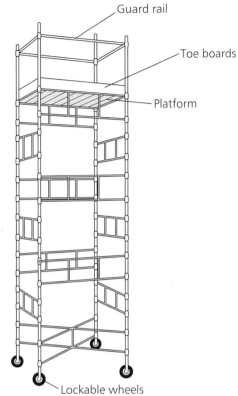

> **Points to note**

If you are required to work from a steel mobile tower, you must ensure that:

■ the working platform has been modified to meet current legislation
■ there is plan bracing every three lifts
■ there is suitable ladder access to the platform
■ all gate sections are free from any defects such as cracked welds, corrosion and bent or loose fitting gates.

Advantages

■ They are strong and durable.

Disadvantages

■ They are heavy and time consuming to erect
■ Plan bracings are often the first components to go missing
■ Castors are not usually adjustable so adjustable base plates have to be used on uneven ground.

> **Points to note**

Before the Tower is Used

The tower must be vertical – square – and all horizontal braces and platforms level.

Outriggers – correctly positioned and secure and in good contact with the ground. Base plate or castor wheels in full contact with the ground. All spigot joints must be fully home and secure.

All bracing members must be located exactly as per the instruction manual.

Guardrails and toe boards must be in position and secure.

All access stairways or ladders must be firmly located.

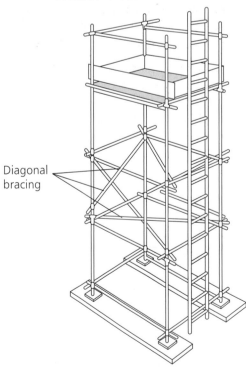

Fig. 4.45 **A steel tower**

Aluminium and Glass Fibre Towers

Most mobile towers available on site or for hire are usually of the aluminium type but glass fibre versions are becoming popular in some industries, particularly petrochemicals.

Advantages

There are many different types available to suit varying demands

They are quick and easy to erect

They are adaptable to different needs and terrain

They can be erected over uneven and sloping ground

They are relatively inexpensive to hire

Glass fibre types are non-conductive, quieter to use and not as cold to the touch in winter conditions compared with their aluminium counterparts.

Disadvantages

Components can be easily damaged with misuse, sections can be dented and split or welds can crack

They are not suitable for work which involves the platform being heavily loaded for example bricklaying.

Sole plates

Adjustable legs

Base plates

Fig. 4.46 **A tower on base plates for greater safety**

Ground Preparation for the Erection of Mobile Towers

When erecting a mobile tower scaffold you must ensure that the ground is firm. If the ground is soft, grass for example, then there is a danger that the wheels will sink causing the tower to lean or topple over. To prevent this happening you must prepare the ground by building the tower off sole plates composed of scaffold boards, ensuring that the wheels are always in the locked position.

When erecting a tower on sloping ground, the tower must always be built perpendicularly. This is achieved by using a spirit level and the adjustable legs of the tower, during the initial stages of building the tower. This avoids having to cope with the excessive weight of the tower when fully constructed.

To construct a tower on sloping or uneven soft ground the ground, must be prepared by digging out level stops and placing the tower on sole boards. The tower is built in the same manner as shown previously in Figure 4.45. As a precaution on sloping or uneven ground, always use base plates on sole boards instead of wheels for greater safety as illustrated in Figure 4.46.

Working Platforms for Mobile Towers

Figure 4.47 shows the guard rail and toe board requirements of a tower scaffold.

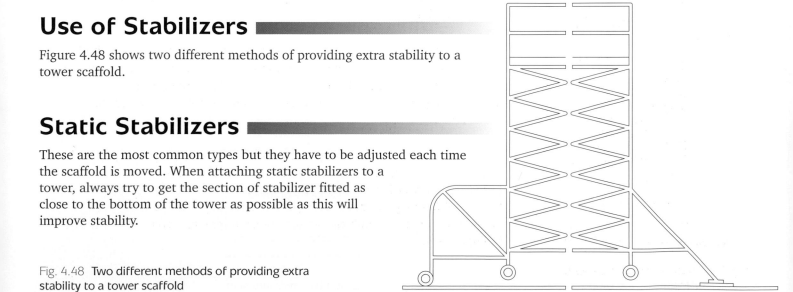

Guard rails

470 mm   Max

950 mm

470 mm   Max

Toe boards

150 mm min

Fig. 4.47 **The guard rail and toe board requirements of a tower scaffold**

Always ensure that guard rails are attached to the horizontal sections of the tower structure. Never attach guard rails to the outside of the vertical section.

The hand rails adjacent to a wall can be removed only if you are working tight up to the wall.

Use of Stabilizers

Figure 4.48 shows two different methods of providing extra stability to a tower scaffold.

Static Stabilizers

These are the most common types but they have to be adjusted each time the scaffold is moved. When attaching static stabilizers to a tower, always try to get the section of stabilizer fitted as close to the bottom of the tower as possible as this will improve stability.

Fig. 4.48 **Two different methods of providing extra stability to a tower scaffold**

Mobile Out Riggers

These allow the scaffold to be moved on hard surfaces with minimal adjustment.

Height to Base Ratio of External Towers

Towers erected outside a building can only be built to a height of three × the length of the smallest base measurement. Therefore, if the base dimensions of a tower measured 2 m × 3 m, then the maximum height of the working platform would be 3 m × 2 m = 6 m.

Towers erected inside a building can be erected to a height of 3.5 × the length of the smallest base measurement. A tower can be built higher on the inside of a building because there is no wind pressure.

If the base measurement of a tower measured 2 m × 3 m the maximum height of the working platform would be 3.5 m × 2 m = 7 m.

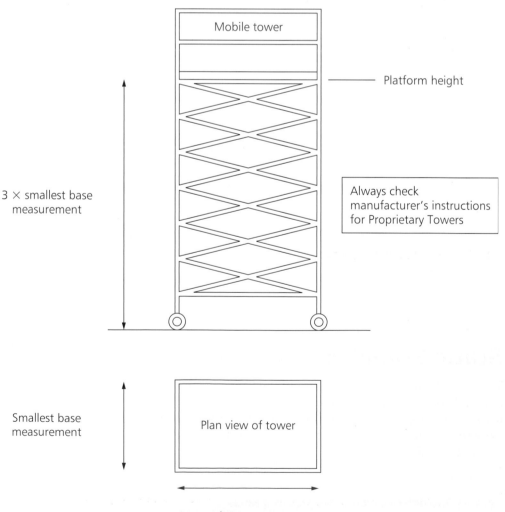

Mobile tower

Platform height

3 × smallest base measurement

Always check manufacturer's instructions for Proprietary Towers

Smallest base measurement

Plan view of tower

Fig. 4.49 **Height to base ratio 1**

Largest base measurement

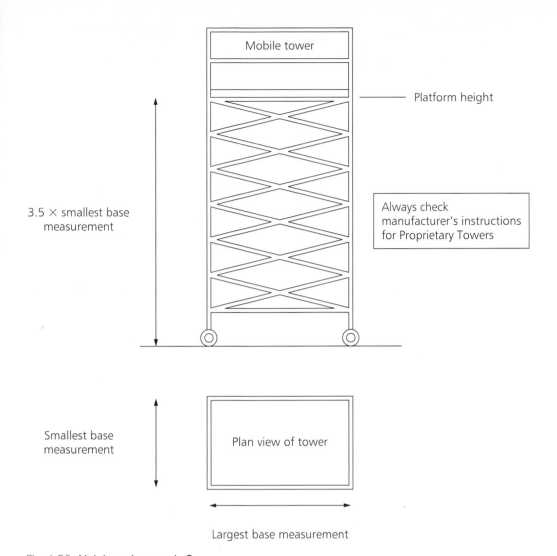

Fig. 4.50 **Height to base ratio 2**

Outriggers and stabilizers increase the dimensions of the base of the tower. This enables the tower to be built to a greater height. Towers fitted with stabilizers, erected outside a building can be built to a height of 3 × the length of the smallest base measurement.

If the base dimensions of the tower measured 3 m × 4 m the maximum height of the working platform would be 3 m × 3 m = 9 m.

Mobile Tower Scaffold Checklist ▬▬▬

When erecting a mobile tower always refer to the manufacturer's assembly instructions. The following checklist is a guide to ensuring that a tower is fit for use.

Checklist

✎ Check and prepare ground conditions if necessary and always avoid overhead power lines

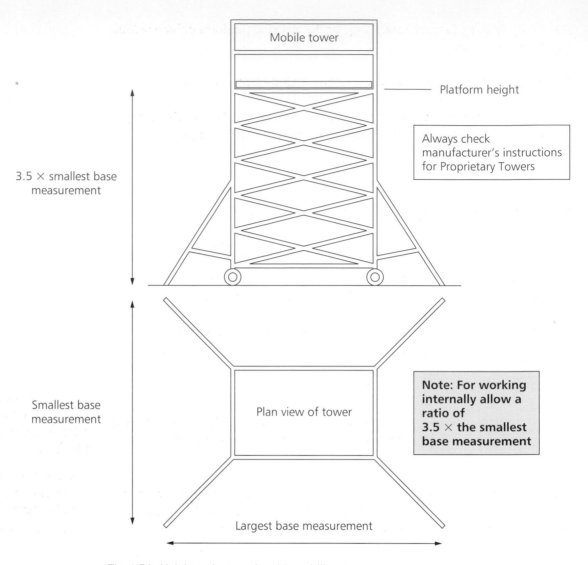

Fig. 4.51 **Height to base ratio with stabilizers**

Inspect components and erected tower prior to use

Check wheels are locked and legs are correctly adjusted

Check that stabilizers are fitted as specified. Remember that it may be necessary to prepare the ground conditions for these components

Check that the tower is upright and that platforms are level

Check the quantity and position of braces

Check that the working platform has sufficient guard rails and toe boards and that the wheel locks are in place.

Safety in the Use of Tower Scaffolds

Mobile towers are often erected properly but are then incorrectly used. The following examples of bad practice are just a small sample of those which are frequently carried out in the workplace.

Do not use another form of scaffolding on the working platform or lean ladders against a mobile tower.

Never try to move a mobile tower by pulling it along from the top.

Mobile towers must be moved by pushing at the base only. Never ride on top of a tower because if the tower encountered soft ground, drains or pot holes it would become unstable.

Safety Requirements in the Use of Mobile Towers

If a mobile tower is in the same location for seven days, it must be inspected by a competent person, and the results of the inspection recorded.

Do not overload a tower with operatives or heavy equipment or move the tower with any equipment left on the platform.

Visually inspect the tower every day before use.

Always climb the tower from the inside using the ladders built into or provided with the tower. Climbing up the outside of a tower can cause it to become unstable.

Never remove components from the tower whilst it is in use. Never dismantle the tower from the bottom. This sounds obvious but it only requires a few braces to be removed to cause the tower to become unstable.

TRY THIS OUT

Carry out research and list the sequence to follow when taking down a ladder from scaffolding or access platforms.

Present your findings to your supervisor and check to see if they match official guidelines.

Quick quiz Quick quiz Quick quiz Quick quiz Quick quiz

❶ Name three defects that could be found in a scaffold board?
❷ What is the minimum overhang for a scaffold board?
❸ What is the maximum height you could build a freestanding static external tower with a base of 2 m × 2 m?
❹ What is the minimum spacing for standards for a tower?
❺ Where is the ladder placed on a tower scaffold?

Proprietary Scaffolds

Tubular System Built Scaffolds

This type of scaffold is made from a range of pre-fabricated components. There are several different types available and they all feature some type of edge system. That is, the components are designed to be assembled with the use of a hammer instead of a spanner as shown in Figure 4.52. Manufacturers produce a range of sizes, shapes and weight bearing capabilities. These systems are light and quick to build, but are expensive to purchase.

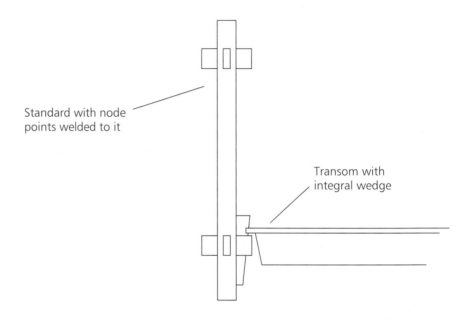

Standard with node points welded to it

Transom with integral wedge

Fig. 4.52 **System built components**

Advantages
- speed of assembly
- low maintenance
- simple to erect
- lighter than conventional scaffolding.

Disadvantages
- expensive
- a wide range of components are required
- components can easily be damaged by an unqualified person.

Handling Requirements

System scaffolds need to withstand adverse weather conditions, rough handling and often poor storage facilities. They need to be adaptable to uneven ground conditions and the variable size and shape of buildings. They need to be quick to erect with all the on-site pressures to meet deadlines. Safety and simplicity are therefore built into these systems.

System scaffolds have been designed to meet these requirements. The key to the success of system scaffold lies in its design features.

➤ Versatility of application

➤ Simplicity of use

➤ Lightness.

Elimination of loose fittings

System scaffolds are a tried and tested access solution that performs successfully on thousands of sites across the UK.

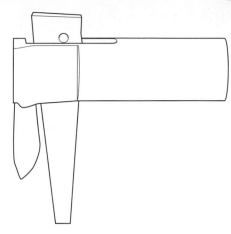

Fig. 4.53 **Wedge fixings**

Types of Systems

The two major types of system build scaffolds in use in the UK are the Cuplock and K-Stage systems.

K-Stage Scaffolding

K-Stage is a modular system scaffold with wedge fixings for all access scaffold requirements. The wedge fixings of the ledgers and transoms, as shown in Figure 4.53, give a simple and fast means of erecting access scaffolding without loose parts.

The rigid four way fixing is designed to give a positive location without movement, as are the spigot and wedge fittings on the standard which is designed to give guaranteed vertical alignment as shown in Figure 4.54.

A typical K-Stage system is illustrated in Figure 4.55.

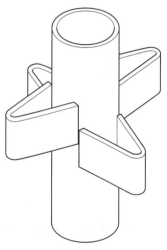

Fig. 4.54 **Spigot and wedge fittings on standards**

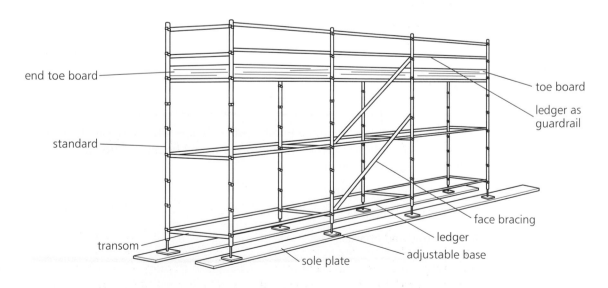

end toe board

toe board

ledger as guardrail

standard

face bracing

transom

ledger

sole plate

adjustable base

Fig. 4.55 **A K-stage layout**

Cuplock Scaffolding System

Cuplock is a multi-purpose scaffold system which can be used for all forms of access and support structures in the construction industry. The Cuplock system provides savings in erection and dismantling times thus reducing on-site costs. When not in use, its modular construction means it can be stored in a minimum of space.

Cuplock's unique node point as illustrated in Figure 4.56 allows up to four horizontal members to be connected to a single vertical member in one simple action – without the use of nuts and bolts or wedges.

Fig. 4.56 **A node point**
Source: K-Lock Scaffolding

Cuplock can be erected for straight, curved and circular configurations for both access and support, and also for independent and mobile towers.

TRY THIS OUT

Working platforms are used in a number of trade specific areas. Create a list of tasks where the following working platforms would be most suited and the trades that would use them.

- stepladders and boards
- trestles and boards
- hop-ups and boards.

Independent Tubular Scaffolds

Tubular Scaffolds

Tubular scaffolding is made up of a variety of components to form either an independent, putlog or system scaffold. The most common type of scaffolding made from tubes and couplers is the independent type shown in Figure 4.57.

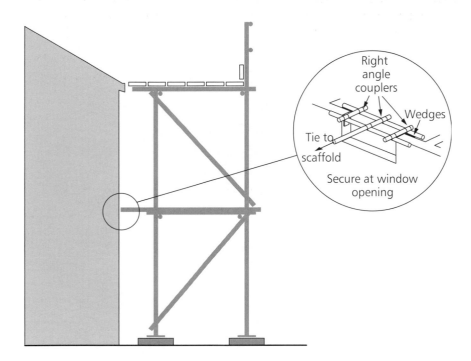

Fig. 4.57 Independent scaffolding

An independent scaffold is designed to carry the weight of people, materials and equipment placed upon it. The scaffold stands clear of the building but it must be tied into the building to provide extra stability.

This form of scaffold is used by all trades when extensive maintenance, refurbishment or construction work is carried out. The main applications for independent scaffolding are:

- access for stonework or masonry buildings
- access to solid or reinforced concrete structures
- maintenance and repair work
- painting
- cladding work.

✓ Good Practice

Independent scaffold must be inspected every seven days, immediately after bad weather, after any alteration, or if the stability has been affected in any way, by a competent person usually a qualified scaffolder.

A scaffold which has two lines of standards, one line supporting the outside of the deck and one inside. The transoms are not built into the wall of the building. It is not free standing, but relies on the building for stability.

Independent Tied Scaffold

Some important components of an independent tied scaffold are illustrated in Figure 4.58.

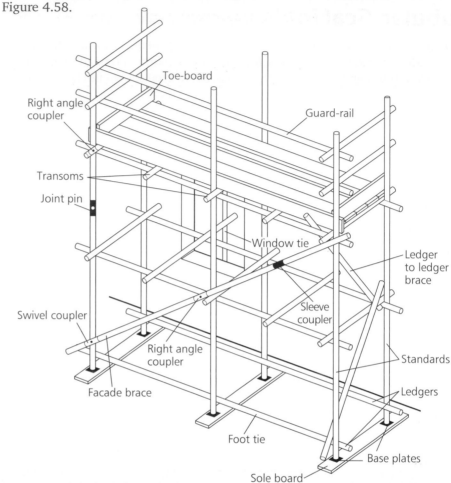

Fig. 4.58 **Tied independent scaffolding**

key terms

Standard – The vertical tubes which carry the load to the ground. Each standard should sit on a base plate which spreads the load, thus ensuring that it does not sink into the ground.

Base Plate – Usually made from steel they have a central spigot which locates the tube. Sometimes the base plate is nailed or screwed to a sole board in order to prevent sideways movement.

Sole Board – Sole boards or sole plates are necessary, particularly on soft ground, to spread the load over a larger area.

Toeboard – A board fixed on edge to prevent tools, materials or feet slipping off the platform.

Guardrail – A tube fixed to the standards to prevent workers falling off platforms.

Ledgers – The horizontal tubes which connect and support the standards and act as the support for transoms.

Lift – The distance between ledgers.

Main Transoms – Tubes positioned at right angles across the ledgers, next to each pair of standards or connected to each pair of standards. Their function is to hold standards in place, help make the scaffold more rigid and act as scaffold board supports.

Intermediate Transoms – Tubes positioned across the ledgers between the main transoms to act as scaffold board supports.

Facade Brace – Tubes fixed to the face of the scaffold to stop the scaffold moving. They should run from the base to the full height of the scaffold at an angle of between 35 and 55 degrees and be fitted at the base and at every lift level, either to the standards or the ends of transoms.

Never alter or dismantle scaffold, this can only be carried out by a competent person.

Do not overload the scaffold. Ensure that any loads carried by the scaffold are well distributed.

Do not throw waste materials off the scaffold. If the amount of waste generated by the works is extensive, a chute into a covered skip must be provided.

Do not fool around. Your actions could put yourself and others in danger.

Points to note
Do not use scaffold if signs state scaffold incomplete.

Scaffold Fittings

The illustrations shown in Figures 4.59 to 4.68 show some important couplers and fittings used to construct non-proprietary scaffolds.

Toe Board Clip

A clip used for attaching toe boards to tubes, usually standards.

Right Angled Coupler

This is used to connect ledgers to standards at right angles, designed and tested to achieve a right-angled connection with a minimum safe working load of 635 kg.

Swivel Coupler

This is used to connect tubes at any angle. It is normally used to connect braces to standards and sometimes to make parallel joints. Swivel couplers should never be used as right-angle couplers.

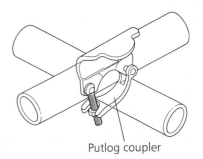

Toe board clip

Fig. 4.59 **Toe board clip**

Putlog Coupler

This is used to connect transoms to ledgers. They are only suitable for light duty use.

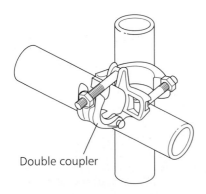

Double coupler

Fig. 4.60 **A right angled coupler**

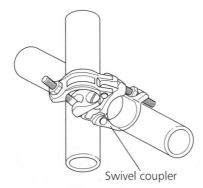

Swivel coupler

Fig. 4.61 **A swivel coupler**

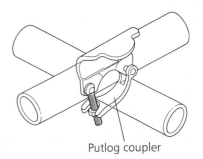

Putlog coupler

Fig. 4.62 **A putlog coupler**

Sleeve Coupler

This is used to join one tube to another coaxially.

Joint Pin or Spigot

An internal expanding pin used to join tubes end to end.

Putlog Adaptor

This is a fitting to provide a putlog blade on to the end of a tube.

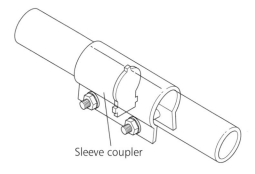

Fig. 4.63 **A sleeve coupler**

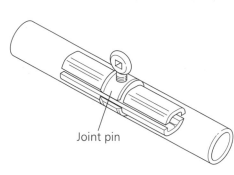

Fig. 4.64 **A joint pin or spigot**

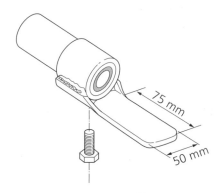

Fig. 4.65 **A putlog adaptor**

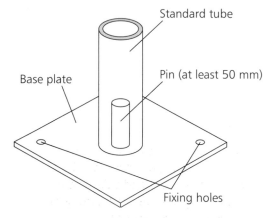

Fig. 4.66 **A base plate**

Base Plate

This is a metal plate with a spigot for distributing the load from a standard or raker or other load bearing tube.

Reveal Pin

This is a pin that is inserted into the end of a tube and adjusted to secure scaffolding in window or door openings.

Castor Wheel

A wheel for use with mobile tower scaffolds.

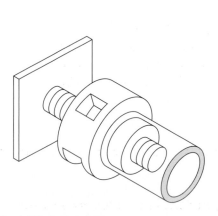

Fig. 4.67 **A reveal pin**

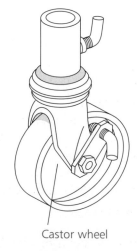

Fig. 4.68 **A castor wheel**

Scaffold Tubes

There are three main types of scaffold tube in use throughout the UK, they are:

- black steel tubes
- galvanized steel tubes
- aluminium alloy tubes.

Black steel tubes and galvanized steel tubes both possess the same inherent properties save that galvanized steel tube is more resistant to corrosion. Aluminium alloy tube is lighter and more flexible than steel tubing, but not as strong.

> **Point to note**
>
> Aluminium and steel scaffold tubing should never be mixed in the same scaffold.

Tube Inspection

Tubes should be checked on a regular basis to ensure that they are:

- straight
- free from cracks, dents and corrosion.

Common faults in tubes

- tubes cut by welding torch
- tubes cut at an angle
- tubes with burred ends
- tubes that are bent
- tubes that have split ends.

Storage of Tubes

Tubes for scaffolding are usually supplied in lengths of 6.3 m. Shorter tubes are available in lengths of 1.5 and 1.8 m.

Scaffold tubes should be stored on level bearers or in racks ranged in their equal sizes.

> **Definition**
>
> A scaffold which has one line of standards to support the outside edge of the deck and utilizes the wall being built or the building to support the inside edge.

Putlog Tubular Scaffolds

This type of scaffold only has one row of standards and it therefore relies on the building to provide additional support. Putlog scaffolding is particularly suited to house building because it can easily be erected as the building increases in height. This type of scaffold can only be used on existing buildings if the holes for the putlog scaffold are cut out of existing brickwork cross joints.

A putlog scaffold must be tied into a building for extra stability with the use of raking struts.

Figure 4.69 shows the first lift of a putlog scaffold, as the building increases in size, the height of the lifts can be increased.

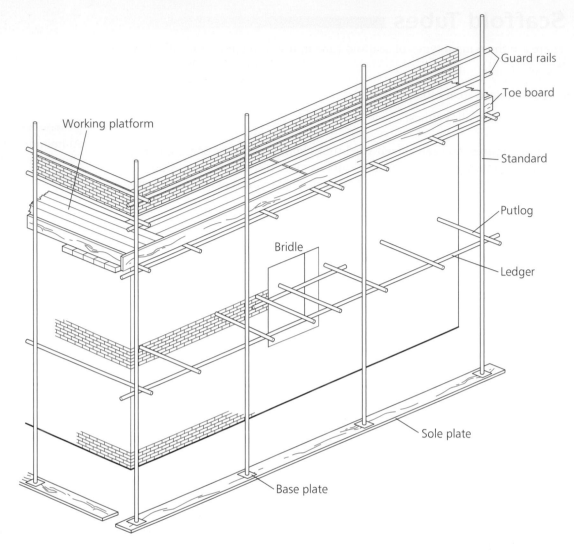

Working platform

Guard rails

Toe board

Standard

Putlog

Bridle

Ledger

Sole plate

Base plate

Fig. 4.69 **A putlog scaffold**

key terms

Bridle – a horizontal tube slung between putlogs for the purpose of supporting intermediate putlogs, where it is impossible to support a putlog in the wall, for example when in front of a window opening.

Raker – a load-bearing tube at an angle to the vertical.

Positive Tie – a tie actually fixed to the building.

Brace – a tube fixed diagonally across the scaffold.

TRY THIS OUT

Write a report comparing the advantages and disadvantages of the use of tower scaffold over independent and trestle scaffolds. Use

■ the library,

■ internet,

■ manufacturers' technical literature

■ builders' merchants for your sources of information.

Present your findings to your supervisor who will find the report useful when planning what access system to use in future operations.

Mobile Elevating Work Platforms

This modern form of plant can provide excellent safe access to high level work. However, in the control of an untrained operative they are potentially dangerous.

If mobile platforms are misused, operatives can be:

- electrocuted by contact with overhead power lines
- knocked off the platform by allowing the platform to protrude into a traffic route
- thrown from the platform by allowing the equipment to overturn while trying to negotiate a slope.

This form of access equipment is becoming a familiar sight in the construction industry. If you are using this type of elevating platform, make sure:

- the operator is competent and fully trained
- the working platform is properly equipped with suitable guard rails and toe boards
- all operatives are aware of the emergency procedures to lower the platform if it fails in the raised position
- the ground conditions are suitable for this type of machine.

Types of Mobile Elevating Machines

There are several types of machine available, some of the most often used types are described below.

Scissor Lift

For use where a large platform area is needed: many can also be driven whilst the platform is raised.

Self Propelled Boom

This machine can be used either internally or externally and can be driven with the platform raised. More versatility is achieved through extra outreach.

Trailer/Push Around

This lightweight, highly manoeuvrable, versatile machine is suitable for most situations.

Truck/Van Mounted

This versatile work platform with a reach of up to 26 m is built on to a non-HGV self-drive truck.

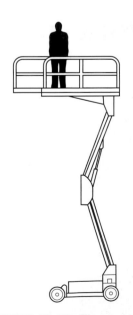

Fig. 4.70 **A MEWP (Mobile Elevated Work Platform)**

Truck Mounted

This is an HGV based high reach work platform with a reach of over 26 m for greater height and outreach capabilities.

Vertical Personnel Platform

This is a compact vertical work platform often used internally or in confined spaces.

Work at Height

When you have worked through this section, you will be able to:

- recognize potentially hazardous situations in the workshop or construction site
- plan, organize and maintain a safe working environment for colleagues.

Health and Safety

The use of any form of scaffolding can be dangerous and your chances of being involved in an accident are far greater if you are working on scaffolding. With this in mind it is worth considering the following points, concerning health and safety.

The Health and Safety at Work Act 1974 (HASWA) makes it the duty of everyone at work, both employers and employees, to set up and maintain a safe working environment. Under the HASWA, employees and employers have responsibilities which if ignored can result in criminal prosecution and, if warranted, a custodial sentence.

The Duties of the Employer

Employers have to ensure, as far as is practicable, the health, safety and welfare of all their employees.

Provide and maintain safe plant and equipment including access equipment and systems of work.

Provide for the safe transport and storage of articles and substances.

Provide for all safety instruction and supervision as is necessary to ensure safe working practice.

Provide for a safe working environment – including safe access and exit.

Provide all the necessary safety equipment.

The Duties of the Employee

To take reasonable care of themselves, work colleagues and the general public who may be affected by what they may do or not do.

To co-operate fully with employers on all aspects of health and safety provision.

Use all equipment and safeguards provided by the employer in a safe and responsible manner.

Never misuse or interfere with anything provided for health and safety.

The Work at Height Regulations 2005

The Work at Height Regulations 2005 came into effect on 6 April 2005. The Regulations will apply to work at height where there is a risk of a fall liable to cause personal injury.

The Regulations place duties on employers, the self-employed, and any person who controls the work of others.

As part of the Regulations, 'duty holders' must ensure:

- all work at height is properly planned and organized
- those involved in work at height are competent
- the risks from work at height are assessed and that appropriate work equipment is selected and used
- the risks from fragile surfaces are properly controlled; and
- equipment for work at height is properly inspected and maintained.

There is a simple hierarchy for managing and selecting equipment for work at height. Duty holders must:

- avoid work at height where they can
- use work equipment or other measures to prevent falls where they cannot avoid working at height.

Falls from Height

In 2003/2004 67 people died and nearly 4000 suffered a serious injury as a result of a fall from height in the workplace.

Falls from height are the most common cause of fatal injury and the second most common cause of major injury to employees, accounting for around 15 per cent of all such injuries. All industries are exposed to the risks presented by this hazard, although the level of incidence varies considerably.

As a result, Falls from Height are a key priority in the Health and Safety Commission Injury Reduction Programme. There objective is to reduce injury rates by 10 per cent by 2010 compared to the 1999/2000 level.

Experience shows that falls from height usually occur as a result of poor management control rather than because of equipment failure. Common factors include:

- failure to recognize a problem
- failure to provide safe systems of work
- failure to ensure that safe systems of work are followed
- inadequate information, instruction, training or supervision provided
- failure to use appropriate equipment
- failure to provide safe plant/equipment.

The HSE recommends that employers:

- follow good practice for work at height (if they do this they should already be doing enough to comply with the regulations)
- follow the risk assessments that have been carried out for work at height activities and make sure all work at height is planned, organized and carried out by competent persons
- take steps to avoid, prevent or reduce risks; and
- choose the right work equipment and select collective measures to prevent falls, such as guardrails and working platforms.

Types of Fall

The construction sector accounted for 40 per cent of falls from ladders in the UK in the last five years.

Types of Fall 2001/2

Total fall from height injuries 1203.

Of these, key categories of fall were:

- falls from ladders 457
- falls from scaffold 171
- falls from floors, pavements and roads 114
- falls from vehicles, plant and earthmoving equipment 89
- falls from building materials such as bricks, tiles and beams 34
- falls from surfaces and structure below ground level 11.

Source: Health and Safety Executive.

Safety Organization

Construction sites should have a safety officer employed by the contractor to ensure that all work areas are safe. On building sites where there is no safety officer, the foreman or supervisor is usually responsible for the implementation of site safety.

Safety programmes and laws are only effective if:

- they are enforced on site
- they are legally enforceable
- all members of staff are aware of safety.

TRY THIS OUT

Prepare a list of safety considerations that site personnel need to observe when erecting, taking down and dismantling access equipment.

Present the list to your supervisor and ask him or her to compare it with the official procedures in order to check the correctness of your findings.

RESOURCES   4.2

In this section you will learn about materials, components and equipment relating to types, quantity, quality and sizes of standard and/or specialist:

- bricks, blocks, mortar, thin joint mixes, wall ties, cavity insulation, damp proof membranes
- hand tools and equipment
- methods of calculating quantity, length, area and wastage associated with the method/procedure to lay bricks and blocks to line.

When you have completed this section you will be able to:

- select the required quantity and quality of resources for the methods of work.

Know and understand:

- the characteristics, quality, uses, limitations and defects associated with the resources
- how the resources should be used.

Bricks

Ordinary bricks are unit blocks manufactured from 'brick earths' and are commonly known as clay bricks.

The characteristics and colours of bricks vary with the method of manufacture, the composition of the brick earth, and the natural position from which the earth is obtained.

Classification

For the purpose of brick classification it is useful to note the difference between types of bricks according to:

- their method of manufacture; and
- the general use for which they are suitable.

Classification by Method of Manufacture

Bricks may be broadly sub-divided under the following headings based upon the process of making and burning:

- Handmade
- Wire cut
- Machine moulded or pressed
- Sand lime and flint lime bricks.

Each of these processes produces in the finished brick certain characteristics, which largely govern the use to which the brick is put: general construction, decorative work, engineering work, etc.

Handmade Bricks

As the name suggests, these bricks are entirely handmade. The mould in which the bricks are made consists of a bottomless box that fits over a board having the frog of the brick formed in the reverse upon it. Clay is thrown into the mould that has been previously wetted or sanded to prevent the clay adhering to the sides. The surplus clay is cut off with a piece of wood known as a striker, or with a length of wire stretched over a wooden frame. The box is then removed leaving the brick ready for drying. When a mould is sanded it produces a sand-faced brick, and also tends to produce a variety of colours.

Wire Cut Bricks

These bricks are partially machine made, the clay in a suitably plastic state being forced by revolving blades through a rectangular opening, which is the length by the width of a brick plus a shrinkage allowance, in one continuous length on to a steel table. A frame containing several wires spaced the thickness of a brick apart is brought down across the clay cutting it into a number of pieces, each piece being the size of a brick before baking. The brick has no frog and the wire marks can be seen on both beds of the brick.

Machine Moulded or Pressed Bricks

If it is desired to give bricks that have been wire cut a sharp arris and a frog the process of cutting off by wire is followed by machine pressing. The bricks are conveyed to a metal mould, the sides and top of which are simultaneously compressed by mechanical means. This produces a good sound brick very regular in shape and size.

Sand Lime and Flint Lime Bricks

Sand lime and flint lime bricks or calcium silicate bricks, as they are more properly called, are made from a mixture of sand, crushed flint, pebbles or rock, or a combination of such materials, with hydrated lime. They are moulded under pressure and hardened by exposure to steam at very high pressure. On cooling, they are ready for immediate use.

Concrete Bricks

These types of bricks are made in a similar way to sand lime and flint lime bricks, except that sand and cement is used instead of sand and lime.

Classification by Use

Bricks may be classified according to their use as follows, bearing in mind that it is sometimes possible for a brick to come under more than one heading:

- Facing bricks
- Common bricks
- Engineering bricks
- Special bricks.

Facing Bricks

Facing bricks are intended to provide an attractive appearance. They are available in a wide range of facing brick types, colours and textures. Some may not be suitable in positions of extreme exposure. Some facing bricks have engineering properties.

The term facing covers a very wide range of bricks since it includes all those used for exterior and interior walls that are to be left as finished work. While it would not be possible to name all the bricks manufactured as facings, brief descriptions of the more general types are given below.

Reds – this type of brick is obtainable in various colours, and differs in character from a soft sand-faced brick to a hard brick with a smooth surface.

Flettons – These are smooth faced regular-shaped bricks and are a mottled pink in colour. While used chiefly as a common brick, they may also be used as a facing brick. They are produced with various surface treatments. They are entirely machine made, being handled only when placing them in and out of the kiln.

Stocks – this description originally referred to handmade bricks in which it was the practice to mix ashes with the clay before moulding to assist in the burning. Similar quality bricks are now often machine-made and burnt in continuous kilns. There are other types of stocks similar in texture and quality, but usually with a variety of reds in the colouring.

Common Bricks

Common bricks are suitable for general building work and are not chosen for their appearance.

These are bricks for ordinary work that is not exposed to view, for example, walls that are to be plastered or are built underground. Nearly all brick makers produce common bricks, which are often manufactured from the same clay as that used for better class products, but which lack the finer preparation and finish. Bricks to be included under this heading would be wire cuts of all descriptions, second and third class stocks, sand lime and flint lime bricks.

Engineering Bricks

Engineering bricks are hard burnt bricks that are very dense. They have a guaranteed minimum compressive strength and minimum water absorption. They are not chosen for appearance. There is no requirement for colour.

These are bricks suitable for ground works, manholes and sewers, retaining walls, or as ground level damp proof course for free standing walls, or in situations where high strength and low water absorption are the most important factors.

Special Bricks

A wide variety of bricks are available in special shapes or sizes, to blend or contrast with most facing bricks.

Squints

These bricks are manufactured to special shapes that enable the bricklayer to build angled corners at 45 degrees or 60 degrees (see Figure 4.71). They are used to reduce the thickness of a wall and still maintain the face texture of the wall or remove the sharp corners from a brick wall or pier.

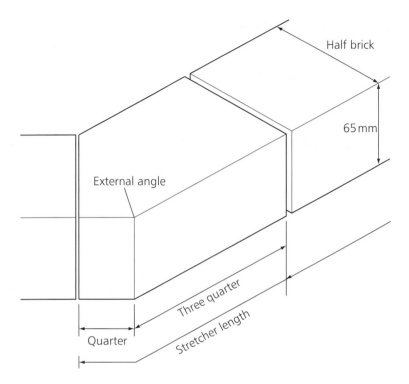

Fig. 4.71 **Properties of a squint brick**

Brick Dimensions

The dimensions and shapes of bricks vary according to the requirements of the purpose that the bricks are intended to serve. Where bricks varying in size are used together, the task of the bricklayer is made difficult on account of the additional care required to produce work of good appearance. To overcome this difficulty, bricks should have standard dimensions, but even the most up-to-date methods of manufacture inevitably produce slight variations in size.

Sizes and Quantities of Bricks

The current British Standard brick size is 215 mm long, 102.5 mm wide and 65 mm thick.

Approximately 60 bricks are required per square metre of half brick walling and 120 for full brick, including 10 mm mortar joints. Table 4.1 may be useful to calculate the numbers required and the mortar needed – but always remember to subtract an allowance for window and door openings.

Table 4.1 Calculating bricks and mortar needed

Wall thickness mm	No. of bricks required per square metre of wall	Volume of mortar per square metre of all (m³)		Volume of mortar per 1000 bricks used (m³)	
		frog up	frog down	frog up	frog down
102.5	60	0.031	0.021	0.52	0.35
215	119	0.072	0.052	0.61	0.44

Notes to table

Note 1 The mix proportions given contain the minimum recommended cement content for durability. If, for any reasons, mortars with greater cement contents are required, then stronger mortars may be satisfactorily used with the London range of bricks

Note 2 The BS5628: Part 3 Table 15 mortar designation is given for each recommended mortar mix to assist these involved in structural design calculations to BS 5628: Parts 1 and 2.

Note 3 For work below finished ground level the mortar may have to be varied depending on the level of the sulphates in the soil or ground water. For details see Table 3. The same mortar should be used for all work up to ground level dpc, or at least two courses above finished ground level.

Note 4 Free-standing walls, parapet walls and chimneys must be finished with an overhanging coping.

Note 5 Retaining walls must have a water-proof backing and an overhanging coping.

Definition of Sizes

Co-ordinating Size – The size of a co-ordinating space allocated to a brick, including allowances for joints and tolerances (see Figure 4.72).

Work Size – The size of a brick specified for its manufacture, to which its actual size should conform within specified permissible deviations (see Figure 4.72).

Sizes

	Length mm	Width mm	Height mm
Co-ordinating size	225	112.5	75
Work size	215	102.5	65

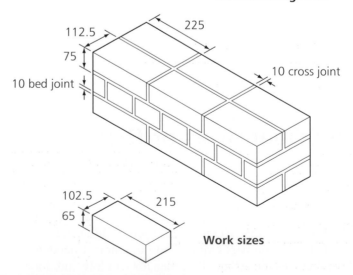

Fig. 4.72 Co-ordinating size and work size

Dimensional Variation

During the brick manufacturing process there is sometimes considerable change in the size of the newly formed brick, as it dries out. For this reason the exact sizes of bricks are difficult to control.

British Standard BS EN 771–i specifies tolerances for both the mean (average) and range (difference between largest and smallest measurement) deviations. (see Figure 4.73).

Durability

Bricks are classified according to frost resistance and soluble salt content. They are given different designations of durability (see Figure 4.74).

The chart shows us that frost resistant bricks (F2) are suitable for use in all normal situations, whilst, moderately frost resistant bricks (F1) may also be used in most situations but should not be used in situations where they remain saturated and are subject to freezing and thawing. Bricks that are not frost resistant (F0) are only suitable for internal use. Low soluble salt content (S2) bricks are advisable in situations where there is a high risk of saturation. There is no requirement for completely protected walls.

Mean value (means of 10 bricks – work size in mm)

	215	102	65
T1	± 6	± 4	± 3
T2	± 4	± 3	± 2
Tm	Deviation declared by manufacturer		

Range (work size in mm)

	215	102	65
R1	9	6	5
R2	4	3	2
Rm	Range declared by manufacturer		

Fig 4.73 Charts showing size tolerances
Source: Ibstock Brick Ltd

Freeze/thaw resistance

F0	Suitable for passive exposure
F1	Suitable for moderate exposure
F2	Suitable for severe exposure

Fig 4.74 Chart showing brick durability
Source: Ibstock Brick Ltd

Active soluble salt content

Category	Total % by mass not greater than	
	$Na^+ + K^+$ (sodium and potassium)	Mg (magnesium)
S0	No requirement	No requirement
S1	0.17	0.08
S2	0.06	0.03

❶ In bricklaying terms what is a frog?

❷ Name the three main types of bricks.

❸ What type of brick would be used for building a retaining wall?

❹ Sketch a king closer.

❺ What is a quarter bat?

❻ Make a sketch of a mitred bat.

❼ Draw a brick, including all terminology.

❽ What materials are bricks manufactured from?

❾ Describe a common brick.

❿ Where would we use common bricks?

Blocks

There is a wide variety in the size and type of block used within the construction industry. Some of these are described below.

Lightweight Aircrete Blocks

Manufactured in various widths of between 75, 100, 150 and 200 mm.

Designed for use in lightweight internal partitions and the inner leaves of cavity walls.

Cellular Blocks

Manufactured in widths of 75, 100 and 150 mm.

Used for lightweight partitions.

Foundation Blocks

Manufactured in widths from 100 mm and above.

They are used below ground to carry cavity walls. They may be lightweight or dense.

> **Point to note**
> Dense foundation blocks should be lifted by two people.

Dense Concrete Blocks

Manufactured in widths of 100, 150 and 225 mm.

Used for loadbearing and exposed work on industrial and agricultural buildings.

Hollow Blocks

Manufactured in one size only – 440 mm long × 215 mm wide × 215 mm deep.

Used for loadbearing and hard-wearing walls in industrial and agricultural buildings.

Fig. 4.75   Aircrete blocks
Source: Celcon

Reveal Blocks

Used to close the cavity at door and window openings.

Lightweight Aircrete Blocks

The block manufacturer Thermalite, introduced the autoclaved concrete block, now known as Aircrete over 50 years ago, and it is now one of the largest producers along with Celcon of building blocks in the United Kingdom.

Aircrete is a lightweight, loadbearing and thermally insulating building material most commonly available in block format, but also as reinforced units. The blocks are light in weight, easy to work, and have excellent loadbearing capabilities (see Figure 4.75).

A combination of strength, moisture resistance and high thermal efficiency makes Aircrete blocks an ideal choice for cavity, solid, internal and party walls. Aircrete blocks are lightweight and easy to work, saving time and money. They are manufactured in widths of 75, 100, 150 and 200 mm.

Over 50 per cent of the raw material used in the manufacture of Aircrete blocks is pulverized fuel ash, a stable by-product of coal burning power stations. This recycled material is mixed with sand, cement, lime and aluminium powder together with processed waste and water, to produce a range of blocks noted for their high thermal insulation properties.

High Strength Aircrete Blocks

High strength aerated blocks combine strength with thermal performance and are lightweight and easy to use.

Larger Sized Aircrete Blocks

The block manufacturers Celcon and Thermalite have a range of larger block sizes available, named Plus and Jumbo in the Celcon range and similar from Thermalite. As illustrated in the work face dimensions chart, Figure 4.76 they are made to a size of 610 mm × 215 mm and 610 mm × 270 mm respectively, normal block size being 440 mm × 215 mm.

Work face dimensions	
Wall blocks	440 × 215 mm
Floor blocks	440 × 560 mm
Foundation blocks	440 × 215 mm
Coursing bricks	215 × 65 mm
Plus blocks	610 × 215 mm
Jumbo Plus blocks	610 × 270 mm

Fig 4.76   **Work face dimensions chart**
Source: Celcon

Foundation Blocks

Foundation blocks are mainly used below ground to carry cavity walls. They may be the lightweight Aircrete type or the dense concrete type depending on circumstances. They are manufactured in a range of thicknesses; 100 mm and above for cavity wall construction and 190 mm and above for solid wall construction (see Figure 4.77). The Aircrete blocks have an excellent thermal performance, and are equally suitable for the support of either cavity, solid walls or frame construction above ground level.

Product	Available block thicknesses (mm)	Available[7] face dimensions (mm)
 Turbo	100 115 125 130 140 150 190 200 215 265 300[3]	440 × 215 440 × 430
 Shield	75 90 100 125 140 150 190 200	440 × 215 440 × 140 440 × 430 540 × 440[4]
 Hi-Strength 7	100 140 150 190 200 215	440 × 215 440 × 430
 Hi-Strength 10[3]	100 140 150 190 200 215	440 × 215
 Smooth Face	100 140 150 190 200 215	440 × 215 440 × 430
Hi-Strength Smooth Face	100 140 150 190 200 215	440 × 215 440 × 430
 Party Wall	100 215	440 × 215 440 × 430
Floorblock	100	440 × 350 440 × 215 440 × 540
Floor Endblock	150 175	440 × 140
Coursing Slip	40 65	215 × 100 (Plan dimensions)
 Trenchblock/ Tongue & Groove	255 275 300 355[3]	440 × 215 440 × 140[5]
 Hi-Strength Trenchblock/ Tongue & Groove	255 275 300 355[3]	440 × 215 440 × 140[5]
Coursing Brick	100 115 125 130 140 150	215 × 65

Notes
(1) BRE Special Digest 1: Concrete in aggressive ground
(2) May be used in situations described in A1, A2, but not in situations described in A3 of Table 13 of BS 5628: Part 3
4 Thermalite
(3) Manufactured to special order only
(4) Compressive Strength 3 N/mm²
(5) Not available with Tongue and Groove jointing
(6) See notes on page 18
(7) Some thicknesses to special order only

Key
✔ = recommended use

Fig. 4.77 Range of block thicknesses

Source: Thermalite

Concrete Blocks

The aggregate concrete block is by far the most commonly-used building block type in the construction industry, representing almost 70 per cent of new construction.

Aggregate concrete blocks are probably the most economical solution for house builders and have the best acoustic properties, provide an excellent fixing background and give unparalleled resistance to fires.

Aggregate concrete blocks are strong, durable, ideal for all wet finishes and for dry lining, and are easy to lay and position on mortar.

A single block type can be used in every situation on site, helping to control costs, improve delivery scheduling and reducing the risk of products being used in error. Aggregate concrete blocks are ideally suited to the building of inner and outer leaves of walling, cavity separating walls, beam and block flooring, partitions and work below the damp proof course. They are manufactured as solid, cellular and hollow blocks.

Aggregate concrete blocks are available in various strengths, weights, sizes, and surface textures. They can be used in the following situations:

- Inner and outer leaves of walling
- Separating walls
- Beam and block flooring
- Below the damp proof course.

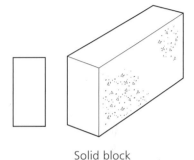

Solid block

Solid Blocks

These blocks are widely used in industrial and agricultural buildings, providing a hard-wearing load bearing structure (see Figure 4.78). Solid blocks contain no formed cavities.

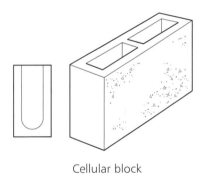

Cellular block

Cellular Blocks

Used mainly for lightweight partitions. They are manufactured in widths of 75, 100 and 150 mm (see Figure 4.78). Cellular blocks contain one or more formed cavities that do not go right through the block.

Hollow Blocks

These mainly concrete blocks are used for load bearing and hard wearing walls in industrial and agricultural buildings (see Figure 4.78). Hollow blocks contain one or more formed cavities that go right through the block.

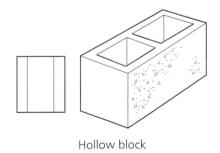

Hollow block

Fig. 4.78 **Solid, cellular and hollow blocks**

Reveal Blocks

These blocks, the majority of which are of the aerated type, are used to close cavities at door and window openings (see Figure 4.79). Closing cavities with aerated blocks provides a number of benefits, both at the design stage and during construction.

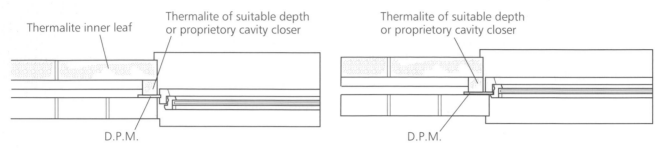

**Window frame overlapping cavity closer
– flush reveal**

**Window frame overlapping cavity closer
– rebated reveal for very severe exposure zones**

Fig. 4.79 Aerated blocks closing a reveal

Good Practice

The Concrete Block Association recommend the following good working practices when block laying.

High standards of workmanship should be encouraged at all times.

All bed and perpend joints should be fully filled with mortar.

Cavities should be kept clear from mortar droppings and other debris.

Partially completed and new work should be protected at all times from bad weather.

Movement should be controlled by the inclusion of movement joints and or bed joint reinforcement appropriately positioned.

To maintain a satisfactory appearance in facing work, wall dimensions should be based on co-ordinating block sizes.

For facing work a sample panel should be built to enable specifications and standards of workmanship to be agreed before construction commences.

Special blocks should be used for lintels, sills and closing cavities.

Energy Conservation and Blocks

Changes to the energy conservation requirements for buildings, mean that areas where thermal bridging may occur should be considered carefully and taken into account in the overall design of the building.

Please note, that the use of bricks and other dense materials for the closing of cavities is now not permitted by the Robust Details Document (this is used in conjunction with the Building Regulations for the specification of materials) The reason being that the use of aerated blocks enables the U-value of the wall construction to be maintained up to the door and window reveals and at roof level.

Daily Lift Heights

Lift heights will be affected by block thickness, weight, type of block, wall type and mortar mix used. Weather conditions will also affect lift heights and they may need to be restricted in bad weather. Generally lift heights should be restricted to seven full block courses, approximately 1575 mm in a working day.

Manual Handling

Careful consideration of the bricklayer's working area can contribute greatly to safe working. Bear in mind the following:

- Blocks should be moved in packs by mechanical means whenever possible
- Blocks should be loaded to just above two block courses in height
- Normal protective equipment appropriate to a building site should be provided and used
- Appropriate eye protection equipment and dust suppression or extraction measures should be provided when mechanically cutting or chasing out blockwork

Protection of Finished Work

Blockwork should be protected from bad weather and when required from other building operations with weatherproof sheeting which must be properly tied down. Care must be taken to cover all new work particularly if there is a likelihood of frost or extreme hot or cold weather.

Laying Blocks

Cold Weather Conditions

Blocks should not be laid when the temperature is at or below 3°C and falling unless it is at least 1°C and rising.

Laying

Solid and cellular blocks should be laid on a full bed of mortar and vertical joints substantially filled. Hollow blocks should be shell bedded with the vertical joints filled.

Do not wet the blocks before laying. Where necessary adjust the consistency of the mortar to suit the suction of the blocks.

---

key terms

Thermal Bridge – a region within a building element, such as a mortar joint or a lintel, where the conduction of heat is higher compared with other parts of the building element.

U Value – The rate of heat loss, in British thermal units per hour, through a square foot of a surface (wall, roof, door, windows, or other building surface) when the difference between the air temperature on either side is 1° Fahrenheit. The U value is 1 divided by the R value.

R Value – A measure of the ability of a piece of material to resist the passage of heat through it. It is equal to the thickness of the material in metres divided by its thermal conductivity.

Reference Panel – A panel of brick or blockwork built at the commencement of a contract to set standards of appearance and workmanship.

Sample Panel – A panel of brick or blockwork which may be built to compare material and workmanship with those of a reference panel.

When laying facing blocks select the blocks, from more than one pack as work proceeds, to reduce the risk of banding or patchiness of colour in the finished walling.

Thin Joint Blockwork Systems

Thin joint masonry is a fast, clean and accurate system of construction using aircrete blocks of close dimensional accuracy with the benefit of 2 to 3 mm mortar joints.

The block manufacturer Thermalite first began trials on thin joint construction in the 1980s, but there is a far longer history of this method of construction in Continental Europe. The increasing demands of the British construction industry for a higher build quality, greater productivity, improved thermal performance, air tightness and waste reduction, mean that the benefits offered by thin joint mortar systems are increasingly relevant.

Thin joint mortar systems have been developed to complement the overall performance of the standard aircrete block. Manufacturers claim that the thin joint system significantly improves productivity to the extent that it is now possible to build the supporting structure to a house in just a few days.

Thin Joint Mixes

Thin joint mortar is a pre-mixed cement based product that only requires adding to water to make an easily applied mortar. It differs from the general use mortar in that it sets far more rapidly, therefore giving early stability to the construction. It provides an alternative to the traditional sand and cement mortar and allows the depth of the mortar to be reduced from at least 10 mm to 3 mm or less (see Figure 4.80).

Benefits of the Thin Joint System

- Building time can be reduced
- Increased productivity
- Follow on trades can start sooner
- Much improved thermal performance
- Reduction of site waste, mortar and aircrete blocks
- Stability achieved earlier during construction
- Accuracy of walls allows thin-coat plaster finishes
- Speed and ease of fixing secondary insulation.

Installation

In common with all types of blockwork walling, the thin joint system should be built to the recommendations of the various British Standard

Fig. 4.80 Materials and equipment for mixing thin joint mortar

Source: Celcon

Codes of Practice for the use of masonry – materials, components, design and workmanship.

Method of Construction

The building techniques employed for thin joint walling are similar to those used when working with general use mortar. It will, for example, remain necessary to maintain regular checks on level and line.

For the inner leaves of cavity walling, a mix of standard, large format and cut blocks can be used to meet design datum levels for floor and wall plate levels. Thicker beds of mortar can of course be used if required to make up a level of a few millimetres or so (see Figure 4.81).

Setting Out the Base Course

The success of the thin joint system depends on the correct setting out of the base or first course. Base course blocks must be bedded in general use mortar

Fig. 4.81 Bricklayer working on a thin joint wall

and laid level, aligned, plumbed and allowed to fully set before commencement of the thin joint construction. Any inaccuracy in the base course cannot easily be corrected in the subsequent thin joint mortar beds.

Planning needs to be made so that any damp proof course can be incorporated into the base course bed joint.

Block and Brickwork Alignment

It is important to understand that thin joint walling combines 2 to 3 mm thick bed mortar with aircrete blocks of close dimensional accuracy. Therefore, bed joints will not align with standard brickwork coursing of the outer leaf as in normal practice, making necessary the use of special wall ties – see Figure 4.82.

Laying Blocks

With thin joint mortar, the construction process can be speeded up greatly. For example, mortar can be applied to the exposed block ends while still in the pack. Alternatively, blocks can be placed on a flat surface and several joint faces can be mortared, to an acceptable standard in one simple operation.

Fig. 4.82 Bricklayer fixing wall ties to thin joint wall

It should be noted that the bricklayer's normal tools are not used for the construction of thin joint walling. Special tools designed specifically for thin joint walling must be used. The use of recommended application tools will deliver the appropriate depth and spread of mortar to the surface bed of the block as well as the cross joint. When building long runs of walling, the thin joint mortar may be applied using a proprietary pumping system.

Subject to reasonable weather conditions, the exposed mortar bed will remain workable for up to 30 minutes. However, once blocks have been laid, initial setting takes place within 10 minutes, and any adjustment to the blockwork should be made during this period (see Figure. 4.83)

Fig. 4.83 Bricklayer using the special tools designed for thin block walling

Wall Ties

To give stability to all types of cavity walls the inner and outer leaves must be tied together. This is achieved by using a metal or plastic wall tie that spans the cavity and is bedded firmly at right angles in both outer and inner leaves of the wall. A drip can be found in the middle of each wall tie. This helps to keep water or moisture away from the inner leaf.

The architect or designer will decide the distance between wall ties. He or she may consider:

➤ How strong the wall needs to be
➤ Where any insulation boards may be placed
➤ The Building Regulations
➤ The Masonry Code of Practice.

It is not always possible for the architect or designer to give the position of every tie placed in a wall. In some situations the bricklayer needs to make common sense decisions.

key terms

Wall ties – A component made of metal or plastic, either built into the two leaves of a cavity wall to link them, or used as a restraint fixing, to tie cladding to a backing.

> **Point to note**
>
> Proposed changes in the Building regulations Part A, recommends that only stainless steel wall ties should be used in external cavity walls.

Density and Positioning of Ties

The distance between the wall ties is measured both horizontally and vertically. The Building Regulations and the Masonry Code of Practice recommends different maximum spacing, as you can see from Figure 4.84.

For walls in which both leaves of masonry are 90 mm or thicker, ties should be used at not less than 2.5 per square metre, which equates to 900 mm horizontal × 450 mm vertical centres. This spacing may be varied when required by the Building Regulations. Wall ties should be evenly distributed over the wall area, except around openings, and should preferably be staggered as shown in Figure 4.85.

Extra wall ties are required to the slope of the gable wall. Vertically: ties need to be placed at a minimum of 300 mm apart; horizontally: ties need to be placed 300 to 400 mm from the roofline. The actual measurement will depend on the angle of the roof slope. Distance from the slope: ties need to be placed within 225 mm of the verge.

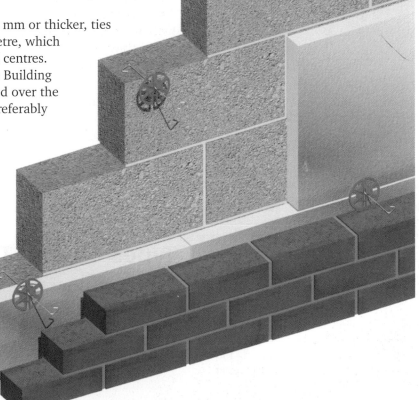

Fig. 4.84 **Wall tie layout**

Source: Celcon

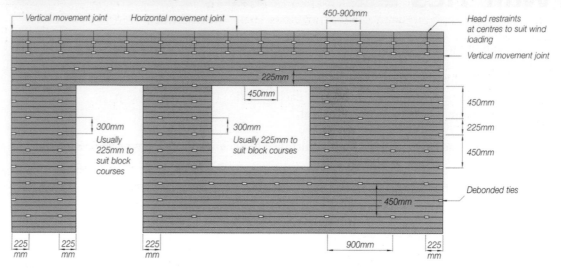

Fig. 4.85 Wall tie layout

Source: Ancon Building Products

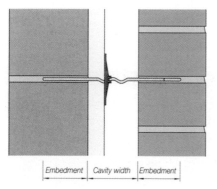

Fig. 4.86 Section of cavity showing correct embedment depths for wall ties

Source: Ancon Building Products

Cavity Width (mm)	Length of Wall Tie (mm)	DD140–2 Wall Tie
50–75	200	HRT4/RT2/ST1
76–100	225	HRT4/RT2/ST1
101–125	250	ST1
126–150	275	SD1
150	300*	ST1

* These wall ties can be used in 126–150 mm cavities if they are embedded further into the inner leaf.

Fig 4.87 Recommended lengths of wall tie for various cavity widths

Length of Tie and Embedment

Wall ties should be of the correct length to ensure they are correctly embedded in the masonry. The tie should have a minimum embedment of 50 mm in each leaf of the wall but also take site tolerances into account for both cavity width and centring of the tie. For this reason manufacturers suggest that tie lengths which achieve an embedment of between 62.5 mm and 75 mm should be used as illustrated in Figure 4.86.

The recommended lengths of wall tie to suit various cavity widths for use in masonry to masonry walls are shown in Figure 4.87.

There are extra wall ties at openings.

If one leaf of masonry is less than 90 mm thick, the maximum spacing of ties is 450 mm.

Types of Wall Tie

There are a wide variety of wall ties available, for traditional brick and blockwork walls. They come in three types:

- Heavy duty wall tie for buildings of any height
- General purpose wall tie for buildings not greater than 15 m in height
- Light duty wall tie for buildings not greater than 10 m in height.

The ties described below are the most commonly available and the most frequently used.

Heavy Duty Tie

Designed by the building products manufacturer Ancon for traditional cavity wall construction, these ties combine ease of use with the expected safety and security standards. The section that spans the cavity has a series of holes to provide water drips. This allows the same tie to be used in insulated cavities as well as open cavities. (see Figure 4.88). This type of tie may be positioned centrally or offset in the cavity provided that they are embedded a minimum of 50 mm on both leaves of masonry.

REMEMBER

In a main wall, ties are required every six courses of brickwork or every two block courses.

Length (mm)	Cavity (mm)
200	50-75
225	76-100
250	101-125
300	126-150

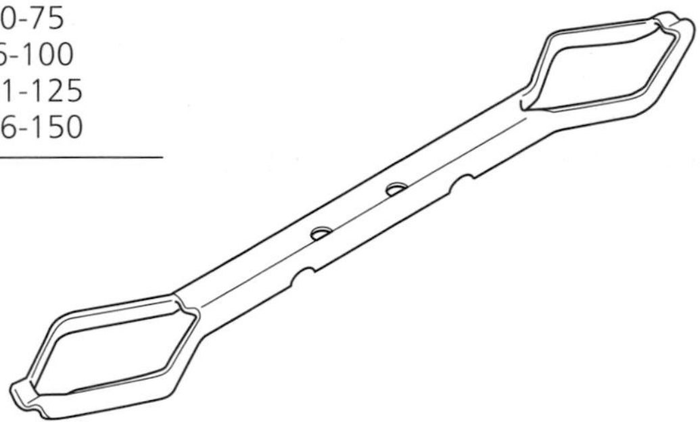

Application
Cavity wall tie suitable for use in the construction of buildings of any height

Fig. 4.88 A heavy duty tie

General Purpose Tie

Designed as before by Ancon for fixing masonry to masonry in cavity walls of domestic houses and small commercial buildings, not exceeding 15 m. The ties are suitable for cavity widths of 50–100mm and should be installed at a density of 2.5 ties per square metre (see Figure 4.89).

Length (mm)	Cavity (mm)
200	50-75
225	76-100

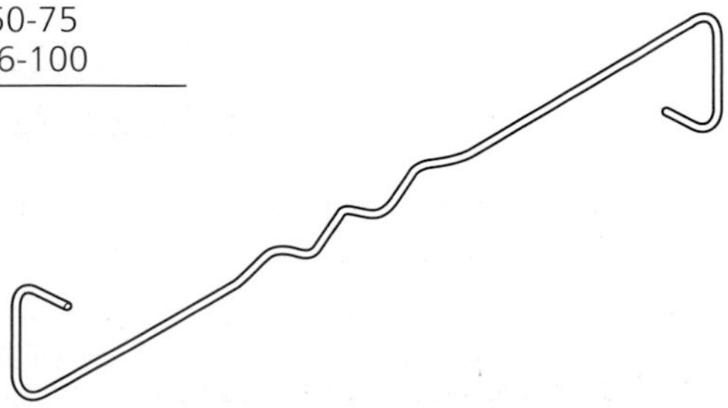

Application
Cavity wall tie suitable for use in the construction of houses and small commercial developments not greater than 15 metres in height

Fig. 4.89 A general purpose tie

Light Duty or Housing Tie

A cavity tie suitable for use in the construction of houses not greater than 10 m in height (see Figure 4.90).

Length (mm)	Cavity (mm)
200	50-75
225	76-100

Application
Cavity wall tie suitable for use in the construction of houses not greater than 10 metres in height

Fig. 4.90 **A light duty tie**

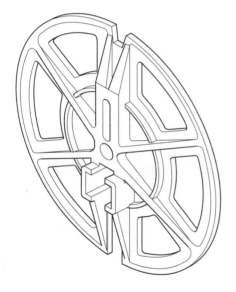

Fig. 4.91 **An insulation retaining clip**

Insulation Retainers

Designed for retaining rigid board or mineral wool and fibreglass insulation material against the inner leaf of the cavity wall. Intended for use with Catnic wire and strip ties, they are, however, flexible enough to use with most systems. The retainers are clipped on to the ties and the flat face of the disc pushed against the surface of the insulation (see Figure 4.91).

Cavity Insulation

Full and Partial Fill Insulation

Cavity insulation can be classified under two headings:

- Full fill
- Partial fill.

Both these methods satisfy the requirements of Approved Document L of the Building Regulations.

Full Fill Insulation

This can be achieved by building in insulation batts as work proceeds or by filling the cavity with foam or granules on completion of the work.

Care is required when considering a fully filled cavity since this can increase the likelihood of water penetration. When choosing an insulant for this application, reference should be made to the relevant British Standards.

Early consultation with a cavity fill manufacturer is advisable, particularly in relation to exposure of the site. Standards of workmanship and site supervision are crucial, as there is no residual cavity to prevent rain penetrating across to the inner leaf, as illustrated in Figure 4.92.

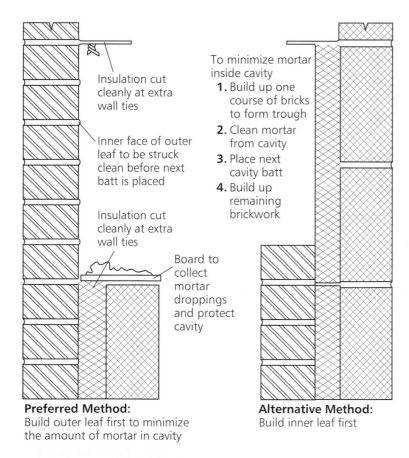

Preferred Method:
Build outer leaf first to minimize the amount of mortar in cavity

Alternative Method:
Build inner leaf first

Fig. 4.92 **A full fill cavity**

The type of insulant and the exposure of the site should be assessed carefully.

Consideration of increasing the cavity width may be appropriate in order to meet thermal and rain resistance requirements.

> *Points to note*
>
> Complete filling of a normal 50 to 70 mm wall cavity with insulant can considerably increase the risk of rain penetration.

Partial Fill Insulation

In partially filled cavity wall construction, a clear cavity of not less than 50 mm must be maintained in order to avoid bridging and to prevent the penetration of wind driven rain.

In order to accommodate the insulation and provide the required residual cavity, longer wall ties may be required together with special clips to fix the insulant securely to the inner leaf, as illustrated in Figure 4.93.

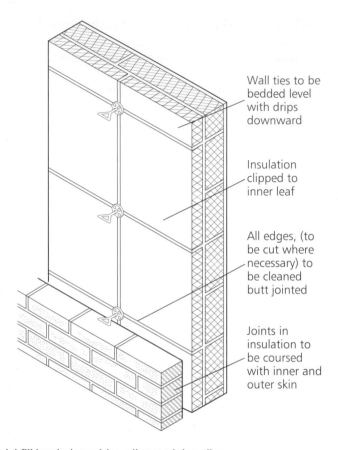

Wall ties to be bedded level with drips downward

Insulation clipped to inner leaf

All edges, (to be cut where necessary) to be cleaned butt jointed

Joints in insulation to be coursed with inner and outer skin

Fig. 4.93 **Partial fill insulation with wall restraining clips**

Insertion of an insulant within a cavity does not affect the durability of the external brickwork, but to reduce the risk of rain penetration to the internal skin, mortar joints should be completely filled, using only curved recessed or weather struck joints.

Building Regulation Requirements

Approved document L of the Building Regulations requires external cavity walls to give a U value of 0.35 W/m square degree K when using the Elemental Method of determination. This can easily be achieved with the range of insulants available. Examples of cavity wall construction with the resultant U values are shown in Figure 4.94.

One of the aims of the Building Regulations is to improve the energy efficiency of all new buildings and existing buildings, when they can be extended or altered. The key objectives can be summarized as follows:

- Reduce carbon dioxide (CO_2) emissions
- Improve design flexibility within the build process

key terms

U Value – The U value is a measurement of the heat loss through a wall, roof or floor. The lower the U value the better the insulation.

K Value – The K value or thermal conductivity value is used in calculating the U value of brickwork construction.

Thermal Conductivity – The measure of the ability of a material to transmit heat.

Elemental Method – Considers the performance of each aspect of the building individually.

Insulation Batt – Rectangular unit of rigid insulation material of uniform thickness used to partially fill the air space in a cavity wall.

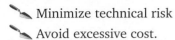Minimize technical risk

Avoid excessive cost.

Please Note: U Values and K values are rather abstract ideas and require explaining thoroughly by your tutor in order to be fully grasped.

THERMAL INSULATION

EXAMPLES OF CAVITY BRICKWORK CONSTRUCTION WITH APPROPRIATE THERMAL INSULATION U-VALUES

U-value	Outer Leaf (Brick Type & Density)	Cavity Insulation Examples	Inner Leaf – Type & Thermal Conductivity 'k' value)	Finish
0.27	Clay Facing Bricks up to and including 2000 kg/m³	50 mm Clear Cavity	100 mm Lightweight block (0.11 k)	50 mm dry lining board on dabs (2.28 R)
0.28	Clay Facing Bricks up to and including 2000 kg/m³	550 mm EPS Board (0.026 k) in 100 mm cavity	100 mm Lightweight block (0.11 k)	13 mm plasterboard on dabs
0.28	Clay Facing Bricks up to and including 2000 kg/m³	50 mm Clear Cavity 48 mm Polyisocyanurate boards (0.019 k)	100 mm Medium density block (0.19 k)	13 mm plasterboard on dabs
0.28	Clay Facing Bricks up to and including 2000 kg/m³	60 mm EPS (0.033 k) in 100 mm cavity	150 mm Lightweight block (0.11 k)	13 mm plasterboard on dabs
0.30	Clay Facing Bricks 1400 kg/m³	50 mm Clear Cavity 50 mm Polyisocyanurate boards (0.019 k)	Handmade Facing (0.38 k)	Fair face
0.30	Clay Facing Bricks up to and including 2000 kg/m³	50 mm Clear Cavity	100 mm Medium density block (0.19 k)	50 mm dry lining board on dabs (2.28 R)
0.30	Clay Facing Bricks up to and including 2000 kg/m³	Bubble insulation in 60 mm Cavity NHBC require 75 mm	150 mm Lightweight block (0.11 k)	13 mm plasterboard on dabs
0.30	Stock Brick 1500 kg/m³	50 mm Injected foam (0.018 k)	Clay Common (0.50 k)	13 mm plasterboard on dabs
0.32	Clay Facing Bricks up to and including 2000 kg/m³	60 mm EPS board (0.033 k) in 100 mm cavity	100 mm Lightweight block (0.11 k)	13 mm plasterboard on dabs
0.33	Clay Facing Bricks up to and including 2000 kg/m³	50 mm Epsx Board (0.032 k) in 100 mm cavity	100 mm Lightweight block (0.11 k)	13 mm plasterboard on dabs
0.34	Clay Facing Bricks 1400 kg/m³	50 mm Clear Cavity 50 mm Insulation batts (0.024 k)	Handmade Facing (0.38 k)	Fair face
0.34	Clay Facing Bricks up to and including 2000 kg/m³	Bubble insulation in 60 mm Cavity NHBC require 75 mm	100 mm Lightweight block (0.11 k)	13 mm plasterboard on dabs
0.34	Clay Facing Bricks up to and including 2000 kg/m³	50 mm Clear Cavity 38 mm Polyisocyanurate boards (0.019 k)	100 mm Medium density block (0.19 k)	13 mm plasterboard on dabs
0.35	Clay Facing Bricks up to and including 2000 kg/m³	50 mm Clear Cavity	100 mm Medium density block (0.17 k)	40 mm dry lining board on dabs (1.73R)
0.38	Clay Facing Bricks 1700 kg/m³	75 mm Mineral Wool batts (0.036 k)	100 mm Heavyweight Block (1.12 k)	13 mm plasterboard on dabs
0.40	Handmade Facing 1400 kg/m³	50 mm Clear Cavity 30 mm Phenolic foam boards (0.018 k)	Handmade Facing (0.38 k)	Fair Face
0.40	Stock Brick 1400 kg/m³	50 mm Clear Cavity 50 mm cellular glass (0.048 k)	100 mm Lightweight block (0.11 k)	13 mm plasterboard on dabs
0.41	Clay Facing Bricks 1700 kg/m³	65 mm Mineral Wool batts (0.036 k)	Clay Common (0.50 k)	13 mm plasterboard on dabs
0.42	Stock Brick 1500 kg/m³	75 mm fibre boards (0.040k)	Clay Common (0.50 k)	13 mm plasterboard on dabs
0.43	Clay Facing Bricks 1600 kg/m³	50 mm Clear Cavity	150 Lightweight Block (0.11 k)	13 mm plasterboard on dabs

Fig. 4.94 Table showing cavity wall construction with resultant U values

Good Practice

Always maintain the specified cavity, placing insulation batts against the inner leaf and secure them with specially designated wall tie clips.

Where a clear airspace of a minimum of 50 mm is maintained, partial fill insulation does not increase the risk of rain penetration and can therefore be recommended.

Where cavity fill insulation is used, the damp proof cavity tray must be provided with stop ends to prevent water running into the cavity and wetting the insulation.

Where batts butt up to reveals and lintel bearings they must be cut accurately to ensure no cold spots.

Where intermediate wall ties occur at reveals the batts can be cut to allow the tie to pass neatly through.

Batts must be closely jointed as condensation will form where gaps appear.

> *Point to note*

Achieving good workmanship is essential when placing insulation materials.

The following points are offered for guidance when handling insulation boards of various types.

- Always carry boards on edge – two men to a board
- Place boards down on their long edge before turning flat
- Use a platform or pallet to support boards when mechanically handling
- Do not carry boards horizontally
- Do not drag boards over each other
- Do not store boards outside unless on a level platform, clear of the ground and securely covered with an anchored polythene sheet or tarpaulin

Damp Proof Membrane

> *Definition and purpose*

A damp proof membrane or barrier is a continuous layer of damp resisting material, the chief object of which is to protect the super-structure of a building against dampness.

Most building materials are liable to be adversely affected by dampness. Consequently, it is essential to provide a suitable means of damp prevention. In addition, the health of the occupants of a damp building may become seriously affected by the conditions that may arise out of dampness.

Prevention of Dampness

The damp proofing of a wall near its base is undertaken to prevent the rise of dampness, which may be drawn from the ground, into the brick or blockwork forming the foundation walling of the building. The placing of a suitable damp proof membrane horizontally in a wall at a level of 150 mm above the adjoining ground level usually fulfils the above requirements.

Since it is essential to protect floors and floor timbers against dampness, it may be found necessary to provide damp proof membranes at different levels and also in vertical positions around the building.

Materials for Damp Proof Membranes

Material for use in damp proof membranes should be permanently impervious to moisture and be durable. When placed in the wall it should be capable of resisting the loads put upon it. These loads which tend to cause crushing or other damage should not induce the wall to develop a sliding action. The latter may arise when the damp proofing material has a smooth surface and the wall is subjected to horizontal or inclined thrusts.

Suitable damp proof membranes may be formed by the proper use of the following materials.

Lead-core Reinforced DPC

A lead-core reinforced damp proof membrane suitable for inclusion in brick, block, stone or concrete walls of both solid and cavity construction. The damp proof membrane is composed of a continuous core of lead reinforced with a tough, high quality Hessian. These layers are coated with a polymer modified bitumen and surfaced on both sides with a silica sand finish.

It can be used as a damp proof course in all masonry walls of both solid and cavity construction. It is particularly suitable for horizontal and cavity tray situations.

Pitch Polymer Damp Proof Membrane

An extremely versatile, high performance, pitch polymer, damp proof membrane. When used alone or in conjunction with self-adhesive waterproof membrane, a continuous barrier against water and vapour can be formed.

Suitable for inclusion in brick, block stone or concrete walls of both solid and cavity construction and in horizontal, vertical, stepped and cavity tray situations, as well as in beam and block flooring.

Liquid Waterproofing Membrane

This is a rubberized bitumen emulsion that dries to form a durable elastic waterproof membrane for floors, walls and roofs. It is usually formulated to be solvent free and to avoid the use of hazardous components such as flammable solvents and coal tar. Liquid waterproofing is a cold applied high performance membrane which when fully dry forms an elastic coating able to accommodate minor structural movements.

Suitable for use on the following building materials:

🛠 Floors – concrete, and sand and cement construction

🛠 Walls – brick, block and concrete

🛠 Roofs – Mastic asphalt, felt, fibre cement, corrugated iron, slates, etc.

Protection Board

This is designed as an important 'tanking' accessory for use with damp proof membranes to meet the tanking requirements of the specifier and contractor. Protection board is an acrylic lacquer coated tough, bitumen impregnated cellulose board, used for the protection of waterproof membranes against damage.

It is designed to protect self-adhesive sheet waterproofing membranes in both horizontal and vertical applications.

Self Adhesive Damp Proof Membrane

Tanking is a critical area of construction where, if failure occurs, it can result in disruption in the use of the building and also expensive remedial work. This tough, self-adhesive waterproofing membrane system can be used on floors as a damp proof membrane and in solid concrete floors. It can also be used in basements as a vertical and horizontal membrane and in internal and external tanking situations.

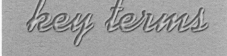

key terms

Tanking – Waterproofing horizontally and vertically, that is, in the form of a tank.

Engineering Bricks ▬▬▬

Two or more courses of engineering bricks suitably bonded and properly bedded in cement mortar.

The above forms of damp proof course materials may be divided into two groups according to their nature:

🛠 Flexible

🛠 Rigid.

The lead, pitch polymer, liquid membrane and self-adhesive membrane constitute the flexible type while the dry lining protection board and engineering bricks form the rigid type.

Flexibility is desirable where a damp proof membrane requires to be shaped into a given form and also where it is required to withstand, without fracture, the effect of settlement. Of the rigid type, those formed with such materials as engineering bricks bedded in suitable mortar are capable of withstanding intense pressure, while being extremely durable and practically impervious to moisture. In addition, it is possible to obtain a satisfactory key between the damp proof membrane and the brick or blockwork to prevent possible sliding action.

Hand Tools and Equipment

Bricklayer's Trowel

The bricklayer's trowel is the most important tool used in bricklaying. It is used to pick up and place mortar on bricks and blocks.

Pointing Trowel

A pointing trowel serves the same purpose as a bricklayer's trowel but is used for working places where it would be difficult to use a larger type trowel.

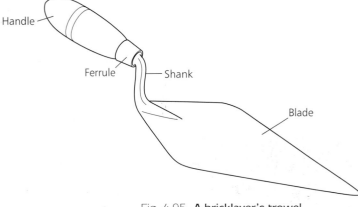

Fig. 4.95 **A bricklayer's trowel**

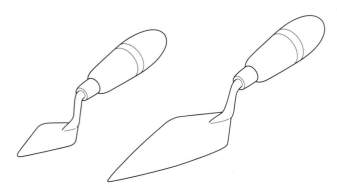

Fig. 4.96 **A pointing trowel**

Spirit Level

The spirit level is a tool which is made of wood or lightweight metal. Spirit levels have at least two vials. One is used for plumbing vertical surfaces and one is used for levelling horizontal surfaces.

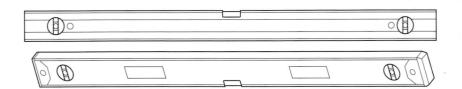

Fig. 4.197 **A spirit level**

Work-based Evidence Required

■ Safe use and storage of tools and equipment

To meet this requirement, obtain a witness testimony sheet from your supervisor stating that you have safely used and stored bricklaying tools and equipment. Place the evidence in your work based evidence portfolio when next in college and map and record it against the syllabus.

Brick Hammer

The brick hammer is a tool designed and manufactured especially for the bricklayer. It is used for breaking, splitting, shaping and trimming bricks and blocks.

Fig. 4.98 **A brick hammer**

Jointer

Jointers are specially designed metal tools used for finishing the exposed cross-mortar joints between bricks and blocks. Finished joints are required in order to seal the joint against mortar penetration and to present a pleasant appearance on faced walls.

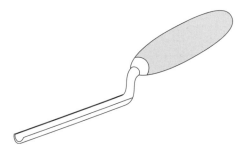

Fig. 4.99 **A jointer**

Runners

Runners are used for the same purpose as jointers except that runners are best suited for finishing the parallel mortar joints.

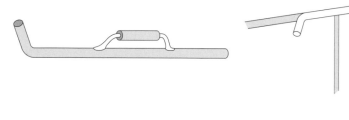

Fig. 4.100 **A runner**

Brick Bolster and Club Hammer

A brick bolster is a type of chisel designed for cutting bricks and similar materials to exact specifications. The bolster is used in conjunction with a club hammer.

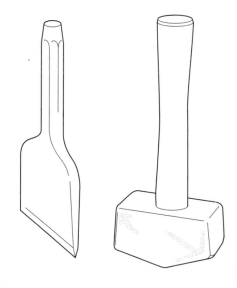

Fig. 4.101 **A brick bolster and club hammer**

Steel Square

The bricklayer's steel square is a tool used for setting out corners or angles of 90 degrees.

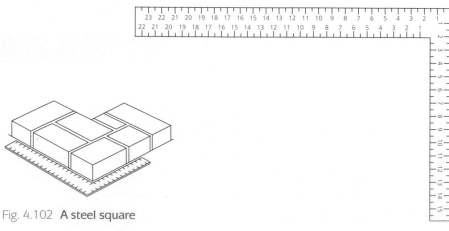

Fig. 4.102 **A steel square**

Bricklayer's Line and Pins

The bricklayer's line and pins are used as a guide for aligning bricks and blocks between established corners. The line can be either cotton or nylon.

Corner Block Line Holders

Corner blocks are used for aligning bricks or blocks laid between established corners. This can be done by using special corner blocks. These blocks are manufactured from light metal or plastic. But, if none are available, you can make them from wood.

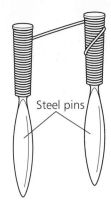

Steel pins

Fig. 4.103 **Bricklayer's line and pins**

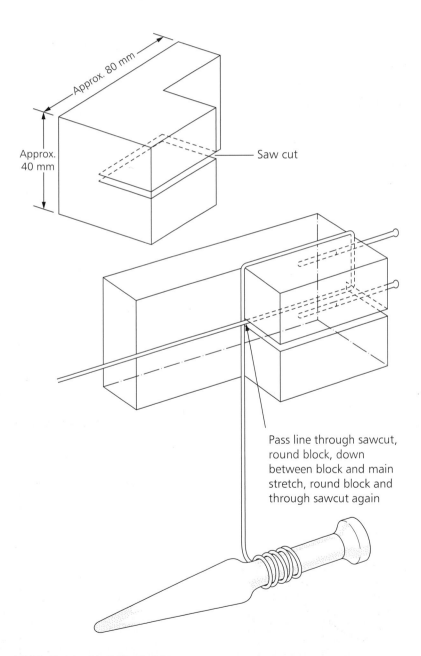

Approx. 80 mm

Approx. 40 mm

Saw cut

Pass line through sawcut, round block, down between block and main stretch, round block and through sawcut again

Fig. 4.104 **Corner block line holders**

Rules

Folding rules are used by bricklayers for measuring and setting out. A bricklayer uses two types of measuring instrument – a wooden or metal folding rule or a metal tape. Tapes extend to an overall length of 2 to 50 m and the folding rule extends to an overall length of 3 m.

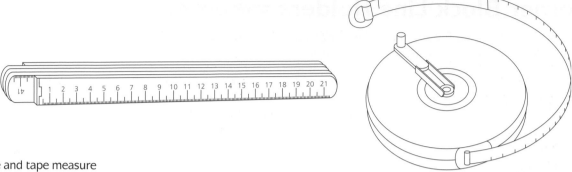

Fig. 4.105 Folding rule and tape measure

Plumb Bob

A plumb bob is used to test or check perpendicular surfaces for trueness, to establish vertical lines and locate points. A plumb bob is a metal weight with a string attached to a centred hole.

For bricklaying purposes a square distance plate is threaded on the line. This plate must have the same outside dimensions and centred hole as the plumb bob.

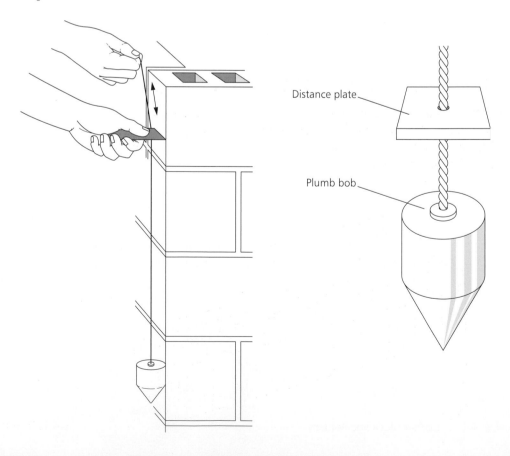

Distance plate

Plumb bob

Fig. 4.106 A plumb bob

Masonry Saw and Blades

A masonry saw is designed for cutting masonry material, stone, concrete, block, brick and tile. This piece of equipment is usually powered by an electric motor. It can be fitted with a water pump which is used for wet cutting. Other types of blades for dry cutting are manufactured with abrasive materials on the cutting surface or edge.

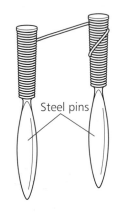

Steel pins

Brickwork
04.04

Fig. 4.107 **A masonry saw**

Wheelbarrow

One of the most strenuous and time consuming jobs required on a building site is moving materials. Using wheelbarrows is the most effective means of moving mortar, brick, block and so on. Wheelbarrows can have solid rubber or pneumatic tyres. The selection is determined by job conditions, spares, repairs, etc. The use of these machines will allow for more efficient handling of materials.

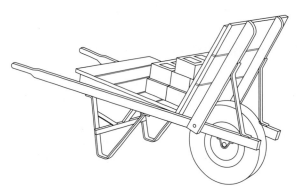
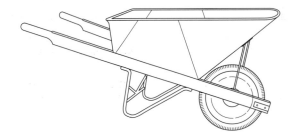

Fig. 4.108 **Wheelbarrows**

Brick Tongs

Brick tongs are manufactured or produced from metal. They are designed to clasp or clamp the load of brick when they are lifted. There are many different designs of tongs but one of the most common is shown in Figure 4.109.

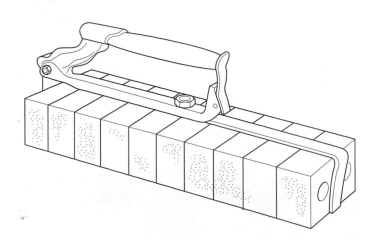
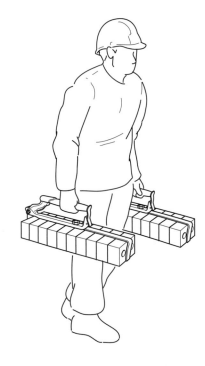

Fig. 4.109 **Brick tongs**

Mortar Boxes

Mortar boxes are containers used for hand mixing mortars or for storing machine mixed mortars. The capacity of mortar boxes range from about 1 to 3 m³. They are usually constructed of metal.

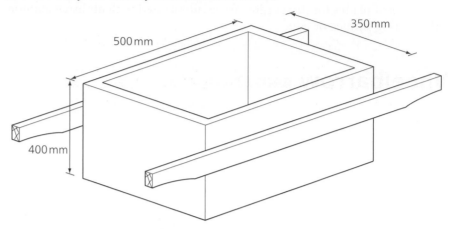

Fig. 4.110 **Mortar box**

Mortar Boards

After the mortar has been mixed it must be placed where the bricklayer can pick it up for laying. Mortar boards serve this purpose. They can be made from wood, steel or synthetic material.

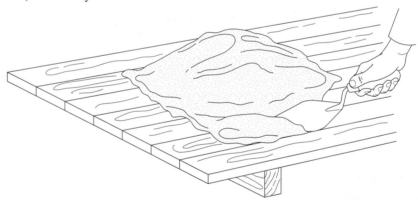

Fig. 4.111 **Mortar board**

Mortar Mixers

When continuous amounts of mortar are required it is sometimes necessary to machine mix for the sake of economy. The capacity of mixers varies from one

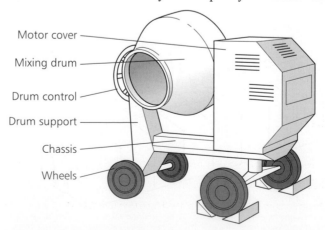

Fig. 4.112 **Mortar mixer**

bag (50 kg) to three bags and can be powered by electric motor or petrol/diesel engine. Job conditions will determine the amount of mortar required. The availability of electricity or fuel will determine your choice of mixer.

Mobile Hoist

On large, economically operated construction sites, mobile hoists are sometimes employed to place material on scaffolds or floors above ground level. Materials can then be quickly positioned for use by general operatives.

Fig. 4.113   Mobile hoist

TRY THIS OUT

Bricklaying Tools

Describe the use of the following tools:

- Line and pins
- Tingle plate
- Spirit level
- Pointing trowel
- Comb hammer
- Laying trowel
- Brick hammer
- Boat level
- Jointer
- Lump hammer and bolster.

Work-based Evidence Required

■ Selection of resources associated with own work:

- ■ Materials and components

- ■ Tools and equipment

To meet these requirements obtain a witness testimony sheet from your supervisor stating that you have selected materials, components, tools and equipment related to brickwork.

When you have received the signed and dated witness testimony sheets from your supervisor, place them in your work-based evidence portfolio when next in college and map and record it against the syllabus.

Quick quiz Quick quiz Quick quiz Quick quiz Quick quiz

1. Explain the term daily lift height.
2. Define the term wall tie.
3. List eight tools used by a bricklayer.
4. What is a plumb bob used for?
5. What two groups may damp proof course materials be divided into?
6. Define the term U value.
7. List three types of wall tie.
8. List three benefits of the thin joint blockwork system.
9. What are aircrete blocks made from?
10. What is the most commonly used type of building block?

Methods of Calculation

Understanding Areas

The area of a wall is the amount of surface that it covers. As a bricklayer you will need to know the areas of walls so you can calculate the number of bricks or blocks you will need for the job.

The calculation of brickwork and blockwork quantities is a problem that you will constantly encounter. However, the procedure is relatively simple. The formula for calculating the area of a square or rectangle looks like this:

🔪 $A = L \times W$

🔪 $A = Area$

🔪 $L = Length$

🔪 $W = Width$

You might need to find the area of a shape that is made up from different rectangles joined together. To calculate this just find the area of each shape and then add them together.

Dimensions on working drawings are usually shown in millimetres but area needs to be measured in square metres. It is easier to convert the dimensions on a working drawing into metres before you calculate the area.

The wall of a building is 7 m long and 4 m high. It has been divided into 1 m by 1 m squares to show you its area. Therefore the area of the wall is 28 square metres.

However, there are more ways than one to calculate an area. A good way is to multiply the length of the wall by its height.

Length by height:

$7 \text{ m} \times 4 \text{ m} = 28 \text{ m}^2$

> REMEMBER
> To convert a dimension from millimetres to metres you divide it by 1000. This is because there are 1000 mm in one metre.
>
> 3000 mm = 3 m because 3000 divided by a 1000 = 3
>
> 8045 mm = 8.045 because 8045 divided by a 1000 = 8.045
>
> Therefore the area of the wall is $A = L \times W$
>
> $8.045 \text{ m} \times 3 \text{ m} = 24.135 \text{ m}^2$

> REMEMBER
> That in the case of a wall, the height would replace the width (w) in the formula.

> REMEMBER
> Sometimes the length is called the base.

TRY THIS OUT

What is the area of the wall shown below?

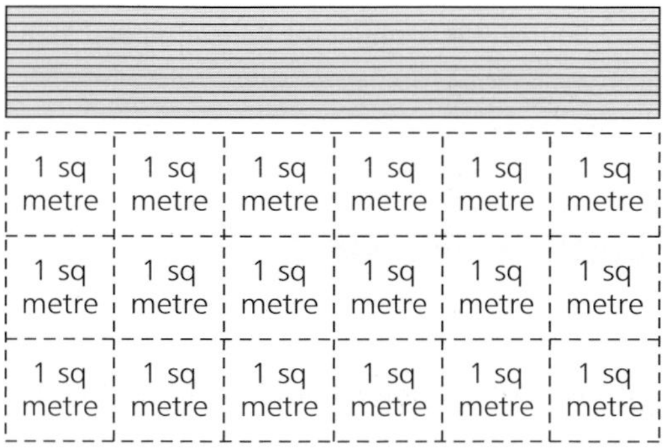

1 sq metre	1 sq metre	1 sq metre	1 sq metre	1 sq metre	1 sq metre
1 sq metre	1 sq metre	1 sq metre	1 sq metre	1 sq metre	1 sq metre
1 sq metre	1 sq metre	1 sq metre	1 sq metre	1 sq metre	1 sq metre

_____ Square metres

Fig. 4.114 **Illustration of a wall**

Show all workings out used in your calculations.

TRY THIS OUT

What is the area of the wall shown below?

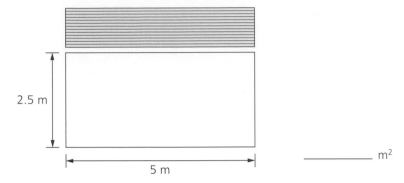

Fig. 4.115 **Illustration of a wall**

2.5 m

5 m

_____ m²

Show all workings out used in your calculations.

TRY THIS OUT

What is the area of the wall shown below? Give your answer to two decimal places.

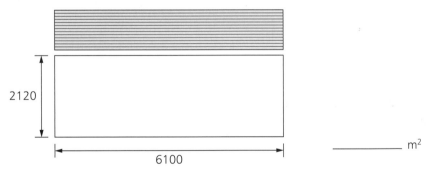

Fig. 4.116 **Illustration of a wall**

2120

6100

_____ m²

Show all working out used in your calculations.

Source: Department for Education and Skills

Calculating Quantities

Stage One

In order to calculate how many bricks there are in 1 square metre of walling we use the following method.

Divide a 1 m horizontal length (1000 mm) by the length of a standard brick and mortar joint, this will tell us how many bricks there are in the length.

Therefore: 1 m divided by 0.225 metre = 4.44 bricks.

Stage Two

Divide a 1 metre vertical length (1000 mm) by the thickness of a standard brick and mortar joint, this will tell us how many bricks there are in the height.

Therefore: 1 m divided by 0.075 m = 13.33 bricks.

Stage Three

Multiply the number of bricks that go into the length of the wall by the number of bricks that go into the height of the wall. This will give us the number of bricks included in 1 square metre of walling.

Therefore: $4.44 \times 13.33 = 59.18$ bricks.

We then round this figure up to the next whole number. Therefore there are approximately 60 bricks in 1 square metre of walling.

Blockwork

We use the same method for calculating the number of blocks in a square metre of walling.

Brick Quantities

In order to work out how many bricks or blocks are required, we use the following method.

Stage One

Calculate how many bricks there are in 1 square metre of brick or blockwork.

Stage Two

Calculate how many square metres of brick or blockwork there are in the building. You will find this out from the measurements on the working drawing.

Stage Three

Multiply the number of bricks or blocks in 1 square metre by the number of square metres of brick or blockwork there are in the building.

Worked Examples for Calculating Quantities

The calculation of brick and blockwork quantities is something that a bricklayer will constantly encounter. The method of calculation is fairly simple, as long as you remember to follow a logical sequence. To calculate the area of brickwork, we follow the following sequence of actions:

Area = length × height

Note: ensure both measurements are in the same quantity, m, mm or cm.

1. deduct the area of any door or window openings

2. multiply the area by the number of bricks per square metre.

Half brick walling = 60 bricks per square metre.

One brick walling = 120 bricks per square metre.

One and a half brick walling = 180 bricks per square metre.

3. Add a percentage to compensate for any damaged bricks.

Percentage waste = common bricks 3 per cent, facing bricks 6 per cent and blockwork 10 per cent.

Example One

A half brick wall measures 5 m long and 2 m high. Allowing 5 per cent waste how many bricks are required to build the wall?

Area = length × height

Therefore 5 m × 2 m = 10 m².

Number of bricks = area × number per square metre

= 10 × 60 = 600

Add 5 per cent waste = 5 divided by 100 × 600 = 30

Total number of bricks required is 630.

If this wall had to be built of blocks instead of bricks, how many blocks would you need?

Remember: there are 10 blocks in 1 square metre of walling.

Example Two

A wall one brick thick measures 8 m long and 5 m high. Allowing 5 per cent waste, how many bricks are required.

Area = length × height

Therefore 8 m × 5 m = 40 m².

Number of bricks = area × number per square metre

= 40 × 120 = 4800

Add 5 per cent waste = 5 divided by 100 × 4800 = 240

Total number of bricks required is 5040

If this wall had to be built of blocks instead of bricks, how many blocks would you need?

Example Three

A half brick wall measures 12.5 m long and 2.4 m high. Allowing 3 per cent waste how many bricks are required.

If this wall had to be built in blocks instead of bricks, how many blocks would you need?

Example Four

A one and a half brick wall measures 10 m long and 2 m high. Allowing 5 per cent waste how many bricks are required.

If this wall had to be built in blocks instead of bricks, how many blocks would you need?

Example Five

If you were building a half brick wall 3 m by 4 m, how many square metres of brick would you need to order?

If there are 60 bricks per square metre of walling, how many bricks will you require for your wall?

It is expected there will be 8 per cent wastage on bricks, how many bricks will you waste building the wall? How many more square metres of bricks would you order to make sure you have enough for the wall?

Example Six

How many bricks do you require to build a wall with a surface area of 16 square metres?

Example Seven

How many bricks do you require to build a structure with a surface area of 55 square metres?

Example Eight

How many blocks do you require to build a wall with a surface area of 28 square metres?

Show all workings out used in your calculations.

Bonding of Brickwork

For further information about the bonding of brickwork, try to obtain the following books which you will find are of great value to your studies.

W. G. Nash wrote a number of books on brickwork notably his series *Brickwork One*, *Two* and *Three*. Probably the best book for the new student would be *Brickwork One*, which in many ways is an introduction to bricklaying. The books (like this one) are published by Nelson Thornes.

Nelson Thornes

www.nelsonthornes.com

Specific Bonds in Brickwork

For further information on specific bonds in brickwork, contact some of the brick manufacturers. They all have technical departments whose job it is to advise and help those planning the design of brick buildings.

Bonding of Blockwork

For further information on the bonding of blockwork why not consult the following text book, which gives valuable information on the topic.

Peter Roper has written a book on the subject of blockwork entitled, *A Practical Guide to Blockwork*. As you might expect the book covers every aspect of blockwork from how blocks are made, properties and performance to site practice. The book is highly informative and extremely comprehensive. The book is published by International Thomson Publishing Limited.

The Concrete Block Association (CBA) produces a comprehensive range of technical datasheets that are freely available. By visiting the CBA website you can view, download or order copies on-line.

CBA

www.cba-blocks.org.uk

Damp Proof Barriers

For more information about damp proof barriers why not visit the websites of the better known manufacturers and suppliers?

For a range of technical information, not only on damp proof barriers but on every aspect of the built environment, contact the Building Research Establishment at the following address.

The Building Research Establishment, Garston, Watford, WD25 9XX. Telephone: 01923 664000.
www.bre.co.uk

Hand Tools

For further information about bricklaying and other tools, why not visit the websites of the better known manufacturers and suppliers?

Ladders

For more information about ladders and stepladders, why not contact the websites of the better known manufacturers and suppliers?

Use of Access equipment

For further information on the use of access equipment, why not visit the websites of the better known manufacturers and suppliers?

Tubular Scaffolding

For more information about tubular scaffolding, why not visit the websites of the better known manufacturers and suppliers?

Mobile Elevating Working Platforms

For more information about mobile elevating working platforms, why not visit the websites of the better known manufacturers and suppliers?

Health and Safety

For more information on health and safety at work, why not visit the following websites.

Health and Safety Executive

www.hse.gov.uk

European Agency for Safety and Health at Work

http://osha.eu.int/

Further information on good safety management practice is available from the Agency's website. All Agency publications can be downloaded free of charge. The Agency site links to member states' sites where national legislation and guidance on construction may be found.

United Kingdom

http://uk.osha.eu.int/

National Access and Scaffolding Confederation

www.nasc.org.uk

Working at Height

The Work at Height Regulations 2005. A brief guide – is available from HSE books. It can be ordered by telephone on 01787 881165 or by post from, HSE Books, PO Box 1999, Sudbury, Suffolk CO10 2WA.

Bricks

For further information about bricks and other associated products why not visit the websites of the better known manufacturers and suppliers, or the following?

The Brick Development Association
www.brick.org.uk

Brick Information Service – 09068 615290.

The Brick Development Association provides a comprehensive range of advice and information on every aspect of brick construction. They are dedicated to promoting the use of brickwork in our environment in the most effective and attractive way. The Brick Development Association also offers a comprehensive consultancy service supported by a wide range of publications and online advice either through professional experts on the phone or via their website.

Blocks

For further information about blocks and other associated products, why not visit the websites of the better known manufacturers and suppliers, or the following?

Concrete Block Association (CBA)
www.cba-blocks.org.uk

The CBA is the trade body that represents manufacturers of aggregate concrete building blocks in Great Britain. The CBA represents an industry of some 50 manufacturers producing around 60 million square metres of concrete blocks per year from over 100 block plants nationwide.

The Thin Joint Blockwork System

For further information about the thin joint blockwork system, why not visit the websites of the better known manufacturers and suppliers.

Tie Wires and Associated Products

For further information about tie wires and other associated products, why not visit the websites of the better known manufacturers and suppliers?

Insulation and Insulating Products

For further information about insulation and insulating products, why not visit the websites of the better known manufacturers and suppliers?

Damp Proof Barriers

For more information about damp proof barriers why not visit the websites of the better known manufacturers and suppliers?

Hand Tools

For further information about bricklaying and other tools, why not visit the websites of the better known manufacturers and suppliers?

Contribute to Setting Out Basic Masonry Structures

NVQ level 1   Unit No. VR 38   Contribute to Setting Out Basic Masonry Structures

This unit, in the context of brickwork and the construction industry work environment is about:

- interpreting instructions
- adopting safe and healthy working practices
- selecting materials, components and equipment
- assisting in setting out basic building structures.

There are two sections in this chapter: methods of work and resources.

This chapter will now cover contributing to setting out basic masonry structures.

METHODS OF WORK   5.1

In this section you will learn about the application of knowledge for safe work practices, procedures, skills and transference of competence, relating to the area of work and material used to:

- assist with setting out basic building structures
- construct and position profiles
- position ranging lines
- transfer levels
- use hand tools and setting out equipment.

You will also learn about team work and communication and the needs of other occupations associated with setting out basic buildings.

When you have completed this section you will be able to:

- comply with the given contract instructions to carry out the work efficiently to the required specification.

Know and understand:

■ how methods of work are followed and problems reported.

Setting out Basic Building Structures

In the initial stages of some building projects, you will see pieces of board fixed in a pattern and embedded in the ground. The boards and the lines which are fixed to them are called profiles because they represent the shape and exact dimensions of the building to be constructed.

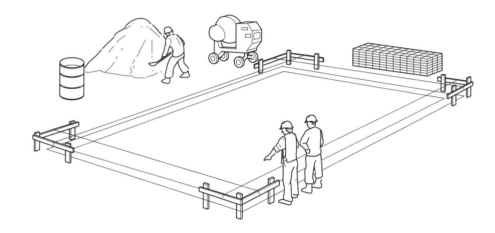

Fig. 5.1 **Profiles and lines on site**

After the foundation of the building has been completed and is ready for the brickwork, it is necessary to transfer the wall outline to the foundation in order to locate and establish the corner profiles for wall construction.

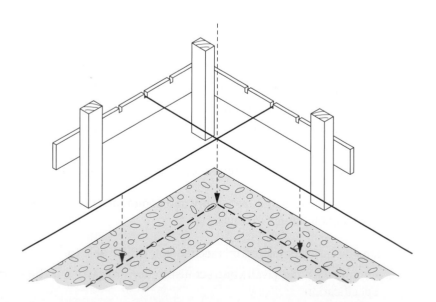

Fig. 5.2 **Transferring wall profile to the foundation**

The lines attached to the profiles represent walls and their locations. If the lines are not fixed to the profiles, ask your supervisor or tutor to fix and position the lines in the correct places.

Once the lines have been attached you can transfer the wall line to the foundation. To do this, you must use a spirit level to plumb down from the external wall line to mark its position on to the foundation concrete.

A spirit level can be used provided the distance from the profile line to the base of the foundation concrete is not greater than the length of the level.

If the distance is too great a plumb bob should be used.

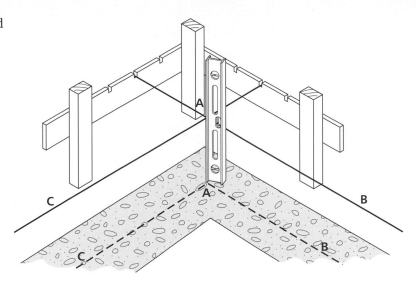

Fig. 5.3 **Plumbing down with a spirit level**

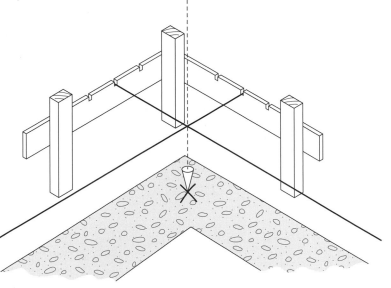

Fig. 5.4 **Plumbing down with a plumb bob**

Using a spirit level, mark out lines A–C and A–B, which represent the angle of the corner.

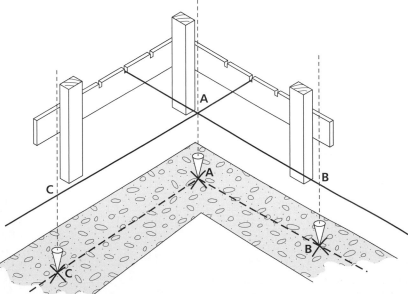

Fig. 5.5 **Using a plumb bob to mark out a corner**

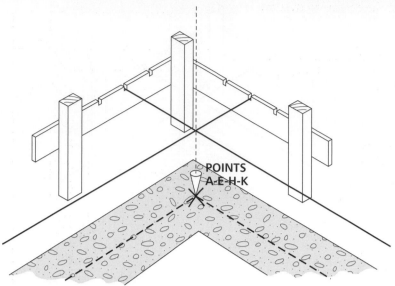

POINTS
A-E-H-K

Fig. 5.6 **Repeat for all four corners**

Repeat this operation until all four corners A E H K, have been marked out.

Another method of setting out for 90 degree angles and walls involves using a builder's square or bricklayer's metal square.

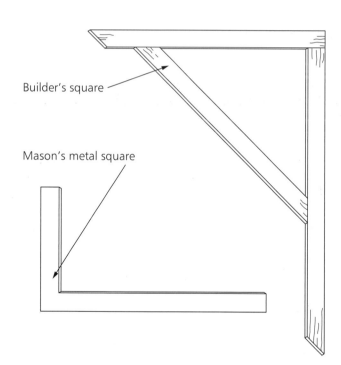

Builder's square

Mason's metal square

Fig. 5.7 **Squares**

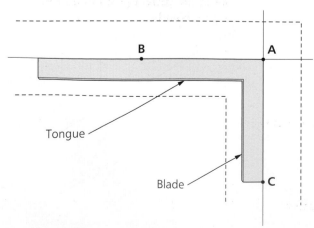

B

A

Tongue

Blade

C

The square is used after you have established points on to the foundation concrete using a plumb bob or spirit level.

Place the heel of the square on the marked point (A) and align one side with point (B). Mark out the side A B.

Fig. 5.8 **Marking out side A B**

You can complete the angle by reversing the position of the square so that the tongue is aligned with points A C.

When points A, E, H, K have been marked out, the next operation is to mark out the wall lines with chalk. To do this, hold or fix one end of the line at point A and extend the other end to point E. Now snap the line.

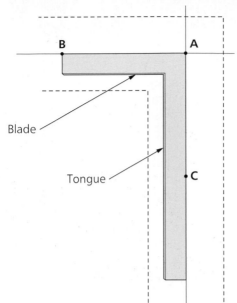

Fig. 5.9 Marking out side A C

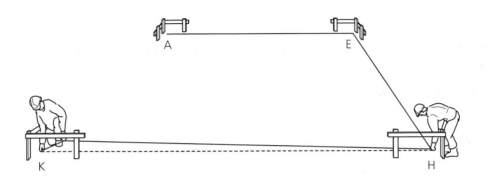

Fig. 5.10 Marking out side A E

Now hold the line from point A and extend the other end to point K. Snap the line. Repeat the marking operation until all the sides have been marked out.

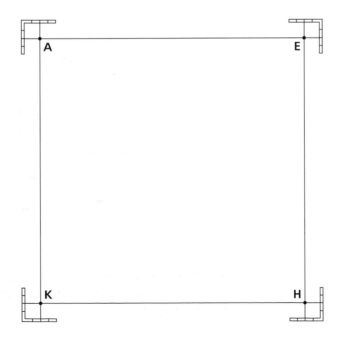

Fig. 5.11 All sides marked out   Source: International Labour Office

> **Point to note**
> Periodically check that your lines are in the correct position on the profile boards.

When you have completed marking all the wall lines on to the foundation concrete, they should be checked for squareness.

key terms

Builder's Square – Constructed from 75 mm × 50 mm timber this is used for setting out right angles.

Building Line – An imaginary line beyond which the face of the building must not project. It is set by the Local Authority.

Diagonals – The final stage to complete the setting involves measuring the diagonals, which must be the same if the building is square. If they are not the same size then a mistake has been made in the setting out process.

Checking for Squareness

There are three methods of checking for squareness:

- the 3–4–5 method
- the builder's square method
- the diagonal method.

The 3–4–5 Method

The 3–4–5 or 6–8–10 method is a system of forming and checking 90 degree angles using a tape measure.

When the working drawings require setting out for walls longer than 5 m, the builder's square is not very accurate as it does not extend far enough along the lines to ensure accuracy.

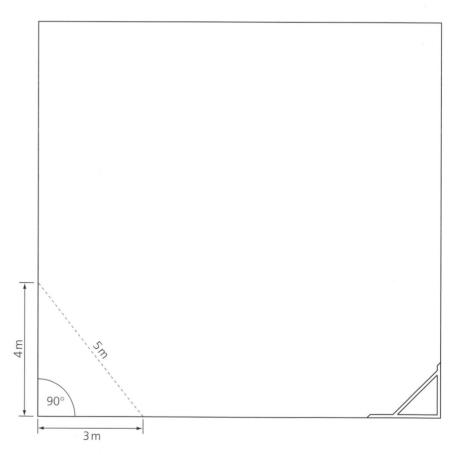

Fig. 5.12 Inaccuracy of builder's square over 5 metres

Therefore, for walls longer than 5 m, the use of the 3–4–5 or 6–8–10 method is employed.

The 6–8–10 and 3–4–5 methods are the same except that the 3–4–5 values are half those in the 6–8–10 method.

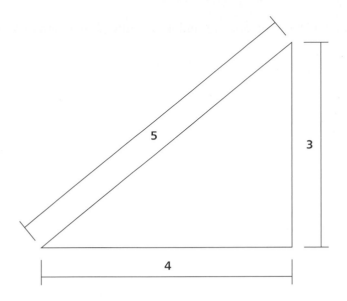

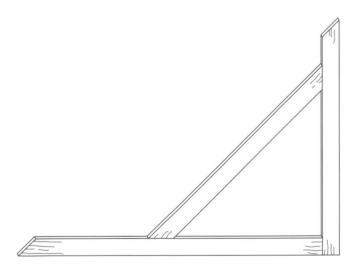

key terms

Profile Boards – Temporary timber boards erected outside the enclosing walls of a structure at corners and used to fix string lines when setting out foundations and walls.

Ranging Line – A line stretched between profiles to mark the position of a wall. Lines are made from nylon or hemp. Nylon stretches more but will retain its tension when strung between pegs or profiles.

3: 4: 5 Method – Used for setting out and checking right angles. It is based on the fact that a triangle, which has sides in the ratio of 3: 4: 5 must contain one angle of 90 degrees.

> *Point to note*

Halving the measurement does not change the angle.

Fig. 5.13 Illustration of both methods (builder's square and use of 3–4–5 or 6–8–10 method)

The procedure for setting out or checking 90 degree angles is exactly the same for both methods.

We will now proceed to set out and check an angle using the 3–4–5 method.

Ask your supervisor or tutor for:

- one roll of line
- one marker pen or pencil
- one tape measure (minimum length 6 metres).

Method

Using bricks or blocks, fix a line between points 1 and 2, a minimum length of 4.5 m.

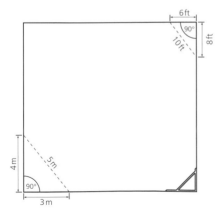

Fig. 5.14 Illustration of procedures for both methods, metric and imperial

Fig. 5.15 Marking out positions 1 and 2

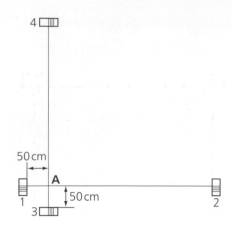

Fig. 5.16 Forming points 3 and 4

Now fix a line between points 3 and 4 to a minimum length of 4 m.

Allow at least 50 cm between the line and the brick as shown in the illustration.

From point A, measure and mark three metres on line A – B.

Now from point A measure and mark out 4 m on line A – C.

You have now formed an angle. Now you must check for the 90 degree accuracy.

Carefully fix the tape at point B. Move the other end of the tape across to point C and read the measurement.

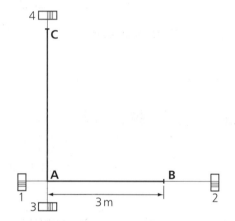

Fig. 5.17 Setting out a right angle 1

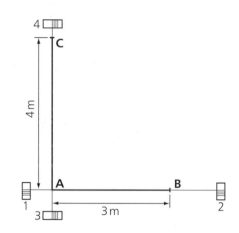

Fig. 5.18 Setting out a right angle 2

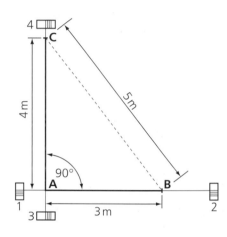

Fig. 5.19 Checking the angle 1

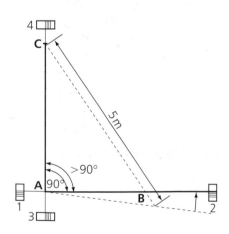

Fig. 5.20 Checking the angle 2

If the measurement B – C is exactly 5 m, you have an accurate angle of 90 degrees.

If the measurement B – C is greater than 5 m, the angle is more than 90 degrees.

Correct the error by moving the line which represents side A – B inward to a position where measurement B – C is exactly 5 m.

If your measurement is less than 5 m, the angle is less than 90 degrees.

Correct the error by moving the line which represents side A – C outward, increasing the angle until the measurement B – C is 5 m, which is 90 degrees.

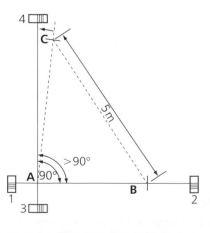

Fig. 5.21 Checking the angle 3

Point to note ▷

If you have any problems forming the angle, ask your supervisor or tutor to observe your method.

The Builder's Square Method

Another way of checking for squareness is to use a builder's square and check each angle for 90 degrees.

The Diagonal Method

To use the diagonal method, proceed as follows:

✎ Using a tape measure from corner point A (diagonally) to point H and from point E to point K

✎ If the measurements A H and E K are the same, your setting out is square

✎ If they differ, the angles must then be checked for 90 degrees using a builder's square or the 3–4–5 method

✎ Make the necessary changes and check it diagonally again; if it is still not correct, ask your supervisor or tutor to observe your checking procedures.

Source: International Labour Office

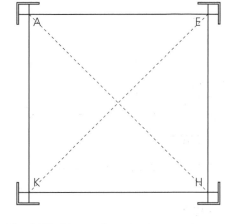

Fig. 5.22 Diagonal method

Construct and Position Profiles

Introduction

Profile boards indicate the position of walls and foundations. Ranging lines are located on to the profiles, which trace out the alignment of walls and foundation trenches.

The overall wall and foundation trench widths are shown on the profiles. The pegs which support the profile boards are positioned on the inside of the profile board cross-pieces. This prevents the line tension pulling the cross piece from the pegs – see Figure 5.23.

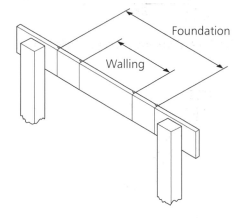

Fig. 5.23 **Pegs and profile board**

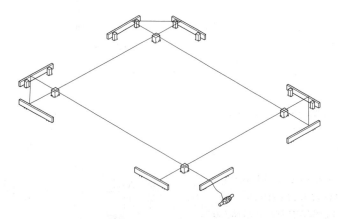

Fig. 5.24 **Final appearance of the setting out of profile boards**

Positioning and Constructing Profiles

Profiles are made from timber pegs and cross pieces.

Pegs

Wooden pegs are used in the setting out of buildings for a variety of reasons:

- to establish the corner points of a building
- to support profile boards
- to establish the level of concrete in a foundation trench
- as a datum peg.

All wooden pegs should be square in section. Sizes can range from 30 mm to 50 mm square, depending on the nature of the soil and the position the peg is to be placed.

Profile Boards

Profile boards are usually made of timber 100 mm × 50 mm in cross-section. Pegs and profile boards are fixed together to construct profiles, as shown in Figure 5.25.

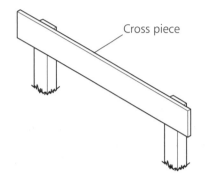

Fig. 5.25 **Pegs and profile board fixed into position**

Method of Assembly

All profiles need to be of rigid construction. The pegs must be firmly placed in the ground.

Nails or screws used for fixing boards to pegs should be staggered diagonally on the board for maximum strength and left proud of the board, as shown in Figure 5.26.

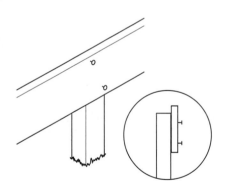

Fig. 5.26 **Fixing board to pegs with screws or nails**

The length of the board used must be long enough to contain the information required, that is, wall and foundation widths, as shown in Figure 5.27.

Two profile boards are needed at each corner of a building, as shown in Figure 5.28.

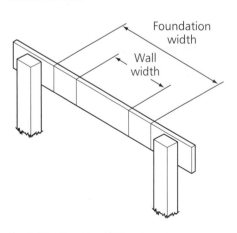

Fig. 5.27 **Boards with wall and foundation widths**

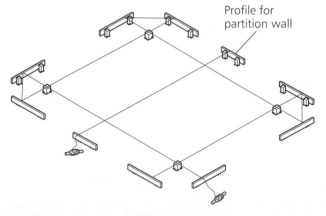

Fig. 5.28 **Profile boards at the corner of a building**

Profiles are also required for setting out any load bearing internal walls.
Ranging lines are then located on to the profiles, which
trace out the alignment of walls and foundation trenches, as
shown in Figure 5.29.

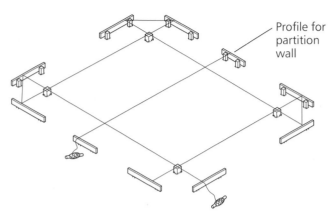

Fig. 5.29 **Profiles for internal walls**

Profiles must be positioned approximately 1 m clear of the intended foundation
excavations, as shown in Figure 5.30.

Points to note
For greater accuracy in setting out,
it is important that all profile
boards are at the same height – see
Figure 5.30.

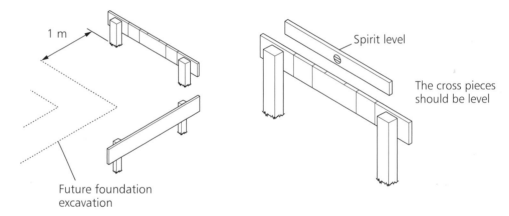

Fig. 5.30 **Profiles positioned 1 m from foundation edge and levelling cross-pieces**

Positioning and Constructing Profiles

One end of a ranging line is located to a corner peg nail. Then the ranging line
is extended beyond the opposite corner peg nail to establish the profile
position.

Method

Stage One
Position a cross-piece clear of the corner peg and at least 1 m clear of the
excavation.

Make an allowance on the cross-piece for the position of the outer edge of the foundation trench excavation. Mark on profile board – see Figure 5.31.

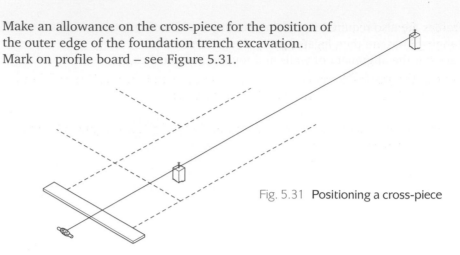

Fig. 5.31 Positioning a cross-piece

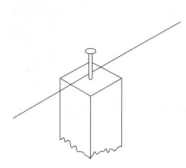

Fig. 5.32 Nail and ranging line on peg

The ranging line should be just touching the nail, as shown on Figure 5.32.

Stage Two

Drive in two pegs to accommodate the cross-piece.

Stage Three

Offer cross-piece into position to determine position of nails.

Stage Four

Partly drive in nails into each end of the cross-piece. Position the nails diagonally to provide rigidity.

Stage Five

Use a sledge hammer to provide support to the pegs when driving in nails. Drive in one nail.

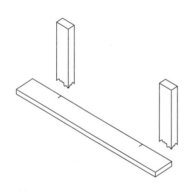

Fig. 5.33 Driving in pegs to accommodate cross-piece

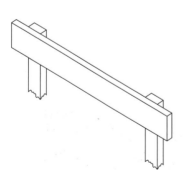

Fig. 5.34 Offer cross-piece into position

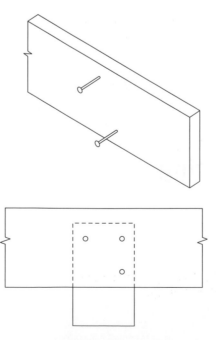

Fig. 5.35 Position nails diagonally to provide rigidity

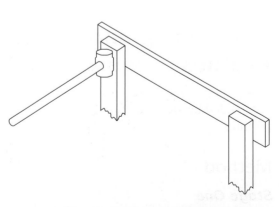

Fig. 5.36 Drive in nails using a sledge hammer to support the pegs

Stage Six

Level the cross-piece using a spirit level.

Drive in the remaining nails. Do not drive the nails fully home. The nail heads left protruding help when dismantling the profiles.

Repeat the process at all corners. The result should look like Figure 5.39 with eight profile boards in place.

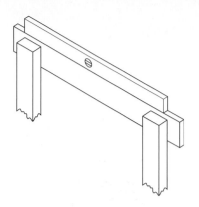

Fig. 5.37 **Level the cross-piece using a spirit level**

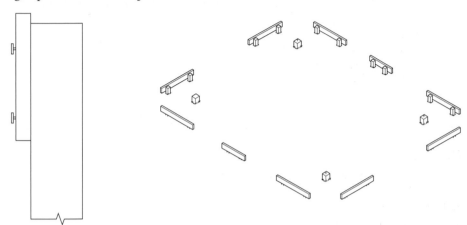

Fig. 5.38 **Nail heads left protruding (helps when dismantling profiles)**

Fig. 5.39 **Eight profiles in place**

Marking Out The Profiles

Method

Stage One

Locate the ranging line on one corner peg, and extend it beyond the next corner peg outside the nail. The ranging line should just touch the nail in the peg.

Where the line crosses the profile board, make a mark with a pencil.

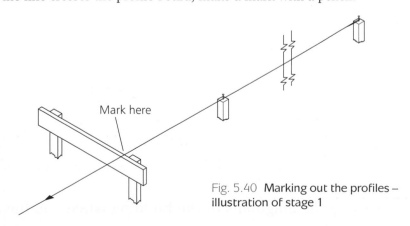

Mark here

Fig. 5.40 **Marking out the profiles – illustration of stage 1**

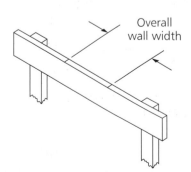

Overall wall width

Fig. 5.41 **Marking out the profiles – illustration of stage 2**

Stage Two

Determine the overall width measurement from the drawing. Mark this dimension on to the profile.

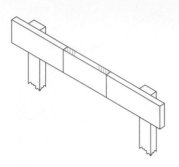

Fig. 5.42 **Marking out the profiles –** illustration of stage 3

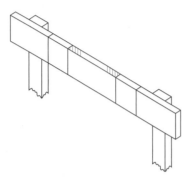

Fig. 5.43 **Marking out the profiles –** illustration of stage 4

Fig. 5.44 **Marking out the profiles –** illustration of stage 5

> **Point to note**

Nails should be inside dimension, saw cuts outside, to ensure ranging line is in correct position.

Stage Three

Hatch an area to the inside of the marks to indicate the walls. The overall wall marks can also be extended onto the vertical face of the profile.

These additional marks clarify the wall position.

Stage Four

The required protection of the concrete foundation beyond the walls is marked on to the profiles. The overall foundation width can also be extended onto the vertical face of the profile.

Stage Five

Partly drive nails into the top of the cross-piece at the wall and trench marks. The nails are used to secure the ranging lines.

As an alternative to nails, saw cuts can be made into the top of the cross-piece.

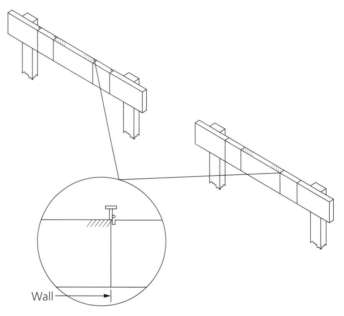

Wall

The process is repeated to mark all eight cross-pieces.

Source: **CITB-ConstructionSkills**

Quick quiz **Quick quiz** Quick quiz Quick quiz Quick quiz

❶ **Why must you take care when setting out?**

❷ **What are profile boards and where would you find them?**

❸ **What information can you find on a profile board and how can it be marked out?**

❹ **What is the purpose of checking the diagonals of the building when you have set it out?**

❺ **What are profiles constructed from?**

Position Ranging Lines

Between the profiles, a ranging line is strung over the points marked on the pegs. The points where it meets the profile boards should be carefully marked on the boards with nails or saw cuts, as previously described. This line represents the front line of the building or the building line; from it, the position of all other walls can be set out.

After these lines have been strung out at right angles from the first two pegs to mark the position of the end walls as shown in Figure 5.45, the length of these walls should be measured off and pegs fixed to mark the back corners of the building.

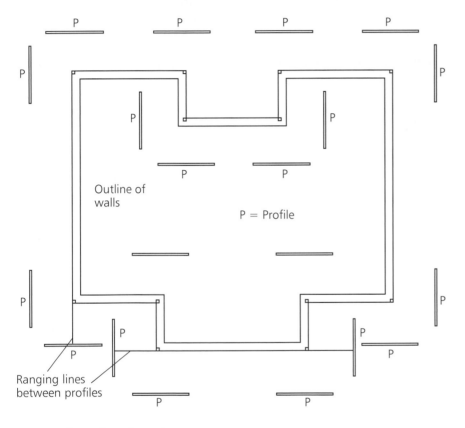

1 Peg out corners

2 Erect profiles

3 Strain lines across pegs and mark position on profiles

4 Mark out profiles and remove pegs

5 Strain lines between profiles as required

Outline of walls

P = Profile

Ranging lines between profiles

Fig. 5.45 **Procedures in setting out**

Lines may now be strained across these pegs in both directions and their position permanently recorded on further profiles.

Cross Walls

The position of any cross walls should also be recorded in the same way, all marks on profiles being fixed by the use of nails or saw cuts. Apart from the face line of each wall, the full width of the foundations should be clearly shown, including the wall thickness.

Transfer Levels

Introduction

Levelling may be defined as a method of expressing the relative heights of any number of points, above or below, some plane of reference called the datum. The site datum is transferred from the nearest ordnance benchmark on to the site by means of transferring levels.

TBM is the abbreviation for a temporary benchmark. A TBM is a known height point from which all other levels are taken.

The TBM can be related to an Ordnance Survey benchmark which is usually found on certain public buildings. On site, the TBM can be surrounded by concrete for protection and a timber fence if additional protection is required, as shown in Figure 5.46. Identification of the TBM is often aided by painting it a bright colour.

All site levels are taken from the top of the TBM peg and, many other different site levels are related to the TBM.

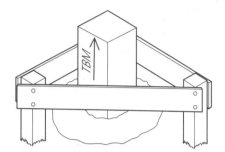

Fig. 5.46 **TBM (temporary benchmark) and protective fence**

Datum Points

A datum height is a level point established in relation to a TBM.

Datums are level reference points for various work activities, for example:

- Damp proof courses
- Invert levels
- Oversite concrete
- Foundations.

Site Datum

It is important to have a fixed point on site to which all other levels can be related. This is known as the site datum, it is located at a convenient height, usually damp course level. The datum itself must be related to some other fixed point, usually an ordnance survey benchmark, or some other clearly visible point, such as a kerb edge or frame cover. Ordnance benchmarks are transferred to the site by means of a series of levels using an optical level and staff.

The site datum is marked by a peg or steel post, concreted into the ground to protect it and located at a convenient point, usually near the site office.

> **Points to note**
> Ordnance Survey benchmarks (OBM) appear on a numerous public buildings, usually cut into walls as shown in Figure 5.47.

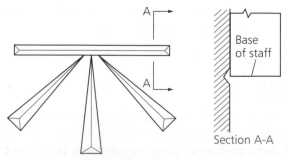

Fig. 5.47 Ordnance survey cut benchmark (OBM)

Transferring Levels

Method

Stage One

Start from the temporary bench mark (TBM). Align a straight edge towards the intended datum point.

Drive in a temporary peg at the full extent of the straight edge, level with the TBM.

Check for level.

To ensure that the spirit level remains in the same position on the straight edge, mark the end of the spirit level (A) on to the straight edge.

Stage Two

Repeat the process to extend the temporary levelling pegs until the final datum peg position is reached.

For greater accuracy, reverse the spirit level and the straight edge at each intermediate levelling stage. Ensure the spirit level remains on mark (A).

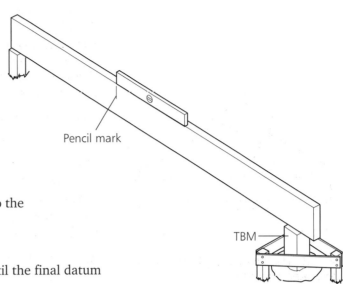

Fig. 5.48 **Transferring levels – stage 1**

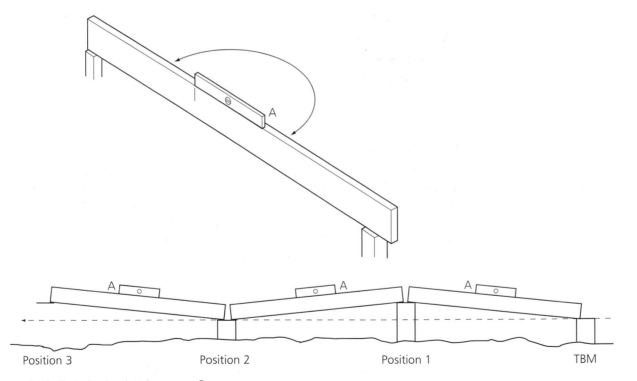

Fig. 5.49 **Transferring levels – stage 2**

Stage Three

Datum pegs are located close to the corner profiles. Datum peg heights may be adjusted in relation to the TBM to suit work activity.

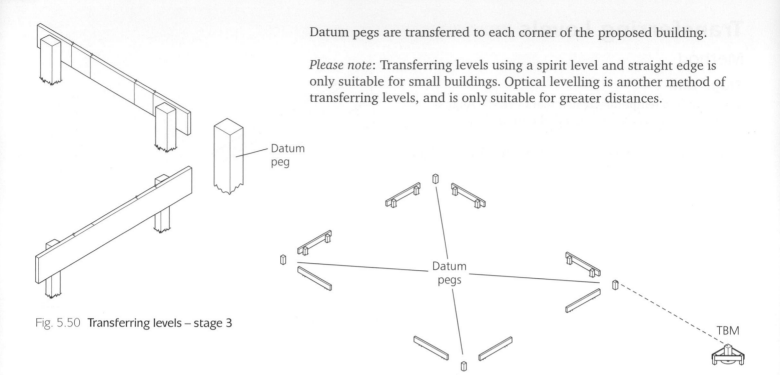

Datum pegs are transferred to each corner of the proposed building.

Please note: Transferring levels using a spirit level and straight edge is only suitable for small buildings. Optical levelling is another method of transferring levels, and is only suitable for greater distances.

Datum peg

Fig. 5.50 Transferring levels – stage 3

Datum pegs

TBM

Fig. 5.51 Illustration of transferring levels

Checking the Accuracy of a Spirit Level

Method

Stage One
To check the accuracy of a spirit level, locate on two known level points – for example, drive in two pegs to a level position.

Stage Two
Reverse the level. The spirit level bubble will show exactly level if the spirit level is accurate.

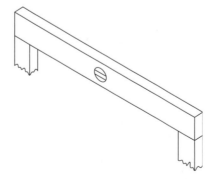

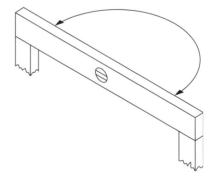

Fig. 5.52 Checking the accuracy of a spirit level –stage 1

Fig. 5.53 Checking the accuracy of a spirit level –stage 2

Source: CITB-ConstructionSkills

Understanding Working Drawings

Construction or working drawings and written specifications must contain the information required for a construction team to be able to convert the design for a proposed building into a completed structure. In order for this to take place, the following information should be included on the working drawings:

- elevations
- external finishes to walls and roof
- positions of windows and doors
- scales
- overall dimensions of the building
- position of internal walls, room sizes and window openings
- position of fitments, baths, sinks, toilets and so on.

It is necessary to draw the building from several different angles or viewpoints. These different views are often shown on the same sheet.

The ability to read and understand working drawings and sketches is an essential function of any bricklayer in the construction industry. As a student you must study this section carefully to fully understand the way working drawings are prepared. To develop the skill of interpreting working drawings and sketches you must practise reading sample drawings provided by your tutor at college and supervisor at work.

Working drawings and sketches are pictures or diagrams used to describe the building specifications and procedures required to erect a building, as shown in Figure 5.54.

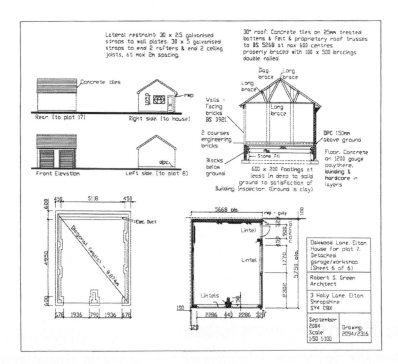

Fig. 5.54 **A working drawing**

In order to give enough information, it is necessary to draw the building from several different viewpoints. These different views are often shown on the same sheet.

Sketches

Sketches are merely freehand pictures that can be drawn by anyone as a method of explaining specific instructions. In brickwork, sketches may be drawn by the bricklaying foreman to describe the size requirements of a building component or a construction procedure.

Scales Used in Working Drawings

The scales used in working drawings differ according to the type of information that is being shown. The most common are as follows.

Section Drawings

Section drawings provide vertical dimensions and constructional details of foundations, floors, walls, roof, damp proof courses and membranes and the height of ground levels.

Plans and Elevations

Plan and elevation drawings or general location plans, identify the positions occupied by the various areas within the building and identify the location of the main elements and components. Scales 1 : 200, 1 : 100 and 1 : 50.

A floor plan provides a view looking down on the building. Floor plans are useful for showing how different levels of the building relate to one another. Elevations are useful for showing how the outside of the building will look once work is completed.

REMEMBER
A floor plan of the foundations shows the position of the footings and a floor plan of the ground floor (or any floor) shows the position of the walls, windows and doors.

Side elevation – provide views of each side of the building

Rear elevation – Provide views of the rear of the building

Front elevation – Provide views of the front of the building.

Block Plans

Block plans identify the proposed site in relation to the surrounding area. Scales 1 : 2500 and 1 : 1250.

Site Plans

Site plans give the position of the proposed building and the general layout of roads, services, drainage and so on. Scales 1 : 500 and 1 : 200.

Assembly Drawings

Assembly drawings show in detail, the junctions between the various elements and components of a building. Scales 1 : 20, 1 : 10 and 1 : 5.

Detail Drawings

Detail drawings show all the information that is required in order to manufacture a particular component. Scales 1 : 10, 1 : 5 and 1 : 1.

Component Drawings

Component range drawings are specific to the proposed building itself and show the dimensions and layout of a standard range of components. Scales 1 : 100, 1 : 50 and 1 : 20.

Quick quiz Quick quiz Quick quiz Quick quiz Quick quiz

1. What information would you find on the following: elevations, plans, sections and site plans?
2. What is the building line?
3. What scale is a detailed drawing usually drawn to?
4. Which drawing would you use when setting out a building?
5. What information would you find on an assembly drawing?

Understanding Scales Used in Working Drawings

Construction drawings are pictures or diagrams used to describe the building specifications and procedures required to erect a building, as shown in Figure 5.55.

Working drawings are usually prepared by architects or designers using manual draughting techniques and computer aided design software. These drawings along with the written specification describe the details of the building.

Construction or working drawings and written specifications must contain the information required for a construction team to be able to convert the design for a proposed building into a completed structure. In order for this to take place, the following information should be included in the working drawings:

- Elevations
- External finishes to walls and roof
- Positions of window and door openings
- Scales
- Overall dimensions of the building
- Position of internal walls, room sizes, door and window openings
- Position of fitments, baths, sinks, toilets, etc.

Scales

The sizes of buildings and construction sites means that drawings need to be scaled down from full size to sizes that will fit on a sheet of drawing paper. This is known as drawing to scale. A scale drawing is different from a sketch because every measurement in a scale drawing has to be in proportion to the real thing and must be exact.

Dimensions can be taken from a drawing by the use of a scale rule.

The main scales used in construction are:

Scale	Drawing is
1: 1	The same size as the object
1: 5	5 times smaller than the object
1: 10	10 times smaller than the object
1: 50	50 times smaller than the object
1: 100	100 times smaller than the object
1: 500	500 times smaller than the object
1: 1250	1250 times smaller than the object

Although imperial measurements are still used in some cases on site, metric measurements are now accepted universally for drawings with the millimetre as the basic unit.

Section Drawings

Section drawings provide vertical dimensions and construction details of foundations, floors, walls, roof, damp proof courses and membranes and the height of ground levels, as shown in Figure 5.56.

Specifications

The specification is a detailed description of all the essential information and requirements that will affect the price of the work but cannot be shown on the drawings. Items included in the specification are:

- Site description
- Restrictions, for example, limited access and working hours
- Availability of services, water, gas, electricity and telephone

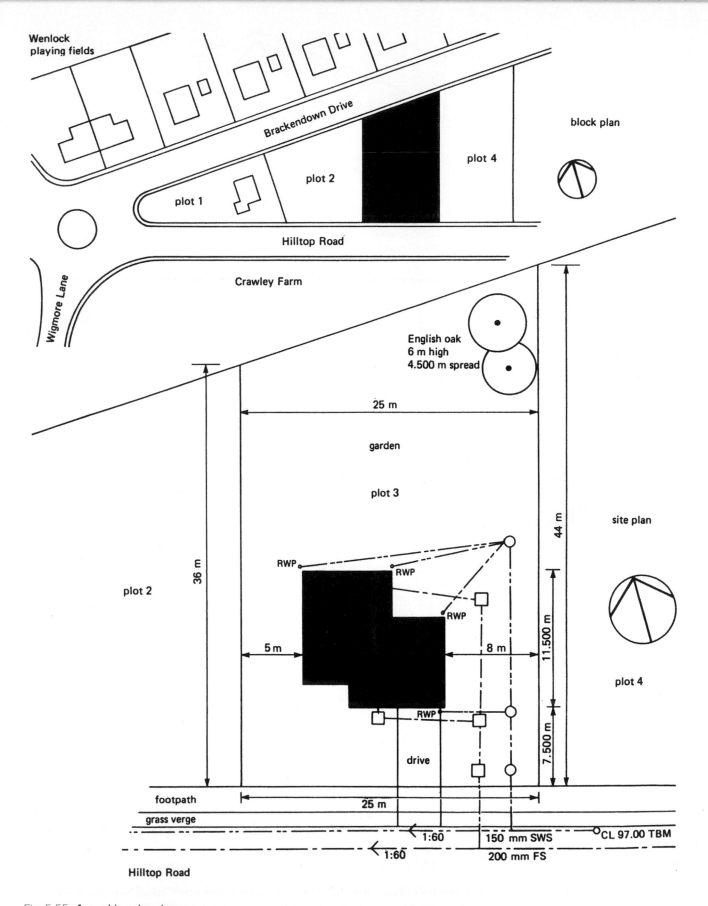

Fig. 5.55 A working drawing

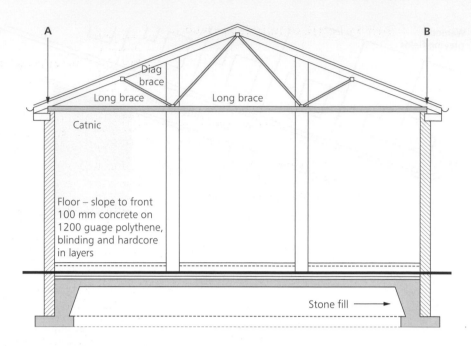

Fig. 5.56 **A section drawing**

🔨 Description of materials, quality, size, tolerance and finish
🔨 Description of workmanship, quality and industrial standard
🔨 Other requirements: site clearance, making good on completion, names of suppliers, names of sub-contractors, etc.

Understanding Symbols Used on Working Drawings

Symbols or hatching is the term that describes the markings on a working drawing, particularly those showing sections through the structure, to denote the material that the building is constructed from – see Figure 5.57. The symbols are official British Standards and can be found in BS 1192 which controls drawing practice across all sections of the construction industry.

You need to know what each symbol means in order to read the information contained in the drawings. Working drawings use symbols to represent different features. The lengths of walls and openings are shown with their actual dimensions. Additional information is provided about the heights of windows and doors.

Examples of Types of Symbols:
🔨 brickwork
🔨 blockwork
🔨 concrete
🔨 stonework
🔨 hardcore
🔨 insulation
🔨 sub-soil.

The symbols illustrated in Figure 5.58 only represent a small sample of those that are used regularly on all standard working drawings.

> **Point to note**
>
> Dimensions are normally shown in millimetres only. This avoids confusion and the repetition of units, for example:
>
> ▪ 10 not 10 mm
> ▪ 215 not 21.5 cm or 0.215 m
> ▪ 1200 not 120 cm or 1.2 m
> ▪ 2100 not 21 m.
>
> Dimensions are normally written above and in the centre of a dimension line to be read from the bottom or right-hand edge of the drawing.

Sectional detail of typical foundation

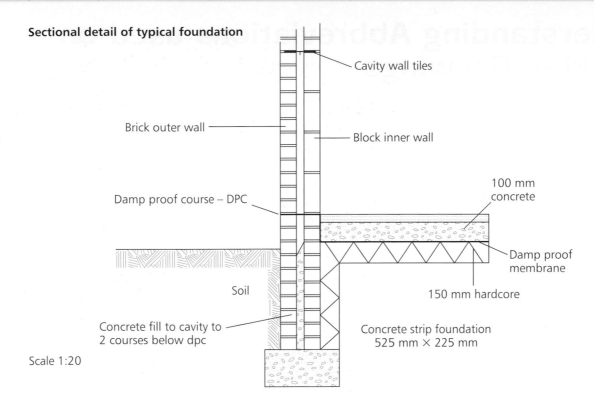

Cavity wall tiles

Brick outer wall

Block inner wall

Damp proof course – DPC

100 mm concrete

Damp proof membrane

150 mm hardcore

Soil

Concrete strip foundation
525 mm × 225 mm

Concrete fill to cavity to
2 courses below dpc

Scale 1:20

Fig. 5.57 A sectional drawing of a foundation

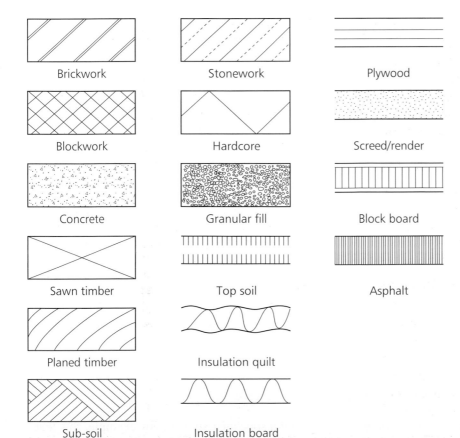

Brickwork

Stonework

Plywood

Blockwork

Hardcore

Screed/render

Concrete

Granular fill

Block board

Sawn timber

Top soil

Asphalt

Planed timber

Insulation quilt

Sub-soil

Insulation board

Fig. 5.58 Symbols used on drawings

REMEMBER

Different symbols are of use to different trades. For example, as a bricklayer you will need to know about the measurements of walls and openings.

TRY THIS OUT

Using the floor plan from a working drawing supplied by your tutor, draw up a list of the materials and their quantities required to construct the building in the drawing.

Understanding Abbreviations used on Working Drawings

Because of the amount of detail shown on working drawings, abbreviations are used for many of the materials or components used. Some of the customary and more common abbreviations used on working drawings are as follows:

Brickwork	bwk
Damp proof course	dpc
Concrete	conc
Foundation	fdn
Insulation	insul
Rainwater gully	rwg
Soil and vent pipe	svp
British Standard	BS
Maximum	Max
Minimum	Min
Finished floor level	Ffl
Setting out point	Sop

To help you find out what different technical words and abbreviations mean I have listed some tips below.

Using a Dictionary

There are a number of ways you can find out or check the meanings of technical words and abbreviations.

Dictionaries are useful for looking up the meanings of everyday words including mathematical terms and abbreviations. For example, max is short for maximum. It means the largest possible size.

> **REMEMBER**
>
> If you are in any doubt about words or abbreviations on a working drawing, ask a colleague or supervisor for help. It is very important to get it right. Mistakes cost time and money.

Using a specialist glossary or website

A specialist glossary is the best place to find out the exact meaning of technical terms such as masonry units or wall ties. You may find additional information by looking on a specialist website.

Glossaries

A glossary contains words about a specialist subject. For example, this text book has a glossary of all the specialist words used in it, together with their meanings.

Work-based Evidence Required

■ Work skills required to:

■ measure, mark out, level, position and secure

■ Use and maintain:

■ hand tools

■ ancillary equipment

To meet this requirement, obtain a witness testimony sheet from your supervisor stating that you have used work skills to measure, mark out, level, position and secure a building, whilst using hand tools and setting out equipment.

When you have received the signed and dated witness testimony sheet from your supervisor, place them in your work-based evidence portfolio when next in college and map and record it against the syllabus.

Quick quiz Quick quiz Quick quiz Quick quiz Quick quiz

❶ Why are graphical symbols used in drawings?

❷ Briefly explain what BS 1192 is.

❸ Draw the symbols for brickwork, blockwork, hardcore, damp proof course and concrete.

❹ Where on a drawing are dimensions usually written?

❺ Why are symbols used on drawings?

❻ What is another term for symbol?

❼ What do the following abbreviations stand for: bwk, dpc, max, conc, fdn?

❽ What is the difference between a glossary and a dictionary?

❾ Why are abbreviations used on working drawings?

❿ If a word has more than one meaning, how do you choose the correct one to use?

RESOURCES   5.2

In this section you will learn about materials, components and equipment relating to types, quantity, quality and sizes of standard and/or specialist:

- hand tools and setting out equipment
- methods of calculating quantity, length and area associated with the method/procedure to assist in setting out basic masonry structures.

When you have completed this section you will be able to:

- select the required quantity and quality of resources for the methods of work.

Know and understand:

- the characteristics, quality, uses, limitations and defects associated with the resources
- how the resources should be used.

Setting Out Materials and Equipment

When you have worked through this section, you will be able to:

Establish lines and levels for construction activities including, using appropriate equipment: tapes, rules, spirit levels, straight edges, lines and levelling instruments.

Hand Tools and Setting Out Equipment

The Builder's square

The builder's square is used for the setting out of right angles on site.

A builder's square is usually made from wood. It is braced to maintain its squareness and one side is longer than the other. When first made, a square's accuracy can be guaranteed, but on site after exposure to the weather and possibly misuse, its accuracy should not be relied upon.

Most builder's squares are made of 75 mm × 30 mm timber half jointed at the 90 degree angle with a diagonal brace, tenoned or dovetailed into the side length as illustrated in Figure 5.59.

When setting out with a builder's square, accuracy depends on lining up the ranging line with the side of the square. Greater accuracy can be achieved when the sides of the square are increased in length.

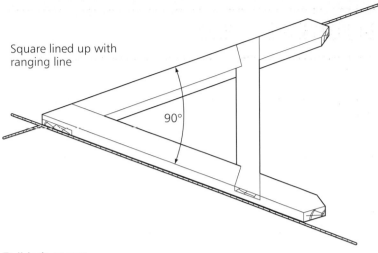

Square lined up with ranging line

90°

Fig. 5.59 Builder's square

Types of Level

Cowley Level

The Cowley automatic level is a simple self-levelling instrument widely used for general site levelling. The level consists of:

- A metal cased box containing a system of mirrors and prisms
- A tripod with a central pin. The metal cased box is placed on to the pin, which then activates the level
- A graduated staff consisting of a sliding target which moves up and down the staff. An arrow on the target gives the precise measurement on the graduated staff, as illustrated in Figure 5.60.

Slope Attachment

A small optical attachment that enables the Cowley level to be used to set out gradients.

There are two models available with ranges 1 in 10 to 1 in 50 and 1 in 60 to 1 in 250 respectively.

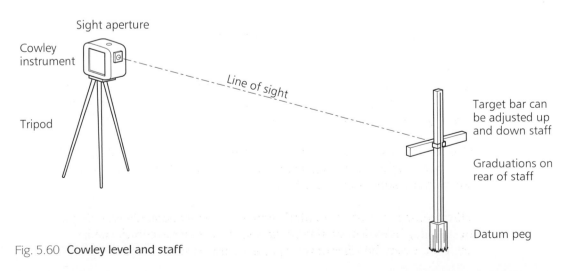

Sight aperture

Cowley instrument

Line of sight

Tripod

Target bar can be adjusted up and down staff

Graduations on rear of staff

Datum peg

Fig. 5.60 **Cowley level and staff**

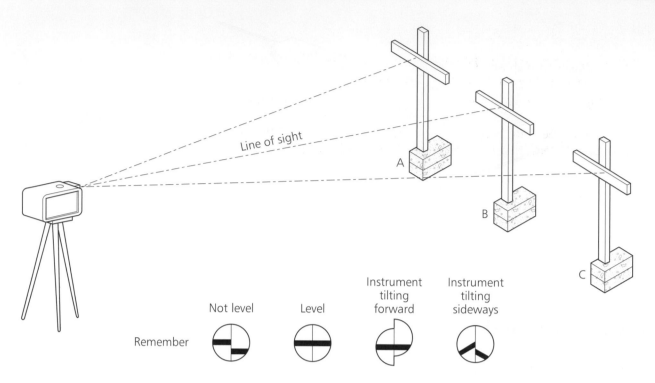

Fig. 5.61 **Levelling exercise using the Cowley level**

Remember | Not level | Level | Instrument tilting forward | Instrument tilting sideways

Optical Site Square

This is an optical instrument used for setting out right angles on site. The site square contains two telescopes set permanently at 90 degrees to each other. They can be adjusted vertically to enable fixing points to be located at convenient spots.

A tripod with adjustable legs and a steel rod which allows the instrument to be set up over a fixed point, for example a saw mark on a profile or a nail in a peg, as illustrated in Figure 5.62.

The site square will give a range from 2 to 90 m.

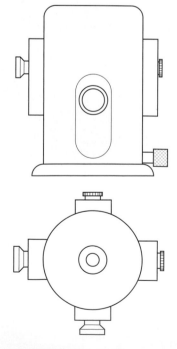

Fig. 5.62 **Cowley site square**

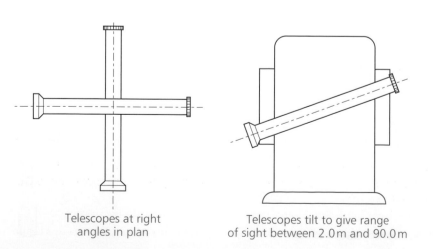

Telescopes at right angles in plan

Telescopes tilt to give range of sight between 2.0 m and 90.0 m

Measuring Tapes

When you have worked through this section, you will be able to:

➤ recognize the different types of tapes available

➤ use tapes as an aid to setting out work for construction activities.

All measuring tapes should be manufactured in accordance with British Standard 4884 Measuring Instruments for Construction Works.

Steel Tapes

For maximum accuracy always use steel tapes. The majority of steel tapes are graduated into metres, centimetres and millimetres and can be read to the nearest millimetre. Tapes are usually available in lengths of 3, 5, 20, 30, 50 and 100 m.

Synthetic Tapes

Synthetic tapes are usually available in 20 and 30 m lengths. This type of tape is liable to stretch or shrink, and is therefore not as accurate as a steel tape.

Good Practice

Care and Maintenance of Measuring tapes

Clean and lightly oil the tape at the end of each working day.

Do not leave tapes lying on the ground, they are liable to be damaged or to kink and break.

Always have the tape wound on its spool when not in use.

When using a tape for measuring purposes ensure it is carried by two people across the site and not dragged.

TRY THIS OUT

You have been using a 30 m plastic tape on site, and you think it may have stretched in parts. How do you check it? Assume you do not have any other equipment available.

Ranging Lines

When you have worked through this section, you will be able to:

🖌 identify a ranging line

🖌 position a ranging line on to profiles for the face line of walls.

A Ranging Line – a stout line used for setting out purposes.

Ranging lines are produced in lengths known as shanks. A bricklayer would have two shanks on a pair of line pins, but for setting out purposes, four or five shanks would be required. The lines themselves are usually made from hemp or nylon. Although it can stretch more than hemp, nylon line will retain its tension when strung between pegs or profiles.

If a line breaks, it should be spliced together as shown in Figure 5.63 and not knotted. The strand of line is opened up to allow the other end of line to pass through. When tension is applied, the strands will tighten up to hold the ends together.

> **Point to note**

The term knot is sometimes used instead of shank when describing line.

TRY THIJ OUT

List the equipment you would use for each of the following setting out activities, as well as any other items of general equipment required.

- ▪ linear measurement
- ▪ angle measurement
- ▪ line levels
- ▪ plumbing and fixing verticals
- ▪ general equipment.

Spirit Levels and Straight Edges

When you have worked through this section, you will be able to:

🖌 use a spirit level and straight edge to transfer levels.

Spirit Levels

A spirit level is a metal straight edge specially fitted with glass tubes containing a spirit and a bubble of air. These level tubes are set into the straight edge so that when the straight edge is placed across two points that are exactly level, the air bubble will be exactly in the centre of the tube, this position being clearly marked with incised lines. In a similar way, tubes are fitted to read correctly with the level held *vertically*.

To check the accuracy of a spirit level it is usual to reverse its length to see if the bubble remains in the same position. If not, it can be adjusted until it does.

Fig. 5.63 Line splice

TRY THIS OUT

Using a spirit level, draw a horizontal, straight line with a pencil or marker between two perpends on a wall that you have built in the college workshop.

Straight Edge

A straight edge is any piece of wood that has parallel sides which can then be used as a straight edge, but not accurately. A purpose-made straight edge is preferable (see Figure 5.64).

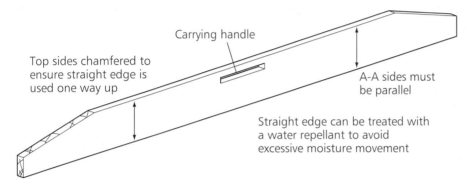

Carrying handle

Top sides chamfered to ensure straight edge is used one way up

A-A sides must be parallel

Straight edge can be treated with a water repellant to avoid excessive moisture movement

Fig. 5.64 **Purpose made straight edge**

When a straight edge is used, it should be reversed each time a level is taken. This will reduce any errors caused by a faulty level or in the straight edge itself.

Work-based Evidence Required

■ **Selection of resources associated with own work:**

■ materials, components and fixings

■ tools and setting out equipment

To meet these requirements, obtain from your supervisor a witness testimony sheet, stating that you have selected resources associated with brickwork and tools and setting out equipment.

When you have received the signed and dated witness testimony sheet from your supervisor, place it in your work-based evidence portfolio when next in college and map and record it against the syllabus.

Quick quiz Quick quiz Quick quiz Quick quiz Quick quiz

❶ Explain how a spirit level can be checked for accuracy.

❷ Why should a spirit level and straight edge be reversed for alternate readings?

❸ What kind of hammer would you use for knocking in the wooden pegs when marking out a site?

❹ Two pegs have been placed too far apart to check for level using a spirit level. What would you use with the spirit level to check that the pegs are level?

❺ What does the term building line mean?

Construction Surveying

For more information on construction surveying, why not contact the websites of the better known manufacturers and suppliers, or the following?

Ordnance Survey

www.ordnancesurvey.co.uk

Setting Out of Buildings

For more information about the setting out of buildings why not visit the following website.

CITB-ConstructionSkills

www.citb-constructionskills.co.uk

Setting Out of Brickwork

For more information about the setting out of brickwork, obtain from the library or your tutor the set of training workbooks produced by CITB–ConstructionSkills. These workbooks give a step by step guide to the various operations involved in the setting out of walls and small buildings.

The workbooks are just one of over 400 aids to training published by CITB–ConstructionSkills. Others include videos, tape slide programmes, open learning packages, books, manuals, training support packages, work sheets and so on.

For a listing of all CITB–ConstructionSkills publications contact: CITB–ConstructionSkills Publications, Bircham Newton, Kings Lynn, Norfolk, PE31 6RH, Telephone. 01485 577800. or visit their website at www.citb-constructionskills.co.uk/publications

Chapter six

Joint Brick and Block Structures

NVQ Level 1   Unit No. VR 39   Joint Brick and Block Structures

This unit, in the context of brickwork and the construction industry work environment is about:

- interpreting instructions
- adopting safe and healthy working practices
- selecting materials and equipment
- jointing and pointing brick and block structures.

There are two sections in this chapter: methods of work and resources.

This chapter will now cover jointing brick and block structures.

METHODS OF WORK   6.1

In this section you will learn about the application of knowledge for safe work practices, skills and transference of competence, relating to the area of work and material used to:

- form jointed finishes in new masonry work
- rake out and form pointed finishes in existing masonry work
- mix jointing/pointing material
- use hand tools and equipment.

You will also learn about team work and communication and the needs of other occupations associated with brick and blockwork.

When you have completed this section you will be able to:

- comply with the given contract instructions to carry out the work efficiently to the required specification.

Know and understand:

- how methods of work are carried out and problems are reported.

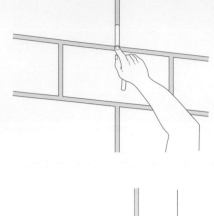

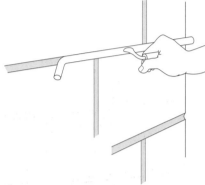

Fig. 6.1 **Tooling mortar joints**

Forming Joint Finishes in New Masonry Work

Definition – Forming the finished surface profile of a mortar joint by tooling or raking as the work proceeds, without pointing.

Tooling Mortar Joints

In order to prevent water from penetrating through a brick or block wall through the mortar joints, it is necessary to seal the joints. Tooling or ironing the joints will seal them as long as the activity is carried out correctly – see Figure 6.1.

Tooling can be described as the process of compacting, smoothing and sealing horizontal and vertical mortar joints – see Figure 6.2.

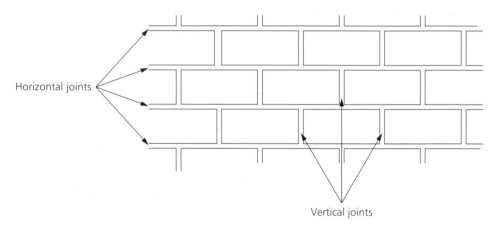

Horizontal joints

Vertical joints

Fig. 6.2 **Horizontal and vertical joints**

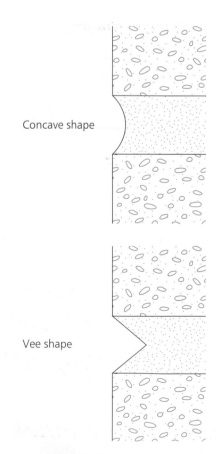

Concave shape

Vee shape

Fig. 6.3 **Concave and recessed joint shapes**

Tooling of mortar joints results in shaped joints:

🔨 Concave shape – see Figure 6.3.

🔨 Recessed shape – see Figure 6.3.

Unless otherwise specified, all mortar joints are tooled to concave shapes.

Mortar joints should be tooled after the mortar has stiffened but before it has hardened. The length of time it takes for the mortar to harden will depend upon:

🔨 weather conditions.

Mortar hardens quicker in warm weather than in cold weather.

🔨 the types of bricks or blocks used.

Mortar hardens slowly when using engineering or glazed bricks.

Mortar hardens quickly when using porous bricks or blocks.

The ability to judge or determine the condition of mortar joints will come as a result of practical experience such as learning to check the readiness of the mortar using your finger-tips.

Ask your tutor to show you this method.

Tooling of the vertical and horizontal joints is carried out using a (S) shaped jointer – see Figure 6.4.

Practise the following procedure and techniques.

First, tool the vertical joints.

Place the jointer at the top of the vertical joint and move it downward in a vertical line – see Figure 6.5.

Fill any voids with fresh mortar and retool. Repeat until the joint is smooth and free of voids – see Figure 6.6.

Fig. 6.4 **A jointer**

> **Definition**

A tool used to form a joint profile.

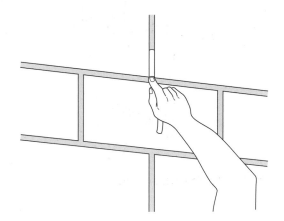

Fig. 6.5 **Tooling a vertical joint**

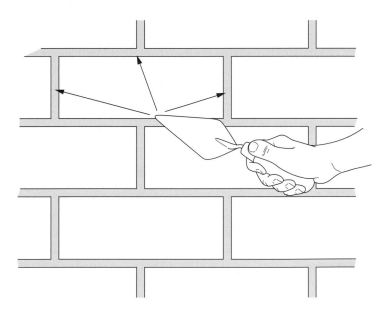

Fig. 6.6 Filling joints with fresh mortar

Next, seal the horizontal joints by moving the jointer back and forth along the top edge of the masonry. Again, fill voids and seal.

Lightly retool the vertical joints.

Use your trowel to remove all loose material from the face and base of the wall – see Figure 6.7.

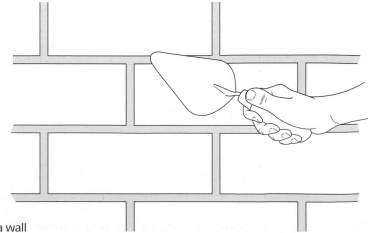

Fig. 6.7 **Removing loose material from the face of a wall**

Raking Out and Forming Pointed Finishes in Existing Masonry Work

Pointing

Pointing is the term applied to the process of raking out the joints in brickwork and refilling them with a mortar of a different character from that used in the body of the wall. The original object was to protect the bedding material of the brick and consequently the bricks also from the effects of the weather.
In more recent times it has been used as a means of varying the appearance of the brickwork.

There are several types of pointing, and these may be carried out in a variety of colours by means of coloured dyes and cements and the use of different sands, the combination making possible an almost unlimited range of finishes.

The type of pointing adopted largely depends on the choice of the architect, particularly when appearance is the primary object, but it can be generally stated that:

- For bricks of regular shape with sharp arrises, a smooth weathered type of pointing should be used as being effective and efficient
- For textured bricks of irregular shape, a pointing with a rough textured finish should be used.

key terms

Pointing – The process of finishing a mortar joint by raking out the jointing mortar before it has set hard, typically to a depth of 15 mm, and filling with additional mortar, to create a specific finish.

Repointing – The raking out of old mortar and replacing with new.

Finishes for Pointing

In addition to the insertion of jointing material after the original joint has been raked out, there are many finishes that may be applied during the process of building. A disadvantage of this method is the difficulty of maintaining an even colour throughout the whole work. This is due to possible variations in the colour and texture of the sand used and to a lesser degree the difficulty of ensuring constant proportions. An advantage of this method of finishing a joint is the fact that that the finish is part of the bedding material. For this reason there is no possibility of the mortar becoming loose and leaving the wall, as sometimes happens in the case of pointing filled into raked joints.

Preparing Walls for Pointing

Joints to be pointed must be raked out to a depth of at least 15 mm, care being taken to remove completely the mortar from all brick edges. In new work, this will, of course, be done as the work proceeds, a piece of wood or metal of the correct width being all that is required, with the addition of a stiff brush finally to remove any loose particles.

When old work is to be pointed, a joint raker will be required to clear the joints and here, also, the wall should be thoroughly brushed down afterwards to remove any dust that would otherwise prevent close adhesion between pointing material and the bricks.

Before pointing is commenced, the brickwork should be thoroughly wetted down, although the extent to which this should be done will depend partly upon the nature of the bricks to be pointed and the climatic conditions at the time. In any case the object is to prevent too rapid absorption of the moisture from the pointing material.

Old brickwork may be revived before pointing by the use of a colour wash matching as nearly as possible the original colour of the bricks.

Joint Finishes and the Use of Hand Tools

Procedure

The handling of all materials will be similar for most types of pointing. That is, the pointing material should be placed on the hawk in small quantities for easy manipulation, and drawn down to a thin edge so that a wedge-shaped piece of mortar may be picked up on the back of the trowel, as shown in Figure 6.8, ready for insertion into the joint.

A 75 mm. trowel is normally used for pointing cross-joints, and a 150 mm. trowel for bed joints.

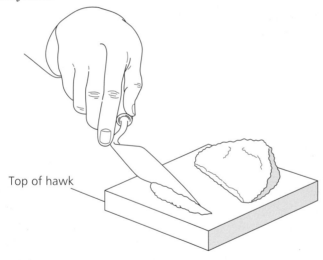

Top of hawk

Fig. 6.8 **Picking up mortar material**

Joint Finishes

Weather Pointing

This is perhaps the most common type of pointing and is used extensively on old and new brickwork. Its object is to prevent any moisture penetrating into the joint. Figure 6.9 shows a section through a bed joint pointed with a weathered joint.

The cross-joints are first filled, pressing the material back on to the existing mortar and pushing in the top and bottom of the joints in order that they shall not interfere with the subsequent insertion of the bed joints (see Figure 6.10). No more cross-joints should be inserted than can be followed with bed joints before they are set hard.

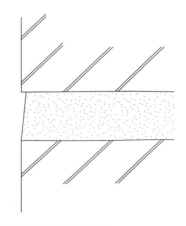

Fig. 6.9 **Weather pointing**

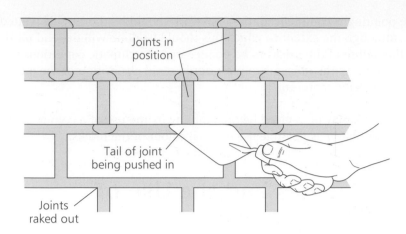

Fig. 6.10 **Placing cross-joints**

The cross-joints should be trimmed with the bedding trowel, every endeavour being made to maintain an even width throughout. It is often found necessary – particularly in old work – to make up the damaged corners of the bricks before commencing the pointing. Figure 6.11 shows a small section of a wall with the cross-joints in place, and the position of the trowel for trimming off ragged edges.

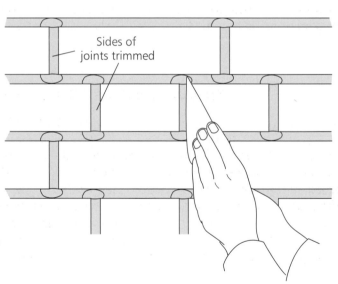

Fig. 6.11 **Trimming cross-joints**

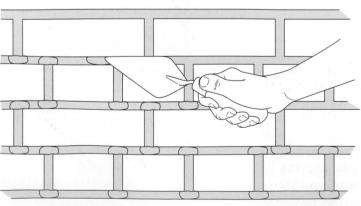

Fig. 6.12 **Placing bed joints**   Source: International Labour Office

After the completion of a number of cross-joints, the bed joints must be inserted, care being taken to avoid marking the face of the bricks. The mortar is taken on the back of the bedding trowel and, working from one end, the joint is filled flush with mortar and finished off with repeated rubbing with the back of the trowel (see Figure 6.12). This is known as ironing in and has the effect of compressing and closing together all the pores of the jointing, thus forming a watertight joint.

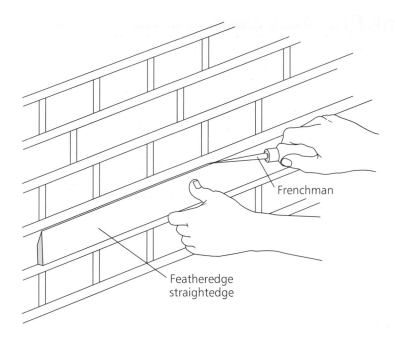

Fig. 6.13 **Trimming bed joints**

Finally, the joint is cut off at the bottom and trimmed at the top with a Frenchman guided by a feather-edge rule, as illustrated in Figure 6.13.

Here again, it will be obvious that, while it is not necessary to cut off each joint as it is inserted, no more joints should be inserted than can be cut off before setting.

Flush Pointing

The preparation for this type of pointing is similar to that described for weather pointing, but the carrying out of the work differs slightly. The mortar is pressed into the joints in the usual way but is not ironed in. Instead, the joints are left rough by dragging the blade of the trowel over the surface, so that the finished texture harmonizes with that of the brick. A piece of wood or sacking is often rubbed over the joints to obtain the same effect. Flush pointing doesn't have the waterproofing property of the weathered joint, but is quite widely used because of the pleasing effect obtained in conjunction with sand-faced bricks. Figure 6.14 shows a section through a bed joint with flush pointing.

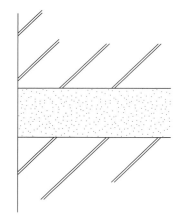

Fig. 6.14 **Flush pointing**

Tuck Pointing

This is purely a decorative treatment to the joints of brickwork and is now generally applied to old brickwork. After the joints have been raked out, the whole of the wall is colour-washed and the joints are then filled flush with a suitably coloured stopping, a further wash being applied in certain cases. A thin white joint of lime putty is then superimposed in the centre of each flush joint, special tools being used for this purpose. It may be easily recognized by the regularly spaced bed and cross-joints forming a thin network over the whole surface of the wall. It is very little used now and, for this reason, the process has not been more fully described. Figure 6.15 shows a section through the joint.

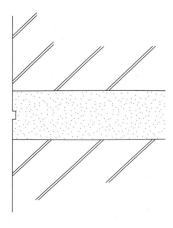

Fig. 6.15 **Tuck pointing**

Joint Finishes

Joint finishes executed during the process of building vary considerably, the principal ones being described below.

Struck Work

This type of joint finish is largely confined to (a) internal brickwork and (b) overhand building and finishing, and is formed by pressing in the joint with the back of the trowel point, the cross-joints being ironed in first. The ease with which this may be carried out will depend upon the fullness of the joints as the work is built, thereby reducing to a minimum any necessity for filling the joints afterwards.

The appearance of a wall having struck joints is very similar to that of a weather jointed wail but lacks the fine finish of the latter. Moreover, if the finish is applied externally, water will be held in the joint. Figure 6.16 shows a struck joint in section.

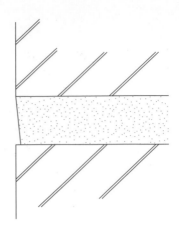

Fig. 6.16 **Struck joint**

Recessed Joints

This joint is not recommended for external walls as moisture can be trapped on the lower surface of the joint – see Figure 6.17.

It is achieved by raking out the mortar joint with a chariot recessing tool or by making a recessing tool from timber and a nail – as shown in Figure 6.18.

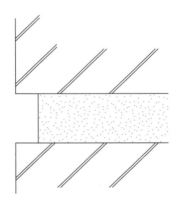

Fig. 6.17 **Recessed joint**

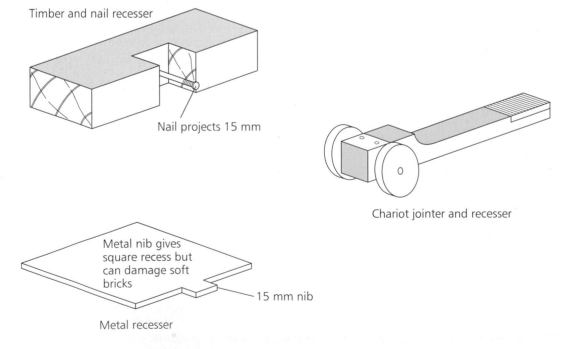

Timber and nail recesser

Nail projects 15 mm

Chariot jointer and recesser

Metal nib gives square recess but can damage soft bricks

15 mm nib

Metal recesser

Fig. 6.18 **Recessing tools**

Half Round Tooled Joint

This joint is produced by ironing the joints with a rounded jointing bar. It is referred to as a bucket handle joint which originated from the use of galvanized bucket handles to achieve the finished joint – see Figure 6.19.

For the joints shown in Figure. 6.17 and 6.19, purpose made tools of reverse shape to the section are used, the joint being pressed back and ironed while still comparatively soft. These finishes are generally confined to bricks of regular shape and sharp arrises.

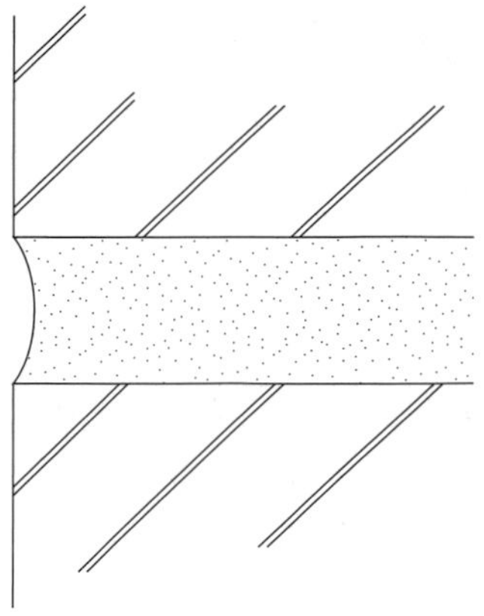

Fig. 6.19 **A half round joint**

Sequence for Pointing

Pointing is one of the most difficult skill areas to become proficient at, it requires a great deal of practice to achieve a satisfactory finish.

There is a set sequence to pointing and it should always be followed.

Sequence of Pointing for Struck Joints

Stage One
Always start at the highest part of the wall.

Stage Two
Taking about 1 square metre at a time, remove any mortar stains or loose mortar from the joints and face of the brick. Care must be taken not to damage the face of soft bricks.

Stage Three
Wet the wall face starting at the top. The amount of water used will depend upon the absorption rate of the bricks. Allow for water to be fully absorbed from the face of the wall before beginning the pointing.

Stage Four
Using a hand hawk and small pointing trowel, apply mortar to the cross joints first. Finish each joint by compressing and ironing the mortar with the trowel until it is slightly indented on the left hand side of the joint. Complete about 1 square metre at a time.

Stage Five
In the same manner, fill the bed joints and compress and iron in with the top of the joint slightly cut back behind the arris of the brick above.

Stage Six
Once the joint has set it should be lightly brushed to remove any surplus mortar.

Use of Brick Cleaning Agents

The practice of washing buildings down on their completion with a brick cleaning agent has become more frequent in recent years.

If you are involved in this operation you must take the following precautions:

➤ Follow manufacturers application instructions to the letter

➤ Wear rubber gloves

➤ Wear eye protection

➤ Wear full cover overalls ensuring no part of your flesh is exposed.

Work-based Evidence Required

■ Work skills to:

■ measure, mark out, rake out, joint and mix

■ Use and maintain:

■ hand tools

■ Joint and point masonry structures to contractors working instructions to:

■ new brickwork and blockwork

■ existing brickwork or blockwork

To meet this requirement, obtain photographs of yourself:

■ measuring, marking out, raking out and mixing

■ using and maintaining hand tools

■ jointing and pointing new brick and blockwork and existing brick or blockwork.

When the photographs have been developed, place them on a photo evidence sheet, then get your supervisor to authenticate them by signing and dating. Place the sheets in your work-based evidence portfolio, when next in college and map and record them against the syllabus.

Quick quiz Quick quiz Quick quiz Quick quiz Quick quiz

❶ What is the difference between pointing and jointing?

❷ List five principal joint finishes.

❸ What is a hawk used for?

❹ Define the term tooling.

❺ How would you prepare a wall for pointing.

RESOURCES   6.2

In this section you will learn about materials, components and equipment relating to types, quantity, quality and sizes of standard and/or specialist:

■ jointing/pointing mixes, sands, cement, limes and additives

■ hand tools and equipment

■ methods of calculating quantity, length, area and wastage associated with the method/procedure to joint brick and block structures.

When you have completed this section you will be able to:

■ select the required quantity and quality of resources for the methods of work.

Know and understand:

■ the characteristics, quality, uses, limitations and defects associated with the resources

■ how the resources should be used.

Jointing and Pointing Mixes, Sands, Cement, Limes and Additives

Jointing and Pointing Mixes

The selection of the aggregate and matrix will depend upon the type of jointing and pointing and the finish required, but the mortar used should not be excessively strong in comparison with the brick as there is a tendency for the brick to wear away and leave the joints projecting.

Mixing Jointing and Pointing Material

To form a mortar that may be easily used, all the materials should be passed through a fine sieve and be thoroughly mixed in a dry state before any water is added. Since, for pointing, the mortar is taken up on the back of the trowel, it is desirable to have it much stiffer than ordinary mortar; therefore, a smaller amount of water is required and the mortar is brought to its correct consistency by beating the materials well together with the back of the shovel. It must also be remembered that an excess of water tends to render the joints porous.

Mix Ratios

The matrix may be cement, lime, or a combination of the two, and is mixed with the aggregate in varying proportions according to the finish required. The following proportions are usually adopted:

- Weather pointing

    1 part cement, 1 part sand for engineering bricks

    1 part cement, 2 parts sand for general building work.

- Flush pointing

    1 part cement, 2 parts sand; or 1 part cement, 1 part lime, 3 parts sand.

Coloured Joints

To obtain a coloured joint, coloured earth pigments are sometimes added to the dry materials or, better still, a proprietary brand of pointing material is used that only requires mixing with water before using. Because of the wide range of finishes that can now be obtained by varying the proportions and materials, it is general practice to prepare small panels of brickwork pointed in a number of different shades of the colour required, so that the architect may make a selection.

Water

Water used in the preparation of mortar should be clean and free from impurities which may impair the necessary characteristics of good mortar. Impurities such as salt and oil are harmful since they reduce the adhesive property.

Sand

Definition – a fine aggregate which forms the bulk of mortar.

Properties of Sand

The properties of sand influence, to a large extent, the quality of mortar. In selecting a sand suitable for jointing and pointing the following points should be observed.

The sand should be

- clean, that is, free from impurities such as those stated for water
- sharp, that is, having angular shaped grains
- well graded, that is, having proportionate amounts of varying sized grains combined to give the required texture: neither too fine nor too coarse.

Sand which is not clean may reduce the adhesive property of the mortar. Dirty sand can usually be made suitable for use by washing with water to separate and remove the impurities from the sand. A simple test for cleanliness can be carried out if a small quantity of sand is stirred in, say, a glass jar containing clean water; if the water becomes discoloured the presence of impurities is indicated. Oil or grease will rise to the surface.

Sharp sand, obtainable from pits or quarries, produces mortar of greater adhesive strength, sand found in sea and river beds has rounded grains due to the continuous action of moving water. These grains are not only round but smooth and consequently cause a reduction in the adhesion between the lime and sand. The use of sea sand should be avoided since it contains salts. With practice, sharpness can be tested by rubbing the grains between the fingers. Well graded sands tends to produce strength and workability with a minimum of lime.

Colour of Sand

Sand obtained from different sources may vary in colour from reddish-brown to pale yellow, while in some cases there is almost a complete absence of colour. Normally, the colour of sand influences the colour of the mortar but where special colour is required the appropriate coloured cement or dye can usually be obtained for the purpose.

Cement

Definition – A fine powdered material which, when mixed with water, sets and binds together to form a hard solid material. It is used as a component of mortar and concrete.

Composition and Manufacture

Cement for jointing and pointing is produced from chalk (or limestone) and clay (or shale) together with small quantities of other ingredients, including iron oxide and magnesium oxide and is strictly known as Portland cement.

The manufacturing process may be briefly described as follows:

The raw materials, in definite proportions, are converted into a liquid state by grinding, mixing and watering; the resulting mixture, termed 'slurry', is conveyed to a kiln for subsequent drying and burning. The burning process changes the slurry into clinker which is afterwards passed on to mills for grinding to a fine powder in its final process. Tests are made from time to time to ensure high quality.

Setting

The setting action of Portland cement commences immediately after the addition of water, consequently, any mortar which contains cement should be used within approximately four hours after mixing, otherwise the value of the cement will be practically lost. Setting will also occur when the cement is exposed to a damp atmosphere; therefore dry storage becomes essential. It is also important to avoid storing over a long period in order to reduce the risk of contact with moisture.

The strength characteristics of the common types of cements are given in Figure 6.20.

Normal Portland cement is a general purpose cement suitable for all uses when the special properties of the other types are not required. It is usually specified for construction of houses, offices and schools.

Types	Strength in days	
	Minimum	Maximum
Normal	7	28
Rapid	3	7
Low-heat	14	91
Coloured	7	28

Fig. 6.20 **Strengths of cement chart**

> *Point to note*

Rapid hardening cement is also quick-setting, so concrete made with it needs to be placed within a shorter time of mixing than usual.

> *Point to note*

Cement heats up as it hardens, specially in large masses, and the heat makes the concrete expand, sometimes causing cracking. But lo-heat Portland cement heats up more slowly than other types, so the concrete made from it expands less and the risk of cracking is reduced.

Rapid-hardening Portland cement is used when a job has to be finished especially quickly, or to offset the effects of low temperature (freezing before hardening).

Low-heat Portland cement is usually manufactured for specific contracts involving mass concrete such as dams or heavy retaining walls.

White and Coloured Portland cements

White cement is made from specially selected raw materials, and cement in a variety of colours can be obtained by mixing suitable pigments with the white cement at the factory.

These cements are fairly expensive and are therefore used mainly for facings, cast stone or rendering, where white or clear, pale colours are required.

Limes

Lime is a fine powdered material, with no appreciable setting and hardening properties, used to improve the workability and water retention of cement based mortars.

Classification of Lime

The varying qualities of lime used for brickwork are classified as:

- high calcium lime
- semi-hydraulic lime
- eminently hydraulic lime.

High calcium lime is also known as 'white' lime and may be classed as quick slaking due to it being a practically pure lime, that is, its composition is almost entirely calcium. An outstanding characteristic of this grade of lime is the high degree of workability which can be obtained.

Semi-hydraulic lime, or 'grey' lime, does not possess the same high calcium content as white lime and consequently has correspondingly less plastic properties.

Eminently hydraulic lime, contains an even greater proportion of impurities than the semi-hydraulic lime and therefore it follows that these impurities reduce the plastic properties making it more difficult to work.

The existence of certain, so called, impurities in lime used for brickwork does not necessarily infer a reduction in quality, in fact, they aid the setting properties and are therefore considered suitable for work where strength is required. In some instances lime contains a comparatively large proportion of magnesia when it is known as magnesian lime and possesses better hardening properties than high calcium lime.

Additives

Plasticizers

There are many types of plasticizer on the market, some of those more commonly used in construction are produced by the Degusa construction chemicals company and are described below.

Febmix Admix Mortar Plasticizer

Description of Product

This is a liquid air entraining plasticizer that replaces lime or other supplements in the mix and reduces the amount of water required to achieve the desired workability.

Fields of Application

Febmix Admix is an admixture for mortars that improves the workability of bricklaying mortars and significantly increases their resistance to freezing and thawing cycles.

Febmix DH Powder Mortar Plasticizer

Description of Product

Febmix DH is a mortar plasticizer in powder form for use as an alternative to lime or as a supplement to lime to aid mortar durability.

Fields of Application

For use as an admixture for mortars to improve workability in bricklaying. Febmix DH aids resistance of mortars to frost attack in both the wet and cured state. It also increases long term durability of cement, sand and cement, lime and sand mortars.

key terms

Plasticizer – A substance that when added to a material (in the case of brickwork, sand and cement) produces a product which is flexible, resilient and easier to handle.

Pigments or Dyes

Pigments or dyes are added to the mix to produce coloured mortars.

Methods of Calculation

Understanding Areas

Area is the space taken up by a flat surface like a wall, most bricklaying is about flat surfaces.

You will need to know the area of the walls so as you can order the materials you need for the job.

The wall in Figure 6.21 is 4 m long and 2 m high.

Point to note

Use accurate and consistent proportions of materials otherwise the mortar and jointing or pointing may not be sufficiently strong and the colour will certainly vary.

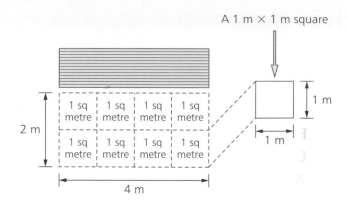

Fig. 6.21 A wall 4 m × 2 m

As you can see this gives you eight 1 m by 1 m squares. Therefore the area is 8 square metres in total.

The easy way to work this out is to measure the length and the width or height and multiply them together. If we use the example in Figure 6.21 it will look like this:

$$4 \text{ m} \times 2 \text{ m} = 8 \text{ m}^2$$

The formula looks like this:

$$A = L \times W.$$

Key:

A = Area

L = length

W = Width

Calculate the area in Figure 6.22.

The area of the wall is . . . . m².

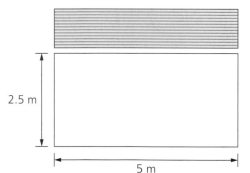

Fig. 6.22 A wall 5 m × 2.5 m

Source: Department for Education and Skills

Work-based Evidence Required

■ **Selection of resources associated with own work:**

■ materials

■ tools and equipment

To meet these requirements, obtain a witness testimony sheet from your supervisor stating that you selected materials relating to pointing and jointing and chose the necessary tools and equipment required to carry out the tasks. Place the evidence in your work-based evidence portfolio when next in college and map and record it against the syllabus.

Quick quiz Quick quiz Quick quiz Quick quiz Quick quiz

❶ What is a plasticizer used for?
❷ List three types of lime used in bricklaying.
❸ From what materials is cement produced?
❹ List three properties of sand.
❺ What mix ratio would you use for weather pointing?

Pointing and Jointing

For further information about pointing and jointing, the following books are both informative, interesting and extremely useful to the student of brickwork.

Books

The BDA Guide to Successful Brickwork (Various Authors) Publisher: Arnold. A member of the Hodder Headline Group, London.

This book has an excellent section about pointing and repointing written by R. Baldwin, which goes much further than I am able to do here in its detail and informative content. The book itself is a must for all those interested in brickwork.

Creative Brickwork (Terry Knight on behalf of the Brick Development Association) Publisher: Arnold as before.

The book has an excellent section about mortar joints and how their design and specification affects the appearance of brickwork. The book also covers the history of bricks in the UK.

Mortars, Cements and Limes

For more information about mortars, cements and limes why not visit the websites of the better known manufacturers and suppliers, or the following?

Mortar Industry Association

www.mortar.org.uk

The Mortar Industry Association since its inception in 1971 has been providing independent advice and technical support to specifiers and users of mortars. Today the association is active in the fields of standardization, the provision of technical data and the implementation of best practice in brick and blockwork specification. The association welcomes enquiries and a range of technical literature will be supplied on request.

Index